OECD PROCEED

GLOBALISATION, MIGRATION AND DEVELOPMENT

ORGANISATION FOR ECONOMIC CO-OPERATION AND DEVELOPMENT

ORGANISATION FOR ECONOMIC CO-OPERATION AND DEVELOPMENT

Pursuant to Article 1 of the Convention signed in Paris on 14th December 1960, and which came into force on 30th September 1961, the Organisation for Economic Co-operation and Development (OECD) shall promote policies designed:

- to achieve the highest sustainable economic growth and employment and a rising standard of living in Member countries, while maintaining financial stability, and thus to contribute to the development of the world economy;
- to contribute to sound economic expansion in Member as well as non-member countries in the process of economic development; and
- to contribute to the expansion of world trade on a multilateral, non-discriminatory basis in accordance with international obligations.

The original Member countries of the OECD are Austria, Belgium, Canada, Denmark, France, Germany, Greece, Iceland, Ireland, Italy, Luxembourg, the Netherlands, Norway, Portugal, Spain, Sweden, Switzerland, Turkey, the United Kingdom and the United States. The following countries became Members subsequently through accession at the dates indicated hereafter: Japan (28th April 1964), Finland (28th January 1969), Australia (7th June 1971), New Zealand (29th May 1973), Mexico (18th May 1994), the Czech Republic (21st December 1995), Hungary (7th May 1996), Poland (22nd November 1996) and Korea (12th December 1996). The Commission of the European Communities takes part in the work of the OECD (Article 13 of the OECD Convention).

Publié en français sous le titre :

MONDIALISATION, MIGRATIONS ET DÉVELOPPEMENT

FOREWORD

This publication brings together a selection of the papers presented at the Conference on "Globalisation, Migration and Development" held in Lisbon on 2 and 3 November 1998. This conference was organised with the support and assistance of the Portuguese authorities. It followed on from the regional seminars organised by the Secretariat between 1996 and 1998 on the themes of migration, free trade and regional integration, in respectively Central and Eastern Europe, the Mediterranean Basin and North America. It also took into account the results of the OECD's work on migration and the labour market in the context of regional economic integration in Asia.

The principal objective of the Lisbon Conference was to invite experts and policy makers to draw the lessons from these regional analyses. The first session presented, with the aid of economic indicators, the relative state of advancement of the process of globalisation in the four regions considered. The second session reviewed different economic models which assessed the impact of free-trade and economic integration on direct investment, employment and migration flows. Two round tables comprised the third session. The first highlighted the economic measures and trade strategies which would help the acceleration of the regional integration processes presently underway. During the second round table the role that migration flows could play in strengthening regional integration and the new directions which employment and migration policies should take in order to attain this objective were further clarified.

Among the measures proposed at the conference to accelerate economic convergence, participants stressed the need for efficient public and financial institutions, the implementation of vocational training programmes and measures to attract foreign capital (including investments by migrants in their home countries) that would ensure sustainable development. In a context of increasing economic convergence, migration policy could play a fundamental role. In this regard, facilitating the exchange of skilled and highly-skilled labour within the framework of a policy seeking greater enhancement of human resources ought to constitute an important element of future migration policies.

This publication was made possible by a financial contribution from the Portuguese authorities. It is published on the responsibility of the Secretary-General of the OECD.

TABLE OF CONTENTS

TABLE OF CONTENTS

INTRODUCTION

The OECD, as a follow-up on the proposals debated at the Conference on Migration and International Co-operation held in Madrid in March 1993 at the initiative of the Canadian and Spanish governments,[1] organised from 1996 to 1998 three regional seminars on migration, free trade and regional integration, in respectively, Central and Eastern Europe (Vienna, March 1996, with the support of the Austrian Federal Chancellery and the WIFO), in the Mediterranean Basin (Athens, October 1996, in co-operation with the Greek authorities) and in North America (Mexico, January 1998, with the support of the Mexican, Canadian and United States authorities).[2] In order to draw the political lessons from these regional analyses and to integrate the results of research undertaken on migration and the labour market in Asia,[3] the OECD organised, with the support of the Portuguese authorities, an international conference on "Globalisation, Migration and Development" in Lisbon, on 2 and 3 November 1998.

The principal objective of the Lisbon Conference was to draw the lessons for policy from these regional analyses, and to discuss them with invited policy-makers and experts. Proposals were formulated to strengthen the links between migration, employment and regional economic integration within the framework of a new partnership between OECD Member countries and between the latter and some non-member countries. This partnership aims essentially at better controlling migration flows and encouraging sustainable development in emigration countries.

The Lisbon Conference comprised three sessions. The first session presented, with the aid of economic indicators, the relative state of advancement of the processes of regionalisation and globalisation in the four large regions considered. The second session analysed the recent policies for regional economic integration and their impact on direct investment, employment and migration. This analysis was completed by an assessment of the modelling that had been done on the different approaches taking into account the impact of free-trade and economic integration on direct investment, employment and migration flows. The third session consisted of two round tables. The first round table highlighted the economic measures and trade strategies, which would help remove the remaining obstacles to an acceleration of the regional integration processes presently underway. The second round table aimed to further clarify the role that migration flows could play in strengthening regional integration and to define the new directions that employment and migration policies should take in order to attain this objective.

---

1. See *Migration and Development: New Partnership for Co-operation* (OECD, 1994).

2. The proceedings of these regional seminars were published under the following titles:
   Migration, Free Trade and Regional Integration in Central and Eastern Europe (OECD-WIFO, 1997).
   Migrations, libre-échange et intégration régionale dans le Bassin méditerranéen (OECD, 1998).
   Migrations, Free Trade and Regional Integration in North America (OECD, 1998).

3. Since 1995, the OECD has also taken part with the ILO in annual workshops on migration and the labour market in Asia, organised in Tokyo by the Japan Institute of Labour and the Japanese Ministry of Labour. The proceedings of these workshops have been published by the OECD,
   Migration and the Labour Market in Asia. Prospects to the Year 2000 (OECD, 1996),
   Migration and Regional Economic Integration in Asia (OECD, 1998).

Since it is not possible to publish complete works and discussions of the conference (reports not included are marked with an asterisk), this publication concentrates on three main issues. The first deals with globalisation, regional integration and migration. The second highlights the links between economic growth, direct investment and migration. The third part shows how migration policies could help accelerate regional integration.

1.   Regional integration trends in the four regions considered

In the document on the indicators for economic processes at work in North America, Asia, Central and Eastern Europe and in the Mediterranean Basin, *Isabelle Bensidoun* and *Agnès Chevallier* compared the evolution of regional economic integration in these four regions. The relative intensity index of trade clearly illustrates the regionalisation of world trade. However, the authors showed that in North America, as in Europe, regional trade reveals deep asymmetries. In Asia, trade by the "South" is greatly differentiated geographically, especially in exports, and "North-South" relations are relatively symmetrical from this point of view. The authors also underline the fact that the countries of the "South", which are the most strongly anchored to the regional centres from a trade point of view, are also more strongly linked in monetary terms.

To conclude, the authors point out that regional integration can only produce dynamic effects if the reforms that must accompany any opening up of the economy are accepted politically and socially. Moreover, in countries where the labour force will continue to grow at a fast rate, employment issues will remain durable. Consequently, one cannot expect the convergence of living standards within regional groupings to be a sufficient means of controlling migration flows. The general comments made by *Yasushi Iguchi* on this paper are followed by three studies on recent developments in the regions under review.

*Norma Samaniego** reviews the impact of the integration process in North America four years after the signature of the NAFTA. In contrast with the European Union experience, the NAFTA did not aim for political union or a common market. The agreement is limited to the creation of a free trade area. The impact of NAFTA on the US and Canadian economies has been modest in the aggregate, while there has been a larger impact on the Mexican economy. According to the author, one conclusion seems clear: economic integration has not been able to mitigate ongoing divergent trends within the economies of the participating countries and it is not yet evident that a cross-country convergence process has been initiated. Increasing trade within the region has not yet significantly affected Mexican labour migration to the United States. If trade liberalisation is not accompanied by measures that promote investment in physical infrastructure and human capital, advanced technological catch-up and a more even development, it can in the medium term lead to a lack of convergence.

Over recent years, economic relations among East Asian countries have became much closer. *Shoichi Ito** examines the initial impact of the recent financial crisis on trade, foreign direct investment (FDI) and international migration. The Asian financial crisis has had various negative effects on their economies, including the rapid rise of unemployment rates. Deteriorating labour market conditions are forcing rural domestic migrant workers, laid off in urban areas, to return to their rural areas. As a result, many foreign workers in rural areas, or in the so-called second category of jobs in urban areas, may loose their jobs and be forced to return to their home countries. In this way, the economic crisis in East Asian countries is causing inverse flows of domestic and international migration.

---

*   Reports not included are marked with an asterisk.

According to *Gudrun Biffl*,* central and eastern European countries joining the EU will have to face a twofold challenge: to cope with the actual or potential out-migration of their skilled labour force on the one hand and to cope with rising inflows of migrant workers from the East on the other. Biffl asserts that the economic benefits of the process of regional integration may outweigh the costs. In order to preserve social cohesion, it will be important to identify the losers, and socialise rather than individualise the adjustment costs. In this context, the provision of a social safety net and of aid to regional and occupational mobility, will be paramount for an increase in the social acceptance of EU-enlargement on either side of the current borders.

2.   Globalisation of migration and regional integration

Putting forward the question of whether one can talk of the globalisation of migration flows, *Georges Tapinos* and *Daniel Delaunay* rejected the widespread conception of a globalisation of international migration flows. Based on an examination of the statistical data, the authors show that migration flows have not accelerated over the past three decades at a pace comparable to those in capital flows and trade in goods and services. Although countries have implemented policies to promote trade and capital flows, they have reinforced their control over migration movements. The authors emphasise however (thereby recognising the validity of the remarks of the discussants, *Dirk Stroband** and *Roger Kramer**) that although it is not possible to talk of a globalisation of migration, the increasing diversity of migrants' nationalities and the migration channels used, as well as the growing proportion of movements of temporary and skilled workers in total migration flows, does show that migration is now taking place in the context of economic globalisation. They add that the interdependence of sending and host countries is stronger than in the past, and that the debate is no longer the impact of migration on the respective countries, but has become inseparable from the issue of human rights, the political and economic development of the country of origin, and the national cohesion and future of the welfare state in the host societies.

Laurence Assous presents an overview of the recent economic literature on regional integration and migration. Assous first summarises the main teachings of the international trade theory. According to some specialists, free trade should lead to a decrease in migration flows. This would imply a relationship of substitution between migration flows and trade flows. However, this decrease is improbable in the short-term, and trade liberalisation alone is not likely to help narrow disparities between countries. Other specialists argue that regional integration may accelerate migration flows. In this regard, trade liberalisation and structural adjustment programmes can also be very disruptive. Assous pursues with a critique of recent studies that don't take sufficiently into account social factors determining the decision to emigrate

3.   Economic growth, regional integration and their impact on the incentives to emigrate

In their document on regional integration, migration, growth and direct investment, *Denis Cogneau*, *Jean-Christophe Dumont* and *El-Mouhoub Mouhoud* studied the substitution of international migration flows by trade flows in the light of the latest theories. The authors analysed the conditions required for speeding the growth of the least-developed countries by an increase in FDI and by regional integration into the immigration country bloc. The authors also showed that North-South regional integration can provide a serious alternative to migration only if it has a fair chance of notably changing the living conditions and expectations of South country populations within a fairly short space of time.

The authors then analysed the new growth theories and showed that it might be deduced from the empirical verification for the South that regional integration has beneficial effects on growth by way of technology transfers and investment. This being granted, and supposing that under certain conditions FDI inflows can foster growth, the authors stressed that the issue of complementarity between export flows and FDI becomes all-important and that present regional integration processes carry the risk of disqualifying countries that are low on human and social capital and have small-sized domestic markets.

Florence Toutain arrives at mostly the same conclusions as the three above-mentioned authors. Focusing essentially on the role played by foreign direct investment, she first presents the recent empirical literature on economic opening and its impact on the growth of emerging economies. Then, she carried out empirical work in order to evaluate the impact of FDI on growth by integrating into her analysis the interactions linking FDI to human capital and to domestic investment. This analysis takes into account the endogenous nature of FDI. The author observes a very high degree of complementarity between the extent of an economy's openness and the inflows of FDI. FDI flows tend to be directed first and foremost towards countries with high incomes but low price levels; this would appear to indicate that these flows are motivated simultaneously by the will to increase market penetration and the pursuit of increased competitiveness. Toutain stresses that, if economic openness can attract FDI, the impact of the latter on economic growth appears to be decisive only when their interaction with domestic investment and human capital is taken into account.

Dealing with the impact that Portugal's entry into the European Community has had on FDI, migration and employment, *Maria Pereira Ramos* described the remarkable economic progress the country has made since 1986. She stressed the increasing globalisation the country's economy, reforms of the public sector, expansion of its social and economic infrastructure, and a high level of job creation and structural reform that has given a strong stimulus to investment and expansion of financial networks. The author clearly showed that the structural funds provided through the "Community Support Framework", from which Portugal has benefited, have served to catalyse convergence of the Portuguese economy towards the economies of the other European Union countries. Portugal has now become an immigration country.

4. Economic development, migration policies and regional integration

Taking into account the geopolitical dimension of regional integration, *Ghazi Hidouci* showed that OECD countries are facing demo-economic constraints which condition their responses to the challenges posed by the issues of development and migration. Population ageing foreshadows labour shortages around 2005; the potential for renewal by means of immigration will no doubt, for want of an alternative, serve as a cushion. According to the author, it is Europe that will have to contend with new immigration flows stemming from the changes attributable to globalisation (Central and Eastern Europe) and the pervading political instability (the Mediterranean Basin and Africa). It is apparently also in Europe and Japan, rather than in North America and the rest of Asia, that behaviour linked with population ageing is reinforcing isolationist attitudes. Such attitudes are all the more harmful when at the same time internal economic forces are structurally affected by ageing.

According to Hidouci, trends in the behaviour of investors and the strategies of firms are at the moment hindering the implementation of stronger regional integration strategies intended to meet the challenges of demographic pressures, poverty and increasing inequalities between developed and developing countries. In the area of research and development these latter suffer from both a weak surrounding infrastructure and a lack of funds. Moreover, the importance of scale economies operates against them due to the limited size of their markets. In conclusion, the author emphasises that the impediments to progress in economic integration, such as concerning the implementation of more liberal migration policies, are in fact located at the level of the immigration countries' distrust *vis-à-vis* the inefficient political and economic systems of the emigration countries. For this reason, he suggests that we take into account this reality rather than propose the limited endeavours of free-trade agreements. Without doubt, the search for lasting solutions must incorporate the strategic preoccupations of peace and integrate them in processes of democratic control.

John Evans describes the different integration processes and explains that a social dimension is crucial for regional integration if there is to be broad support. The current process of globalisation has been accompanied by growing inequality and poverty both between and within countries. Not all these developments can be blamed on globalisation, but there has been a tendency by both companies and governments to say that they have no responsibility for their actions, because outcomes are determined by global markets, over which they have no control. Recent events may suggest that this is no longer a satisfactory response and governments now have to develop effective public policy responses to problems created by their own policies and by global markets. According to Evans, and from a trade union viewpoint, the central objective of policy must now be to re-link the potential of global markets with the achievement of social progress. The failure to achieve this may lead to a rejection by many parts of society of the globalisation process itself.

Demetrios Papademetriou organises his paper into three broad categories. The first one focuses on the relationship between regional integration and migration. The second explores briefly the burdens and opportunities that labour mobility places on policy making in the human resources development area *both* for labour senders and labour receivers. The third one reflects on a handful of "rules of the game" for societies that choose to or are considering engaging in regional integration arrangements in some part as a means of relieving regional migration pressures. According to Papademetriou, in order for liberalisation to lower such pressures in significant ways, it must lead to large scale and sustained investments that promote steady growth. It must also be accompanied by fundamental changes in the way the immigrant-sending societies that are party to these initiatives are organised socially and economically, as well as in the way in which they govern themselves.

PART I

GLOBALISATION, REGIONAL INTEGRATION AND MIGRATION

INDICATORS OF REGIONALISATION IN NORTH AMERICA, ASIA, CENTRAL AND EASTERN EUROPE AND THE MEDITERRANEAN BASIN

by

Isabelle Bensidoun and **Agnès Chevallier**

Economists at Centre d'études prospectives et d'informations internationales (CEPII), Paris

The opening up of developing and transition economies, which has been taking place since the 1980s, and the collapse of the Berlin Wall have given globalisation a pan-world dimension. The structure of economic relations within regional groups is at the same time being reinforced. The forms and objectives of regionalisation, as well as their relationships to globalisation, vary from case to case. This paper seeks to furnish some quantitative indicators of North-South relations, within each of these regional groups, in order to present a development outlook for the countries of the South. This will be done by focusing on regions that have already been the object of past OECD seminars.[1]

1.   Emergence and regionalisation

During the 1970s, two-thirds of the world's population lived in countries that were largely outside the world economy, whether in socialist economies or in economies protected by trade barriers. At the turn of the century, this proportion is expected to drop to 10%. The opening up of China to foreign companies and capital and the collapse of the Soviet bloc have eliminated the most important obstacles to the expansion of capitalism.

The integration of developing countries into the world economy has taken place as result of political, economic and technical changes. The political decisions which allowed numerous countries to reduce their trade barriers have been accompanied by similar choices in the field of finance, and have blended well with the major technical changes that have occurred in the fields of communications and industrial production. The capacity to standardise core products while differentiating their appearance has played a decisive role in globalisation. It has permitted companies to benefit from economies of scale in mass production while at the same time meeting specific market constraints ever more closely (Duval, 1998).

The sectoral complementarity, which traditionally existed between North and South, has given way to a complementarity within manufacturing activities. Trade in manufacturing products, between emerging and developed countries, has been the most dynamic component of international trade in recent years. These trends, coupled with shifts in real prices, have led to a strong progression in the share of manufactured exports by emerging and transition countries. For the regions examined here, this share ran from 30% for the Mediterranean to 58% for Central Europe, rising, respectively, to 50% and 83% by 1996.

---

1.   NAFTA, EU-CEECs, EU-Mediterranean Countries, Eastern Asia. Countries in each region are listed in Appendix 1.

Companies from the North have been able to extend their profit sources by enlarging their production networks to countries of the South. Companies in the South can enter these networks thanks to the cost advantages they have in terms of wages (Figure 1). They, however, must also react to the progress taking place in the North, for example (World Bank, 1997): just-in-time purchases now account for almost half of all purchases in textiles, compared with a quarter in 1987; order cycles in the US electrical and electronics industry have been reduced from some five months in 1980 to seven weeks in 1990 and to close to two weeks today. Competitive pressure, especially that from low-wage economies, has forced companies in the North to make productivity gains, which in turn compelled countries in the South to improve their efficiency. Response times (cutting back production delays of all sorts) are one of the principal means by which competing companies try to differentiate themselves. The more costs related to geographic distance fall, the more time constraints become important. Trade liberalisation and cost reductions related to geographic distance, therefore, do not annul the advantages of proximity. Geographic and cultural proximity continue to have a strong influence on trade flows, notably when they favour such reactiveness. "Trade and contact networks exist which constitute material and above all immaterial investments – habits, confidence networks, diasporas, distributions systems – which guide and stabilise trade flows" (Veltz, 1997).

The regionalisation of trade flows is even more apparent when focusing not only on the bilateral level of flows, but also on their relative intensity, which ignores the absolute size of the partners. For example, the indicator for the intensity of exports from country i to country j is 2, if country j imports 1% of world exports and 2% of exports from country i (for the definition of this index, see Appendix 2). The intensity of North-South trade thus sets out major regional groupings around three hubs: North America, the European Union and Japan (Table 1). Outside these groupings, intensity levels for bilateral trade are less than 1%, with the exception of trade flows between the United States and Asia, which highlight the importance of integration in the Pacific.

Regional integration creates major economic groupings in terms of production and market size. The three groupings set out here account for about 80% of world GDP and are of similar economic size. In contrast, they only cover about half the world's population (Figure 2). Other developing or transition countries are not a part of the process of regional integration linking them strongly to one of these main centres of development, either because of their geographic situation or their low insertion in globalisation.

The logic of regional integration should not be confused with that of opening up. As Charles Oman points out, if globalisation is a centrifugal process, then regionalisation is in turn a centripetal one that involves the movement of two or more economies, that is, two or more societies, towards greater integration with one another (Oman, 1997). Regional integration takes place according to particular forms and with different objectives. In certain cases, regionalisation may constitute a defensive response to globalisation, or it may be a stepping-stone to a strategy of globalisation. Regional integration may result from the *de facto* polarisation of foreign trade and financial flows. In other cases, regionalisation may be based on *de jure* agreements that include more or less formal commitments and more or less developed institutional measures. The four processes of regional integration analysed here are therefore different in various respects.

2. Different forms of regional North-South integration

Differences in regional integration processes are not to be found so much in the scale of contrasts between North and South, which exist in each case. Instead, they lie more in the role of the North as a development centre or regional leader, and the South's form of insertion. These differences also explain the content and scope of differences in *de jure* integration.

North-South contrasts are relatively comparable from one region to another. In 1997, the average income per capita in zones of the South (excluding China) represented between 25 and 32% of zones in the North.[2] Likewise, working population characteristics clearly separate North and South in each of the regions. From a sectoral viewpoint, much of the working population in the North is concentrated in services, whereas in the South a large share of the working population is still in agriculture (Appendix 3). Between 2000 and 2010, growth in the working population of the South will remain strong. In the North however, it is expected to be small: some European countries and Japan will even experience a fall in numbers. It is clear, nevertheless, that the averages hide important differences across countries. This is true both in Europe and in Asia where a kind of continuum exists. Countries of central Europe, as well as Korea in Asia, appear to be relatively close to the North, especially concerning their working populations.

The geographic structure of trade and the choice of currency anchors – whether for fixed or crawling pegs – reveals the different roles regional development centres play and the distinctive modes of global integration by countries of the South.

In America as in Europe, regional trade bears out profound asymmetries (Table 2). In both cases, countries of the South carry out most of their trade with the regional centres, though their place in these trade flows is relatively weak. In Asia, trade in the South is greatly differentiated geographically, especially in exports, and North-South relations are relatively symmetrical from this viewpoint.

Countries of the South that are the most strongly anchored to their regional centres from a trade viewpoint are also most strongly linked in monetary terms. Since the end of the Bretton–Woods system, many countries have abandoned fixed exchange rates in favour of crawling parities or currency floats. Still, where crawling pegs or managed floating exists, the choice of currency anchor defines *de facto* the membership to a currency zone (Bénassy-Quéré, 1995). The Mexican peso, therefore, is pegged to the dollar,[3] whereas the currencies of Tunisia, Morocco, Malta, Cyprus and, henceforth, the majority of central and eastern European countries are pegged to the European Monetary System (EMS) (Table 3). In contrast, Mediterranean countries whose trade was less concentrated geographically in Europe, did not seem to be anchored to a particular currency in the early 1990s – only recently has their currency been pegged to the dollar. The yen is not a currency anchor for any country, as Asian currencies have been linked to the dollar, at least up until the present crisis.

Neither the structure of trade nor foreign indebtedness (spread between the yen, the dollar, and to a lesser degree, among European countries) indicated that the dollar was likely to be a currency that could provide Asian countries with greater stability. But in the absence of organised regional co-ordination, the dollar peg, which existed up until the crisis of 1997, assured an implicit form of co-ordination, which put limits on bilateral parity fluctuations and helped avoid competitive devaluation. Such co-ordination by default reached its limits with the appreciation of the dollar.

In Asia, regionalisation arose as a result of rather similar development strategies, whose success in terms of export performance and growth translated into rising trade interdependency. From

---

2. "North" and "South" refer to economic criteria. For the geographical composition of North and South in each region, see Appendix 1.

3. The nominal pegging by a country k is evaluated by comparing the volatility of the variations of its nominal exchange rate with respect to the dollar, the mark or the yen. The currency k is considered to belong to the dollar zone if the volatility of its exchange rate is clearly lower with respect to the dollar than with respect to the two competing currencies. See Appendix 4 for a more detailed presentation of this methodology.

the 1960s onwards, Korea, Hong Kong (China), Singapore and Chinese Taipei, following Japan, constituted the second wave of the V model of flying geese.[4] They were followed by a third wave, including Thailand and Malaysia, during the second half of the 1970s (Contamin and Lacu, 1998). In 1978, China too initiated a policy of economic reform and liberalisation. More recently, Indonesia and the Philippines have formed the fourth wave, thus enlarging the regional hierarchy. The volumes of intra-regional foreign direct investment have in turn risen in tandem with a state of advanced development in several countries. These volumes have made it possible to bolster the dynamics of complementarity in the region. But they have also led to the building-up of overcapacity in certain sectors. An example of this, observable since 1996, has been the saturation of the market for semi-conductors which has provoked a price collapse and a sharp slowdown in the growth of Asian exports.

In Asia, the goals of economic opening and integration into the world economy preceded those linked to regionalism. Trade liberalisation has had a unilateral character. It has taken place within national development strategies, without reference to international negotiations, be they multilateral or regional. Although ASEAN's first priority is political, the members of the Association did nevertheless commit themselves in 1991 to creating a free-trade zone (the ASEAN Free-Trade Area) in fifteen years. This was in response to concerns generated by NAFTA and the European Single Market.

The character of power relations in Asia must be mentioned in any discussion of regional integration and leadership within the zone (Chaponnière and Dourille-Feer, 1998). In contrast to Europe and America, there is practically an inverse relationship in the region between size and per capita income. Japan, which has the most dominant economy, has only one-tenth of the population of China. China and Indonesia, with 1 230 and 210 million inhabitants, respectively, are the poorest countries in the region. In contrast to the other experiences of regional integration discussed here, integration in Asia is not a question of least developed countries joining a far more important grouping. Instead, the situation is much more characterised by interdependencies between countries at different levels of development.

In North America, as well as in the European Union and Mediterranean countries, regional integration of less developed countries is peripheral in nature. Historical links and geographic proximity have forced these countries to have a strong economic dependence with their powerful neighbours. Direct contact between North and South, which exists in these two parts of the world, however, generates regional relations that are of special political and human density, reinforced by past and recent migrations. The North is preoccupied primarily by issues of stability and a desire to control immigration. This is the principal objective of *de jure* regional integration created by NAFTA and the Euro-Mediterranean association agreements. But globalisation is also leading northern countries to seize the opportunities offered by geographic and cultural proximity of less developed countries in order to improve their global competitiveness. For southern countries, agreements reached with the North are foremost a guarantee of market access. But they also perceive the creation of a free-trade zone as a means to integrate the world economy and attract more foreign direct investment. Apart from the static effects of such agreements, which are necessarily limited, it is the dynamic benefits which improve productivity and growth that are the most sought-after.

The agreement between the United States, Canada and Mexico allowed Mexico to enter a free-trade zone that already existed between the former two countries. Tariff and non-tariff barriers to trade in goods and services were reduced substantially on 1 January 1994, and will be totally removed by 2009. Mexico will abolish the remaining obstacles relating to the protection of intellectual property

---

4.   The general idea of this model, developed by Akamatsu (1961), is that growth in a region is based on a dynamic cycle of export production; production is transmitted from the initiating country to the country further behind as the first reaches a more advanced development phase.

and will soften rules on foreign direct investment. The year NAFTA came into force was also the year of the Mexican financial crisis, which led to a sharp recession, a rapid, renewed rise in inflation, and a brutal readjustment of foreign trade. These macroeconomic shocks make it difficult to analyse the impact of NAFTA on North-American trade. Some authors, however, have noted that tighter links between the United States and Mexico – borne out especially by American financial support – have without doubt helped Mexico avoid adopting protectionist measures. The credibility of Mexico's policy for opening up its economy has not been damaged, which has helped bring about the rapid return of foreign finance and has eased the ending of the crisis (Gould, 1998).

The ambitions of the Euro-Mediterranean association agreements go beyond the creation of a free-trade zone. Given the contents of previous co-operation agreements as well as the political situation of certain countries (open or latent conflicts, the absence of democracy, and so forth), the association agreements have a political and security dimension, a cultural dimension, and provide finance on condition of trade and economic liberalisation. The freeing of trade and extension of liberalisation should progress within this framework. Apart from the requisite microeconomic reforms, the success of regional integration will depend on the ability of macroeconomic policies to accompany such liberalisation, especially the exchange rate policy. It will also depend on how regional integration is developed, especially in the fields of service liberalisation and establishment rights. If integration were restricted to razing barriers at EU frontiers, then it would have little effect in stimulating the development of exporting activities and foreign investment. Under these conditions, the costs of liberalisation, which make themselves felt by the elimination of activities subject to foreign competition, could be greater than the benefits.

The economic and liberalisation policies that Central and Eastern Europe Countries (CEECs) have pursued since 1989 have sparked off their re-emergence in western trade.[5] The association agreements with the European Community set out an asymmetric opening of markets (access to the Community market for manufactured products from the CEECs, with no tariffs or quotas as of the 1 January 1998), leading to open access to CEEC markets by 2002 and to a free-trade zone.[6] The European Union, therefore, finds itself faced with an enlarged periphery in the East and the South, with countries whose trade orientation and levels of income are highly comparable. But the decision to accept the CEECs into the union will deepen differences. The Council of Copenhagen, in 1993, did indeed recognise the possibility of the CEECs integration into the EU as soon as they met the requisite economic and political conditions. From this point of view, the European Commission put forward a white paper setting out in detail all the measures necessary to prepare their entry into the single market.

Enlarged membership will occur in several waves. The five countries (Cyprus not included) which have already entered membership negotiations (Hungary, Poland, the Czech Republic, Slovenia and Estonia) are those which are closest to the union, both economically and geographically (with the exception of Estonia). Within the logic of pre-admission, these countries will be increasingly constrained in their liberalisation and harmonisation by European rules. The adoption of the *acquis communautaire* is in fact one of the conditions to their entry into the single market, even if their membership in the EU, by the years 2002-2003, will inevitably imply certain temporary derogations.

The danger is that these new frontiers will create a demarcation line between an ordered and stable Europe and an eastern Europe characterised by instability and poverty. Some of the candidates that were not included in the first wave will take time to fulfil the political and economic commitments on which depend the liberalisation and the progress of negotiations. Furthermore, the costs of the first

---

5.   The following sentences borrow from Chevallier *et al.* (1997).

6.   Agricultural products remain outside free trade. This is also the case for the Mediterranean countries.

wave of membership (budgetary and administrative costs, tensions linked to institutional reforms) will bear down on the capacity of the EU to integrate further members. Concerns over how to manage the internal stability of the union will lead to the spreading out over time of other countries' candidacies.[7] Countries that are more or less durably "excluded" from the EU will be freer to pursue exchange rate policies that could favour their short-term competitiveness. They could better benefit from their comparative advantage in labour-intensive industries and from their proximity to the union than "selected" countries. In contrast, "selected" countries, with support from structural funds, will be engaged on a convergence process with Member States that will develop new trade specialisations which depend less on North-South complementarity.

3. Specialisation, growth and catch-up

Regional integration can have a positive impact on growth in the South by favouring the evolution of specialisation patterns. Regional liberalisation may of course lead to more direct but less advantageous effects than multilateral liberalisation. The benefits of free access to cheaper imported products may diminish as a result of the trade diversion favouring a regional partner, at the expense of extra-regional suppliers, whose products continue to be taxed at borders. But it is generally admitted that the indirect effects of liberalisation, because of the productivity gains they engender, are certainly more important than the direct effects, and that such effects can be reinforced within the framework of regional integration. The process of regional integration may improve the response to the shock of competition brought about by liberalisation and may facilitate the reallocation of factors across sectors by guaranteeing access to regional markets; by favouring inflows of foreign public and private capital and the transfer of technology; and by encouraging internal reforms and reinforcing their credibility.

Accompanying the industrialisation of the less developed countries, North-South trade, traditionally inter-sectoral, has become intra-branch. This can be seen in the four cases examined here, albeit to differing degrees (see Table 4). Euro-Mediterranean trade remains generally marked by the traditional complementarities and, over the course of the last ten years the difference in the sectoral structure of trade in manufactures has narrowed only slightly.

The particular nature of Euro-Mediterranean trade also stands out when comparing the sectoral structures of trade by southern zones with their different partners (Figure 3). Exports from most of the southern zones have a sectoral structure that is less and less characterised by the specific nature of the regional division of labour. Such exports increasingly resemble exports from these zones going to the rest of the world and imports from their regional partners coming from the rest of the world. From this viewpoint, exports from North Africa to the European Union appear to be very particular. Their sectoral structure resembles neither the "supply" of North African products to the rest of the world, nor the European "demand" directed towards other exporters to the Union. The preferential, non-reciprocal trade regime, from which North African countries benefited in their traditional European market, has not favoured the evolution of their export structures to become better adapted to European demand.[8] Provided that it leads to greater regional integration, above and beyond simple free trade, the Euro-Mediterranean association could direct the production activity of Mediterranean countries to areas of greater value-added and stimulate their growth.

---

7. Slovak Republic, Latvia, Lithuania, Romania and Bulgaria.

8. The nature of trade determines the nature of competition between partners and the effects of such competition on employment. The concentration of North African exports in a small number of branches perhaps explains why the Euro-Mediterranean accords – at the end of which the Mediterranean countries must adopt European competition rules – nevertheless still make it possible to apply anti-dumping measures against these countries.

In the last forty years, countries of the South have not on average (with the exception of Asian countries) been able to reduce the income gap relative to the North (Figure 4). Average income per capita in Mediterranean countries remains at about 30% of that of the European Union, with demographic growth compensating for economic growth differences (Appendix 7). At the beginning of the transition, the CEECs suffered a fall in their living standards, which widened the gap with western Europe, bringing them closer to the Mediterranean countries. Since 1992, however, CEECs have begun to catch up: growth per capita in the CEECs has, on average, been faster than in the European Union. In the Americas, the situation is extremely varied. The debt crisis overturned Mexico's catch-up process of the 1970s. The improved situation of the early 1990s was likewise interrupted by the financial crisis of the middle of the decade. In Asia, the northern countries that were catching up with the industrialised countries experienced very fast growth in the 1960s, so that the gap between the North and South widened. Since the beginning of the 1980s, the southern countries have demonstrated dynamic growth, which has permitted them to close the gap with the North. Thus, while the Asian zone is characterised by the greatest spreads in income between North and South, it is also the only zone in which there has been some convergence in living standards for nearly two decades.

The insertion of a developing country in a regional zone is likely to favour its economic catching up. In Asia, such regional integration results from national development strategies and the dynamism of private goods and capital flows. Regional integration has favoured the catching-up of least developed countries. The present crisis, however, highlights the fragility stemming from insufficient regional co-operation, especially in the financial and monetary fields. In other regions, the intensity of economic relations has not been able to ensure catch up. The institutional processes at work today stem from a political decision: one of their objectives is to use the dynamics of regional integration in order to favour the convergence of living standards. In Europe, the convergence of Spain and Portugal towards the living standards of their partners offers the best illustration of the positive effects of integration.

This experience, and in a certain way the counter-example of Greece, make it possible to draw three lessons. The institutional integration of countries with lagging development will only have a positive effect on their growth if it is accompanied by the necessary financing to increase their human and physical capital. Regional measures have a role to play, either directly through financial transfers made from richer to poorer partners, or by favouring private capital flows to the latter. Indeed, capital is all the more likely to flow into such countries if their regional integration is considered sound. From this viewpoint, the perspective of EU membership for the CEECs leads to anticipatory effects which put them in a position that is clearly favourable with respect to the Mediterranean countries. The second lesson is that trade liberalisation and the inflow of capital are not enough to modify the path of growth. This factor is especially important for countries that commit themselves to pursuing (previously limited) liberalisation by joining regional integration processes. Regional integration can only produce dynamic effects if the reforms, which must accompany any opening up of the economy, are accepted politically and socially. Such doubts exist especially with respect to the real commitment of certain Mediterranean countries to the process of liberalisation. An analysis of the Spanish process of catch up highlights the difficulty of reconciling productivity and employment: the catching-up of productivity spontaneously runs counter to the rate of employment (Fayolle, 1996). Employment challenges are likely to persist in countries where the working population will continue growing at a fast rate. From this viewpoint, seeking a resolution to migration issues via the convergence of living standards within regional groupings must therefore not be expected.

BIBLIOGRAPHY

AKAMATSU, K. (1961)
"A theory of unbalanced growth in the world economy", *Volkswirtshaft Archives*, No. 86-2, (first published in Japanese, 1937).

BÉNASSY-QUÉRÉ, A. (1995)
"Ni change fixe, ni change flexible", *La Lettre du CEPII*, No. 133.

BENSIDOUN, I. and CHEVALLIER, A. (1996)
Europe-Méditerranée : le pari de l'ouverture, Economica, Paris.

CHAPONNIÈRE, J.R. and DOURILLE-FEER, E. (1998)
"Le poids de l'économie dans les rapports de puissance en Asie orientale", mimeo.

CHEVALLIER, A., LEMOINE, F. and NAYMAN, L. (1997)
"L'Union européenne et ses voisins de l'Est et du Sud", *La lettre du CEPII*, No. 162, November.

CONTAMIN, R. and LACU, C. (1998)
"Origines et dynamiques de la crise asiatique", *L'année de la régulation*, La Découverte, Paris.

DE MELO, J. and PANAGARIYA, A. (eds.) (1993)
New Dimensions in Regional Integration, Cambridge University Press, Cambridge, MA.

DUVAL, G. (1998)
L'entreprise efficace, à l'heure de Swatch et McDonald's : la seconde vie du taylorisme, Syros, Paris.

FAYOLLE, J. (1996)
"Rattrapage, convergence, intégration : quelques enseignements à partir du cas espagnol", in J. Le Cacheux (ed.), *Europe, la nouvelle vague. Perspectives économiques de l'élargissement*, Presses des sciences politiques, Paris.

FREUDENBERG, M. and LEMOINE, F. (1998)
"Les dix pays candidats et l'Union européenne : l'intégration en marche", *La Lettre du CEPII*, No. 169, June.

FREUDENBERG, M., GAULIER, G. and ÜNAL-KESENCI, D. (1998)
"Regional patterns of international trade", *Economie internationale*, No. 74, 2nd Trimester, pp. 15-41.

GALAL, A. and HOEKMAN, B. (1997)
Regional Partners in Global Markets: Limits and Possibilities of the Euro-Med Agreements, CEPR-ECES, London, Cairo.

GOULD, D.M. (1998)

    "Has NAFTA changed North American trade?", *Economic Review*, Federal Reserve Bank of Dallas, Dallas, 1st Quarter, pp. 12-23.

HOEKMAN, B.and DJANKOV, S. (1995)

    "Catching up with Eastern Europe? The European Union's Mediterranean free trade initiative", CEPR Discussion Paper No. 1 300, November, p. 40.

KRUGMAN, P. (1991)

    Geography and Trade, Gaston Eyskens Lecture Series, MIT Press, Cambridge, MA. and London: Louvain University Press, Louvain, Belgium, pp. xi, 142.

OMAN, C. (1993)

    Globalisation et régionalisation, Development Centre, OECD, Paris.

OMAN, C. (1997)

    "The policy challenges of globalisation and regionalisation", *Migration, Free Trade and Regional Integration in Central and Eastern Europe*, OECD, Paris.

VELTZ, P. (1997)

    "Une organisation géoéconomique à niveaux multiples", *Politique étrangère*, summer.

WORLD BANK (1997)

    Global Economic Prospects and the Developing Countries, Washington, D.C.

Table 1. Relative trade intensity index[1], 1996

Manufactured products

	Europ. Union	Maghreb	Other Med.	CEECs	North NAFTA	South NAFTA	North Asia	South Asia	China
Europ. Union		**2.6**	**1.9**	**2.5**	0.7	0.3	0.7	0.6	0.5
Maghreb	**3.6**		0.7	0.1	0.1	0.0	0.0	0.0	0.0
Other Med.	**2.0**	**2.3**		**1.3**	0.7	0.1	0.3	0.4	0.2
CEECs	**3.0**	0.7	**1.2**		0.2	0.0	0.1	0.1	0.1
North NAFTA	0.9	0.2	0.8	0.1		**4.1**	**1.2**	0.9	0.7
South NAFTA	0.1	0.0	0.0	0.0	**3.7**		0.1	0.1	0.0
North Asia	0.7	0.1	0.4	0.1	**1.3**	0.3		**2.1**	**2.1**
South Asia	0.6	0.2	0.5	0.4	1.0	0.3	**2.1**		**1.8**
China	0.9	0.3	0.3	0.3	**1.4**	0.2	**1.8**	0.8	

1. See Appendix 2.

Source: Authors' calculations from CHELEM database, CEPII.

Table 2. Geographical breakdown of manufactured trade, 1996

North's share in South trade (%)

	South NAFTA	Maghreb	Other Med. countries	CEECs	South Asia
Exports	87.3	79.3	44.7	60.4	24.0
Imports	75.0	79.8	56.5	69.5	38.6

South's share in North trade (%)

	North NAFTA	European Union			North Asia
		Maghreb	Other Med. countries	CEECs	
Exports	7.6	0.8	2.4	3.7	28.8
Imports	8.3	0.5	1.0	2.8	29.8

Source: Authors' calculations from CHELEM database, CEPII.

Table 3 **Currency anchor**

	1990-96	1997-98/06
Canada	Dollar	Dollar
Mexico	Dollar	Dollar
Israel	None	Dollar
Jordan	None	Dollar
Lebanon	None	Dollar
Syria	None	Dollar
Egypt	Dollar	Dollar
Algeria	None	Dollar
Turkey	Dollar	None
Morocco	EMS	EMS
Malta	EMS	EMS
Cyprus	EMS	EMS
Tunisia	EMS	EMS
Bulgaria[1]	None	EMS
Czech Rep.[1]	EMS	EMS
Slovak Rep.[1]	EMS	EMS
Hungary	None	EMS
Poland	None	EMS
Romania	None	None
Hong Kong (China)	Dollar	Dollar
Indonesia	Dollar	None
Korea	Dollar	None
Malaysia	Dollar	None
Philippines	Dollar	None
Singapore	Dollar	None
Thailand	Dollar	None
China	None	Dollar

Note: For countries in bold, calculations were carried out on different periods. Indeed, these countries have experienced currency crises that have forced them to undertake strong corrections. For Mexico the two periods are 1990-94/10 and 1995-98/06, for Turkey 1990-93/12 and 1994/04-98/06, for Bulgaria the last period is 1997/07-98/06 and for Egypt calculation is made on 1991/02-98/06.

1. The first period starts in 1990/12 for Bulgaria and 1993/01 for the Czech and Slovak Republics.

Source: Authors' calculations from IFS, IMF.

Table 4 **Intra-industry index, 1985 and 1996**

	All products		Manufactured products	
	1985	1996	1985	1996
NAFTA North-South	0.48	0.60	0.64	0.65
EU-Mediterranean	0.24	0.36	0.42	0.47
EU-CEECs	0.48	0.65	0.58	0.66
Asia North-South	0.28	0.51	0.49	0.60

Note: The degree of intra-industry trade is calculated on the basis of the Aquino coefficient. This coefficient takes a value of 0 if trade flows are uniquely *inter*-industry, and 1 if trade flows are uniquely *intra*-industry. For details on the definition of the indicator, please refer to Appendix 5.

Source: Authors' calculations from CHELEM database, CEPII.

Figure 1. **Hourly labour costs in textile industry, 1996**

Dollars

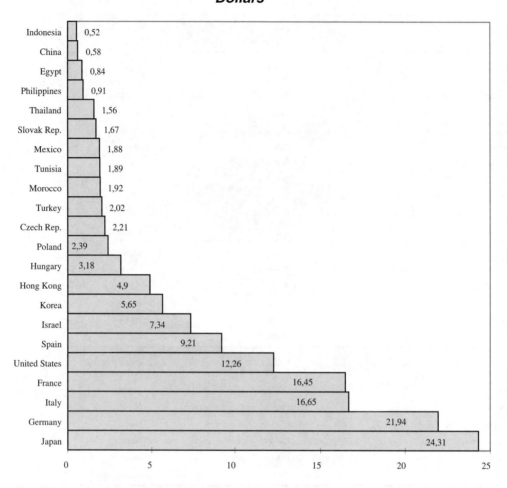

Indonesia 0,52
China 0,58
Egypt 0,84
Philippines 0,91
Thailand 1,56
Slovak Rep. 1,67
Mexico 1,88
Tunisia 1,89
Morocco 1,92
Turkey 2,02
Czech Rep. 2,21
Poland 2,39
Hungary 3,18
Hong Kong 4,9
Korea 5,65
Israel 7,34
Spain 9,21
United States 12,26
France 16,45
Italy 16,65
Germany 21,94
Japan 24,31

Note: Wage and social contributions, May 1996 exchange rate.
Source: Werner International.

Figure 2. **Shares of the different regions in world GDP and population, 1997**

GDP in purchasing power parity

Population

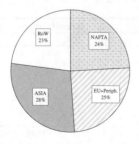

RoW = Rest of World
Source: Authors' calculations from CHELEM database, CEPII.

Figure 3. **North-South regional trade: similarity with extra-regional trade, 1980 and 1996**

Manufactured products

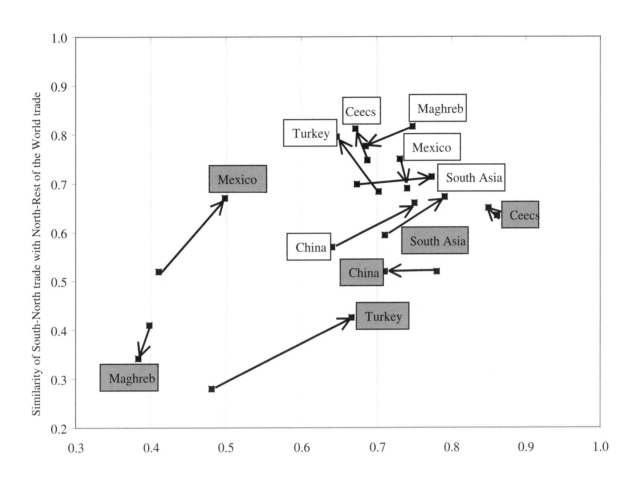

Similarity of South-North trade with South-Rest of the world trade

South exports = North imports ☐ South imports = North exports

Note: The arrow goes from 1980 to 1996. The "South" Asia aggregate excludes China in this figure. For detail on the definition of the indicator, please refer to Annex 6.

Source: Author's calculations from CHELEM database, CEPII.

Figure 4. **GDP per capita of "South" zones, 1960-1997**

In purchasing power parity

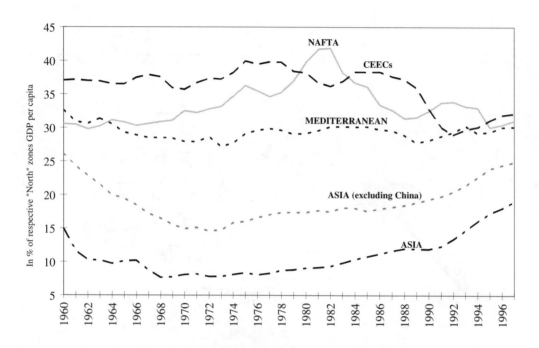

Source: Author's calculations from CHELEM database, CEPII.

	NAFTA	**EUROPEAN UNION –PERIPHERY**		**ASIA**
North	Canada United States	**European Union 15**		Japan Hong Kong (China) Singapore
South	Mexico	**Mediterranean** ***Maghreb*** Algeria Morocco Tunisia ***Other Med.*** Cyprus Egypt Israel Jordan Lebanon Malta Syria Turkey	**CEECs** Bulgaria Hungary Poland Romania Czech Rep. Slovak Rep.	China Korea Indonesia Malaysia Philippines Thailand

Appendix 2. **Relative intensity index**

These indices[9] are used to compare the weight of a country in the trade of a partner country relative to its weight in world trade (W).

It is computed as follows, for exports (X) of i to j (imports of j from i):

$$\frac{Xij}{Xi.} \Big/ \frac{Mj.}{W}$$

and for imports (M) of i from j (exports of j to i) :

$$\frac{Mij}{Mi.} \Big/ \frac{Xj.}{W}$$

Indices equal 1 when bilateral flows are strictly proportional to the weights of both partners in world trade. When the index equals 2, this means that the bilateral flow is twice as intensive as should be allowed for by the partners' weights in world trade alone.

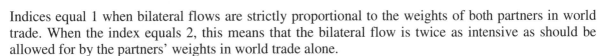

---

9. For further details, see Freudenberg, Gaulier and Ünal-Kesenci (1998), "La régionalisation du commerce international: une évaluation par les intensités relatives bilatérales", CEPII Working Paper n°98-05.

Appendix 3. **Labour force**

Sectoral breakdown, 1990 (*in %*)

	Agriculture	Industry	*Manufactured industry*	Services
United States	2.8	26.0	*17.7*	71.2
Canada	3.4	25.2	*16.2*	71.5
Mexico	27.8	23.7	*15.9*	48.5
Northern Europe	4.8	30.0	*20.8*	65.1
Southern Europe	14.4	32.5	*22.9*	53.1
Western Europe	4.7	33.6	*25.8*	61.8
Eastern Europe	17.5	40.9	*27.5*	41.6
Northern Africa	42.9	21.8	*12.2*	35.3
Turkey	53.4	18.1	*12.0*	28.3
Japan	7.3	34.2	*24.0*	58.5
Korea	18.1	35.6	*27.0*	46.5
Indonesia	55.2	13.6	*10.4*	31.2
Malaysia	27.3	23.1	*16.4*	49.5
Philippines	45.8	15.3	*10.2*	38.9
Thailand	64.1	14.0	*10.1*	22.0
China	72.2	15.1	*11.2*	12.7

Prospects to 2010

	2000	Increase 2000-2010	
	millions	millions	annual growth (in %)
United States	143	11.5	0.77
Canada	16	1.0	0.6
Mexico	41	10.0	2.21
Northern Europe	48	-0.2	-0.05
Southern Europe	66	-0.5	-0.08
Western Europe	88	0.6	0.07
Eastern Europe	160*	0.8**	0.05
Northern Africa	66	21.8	2.9
Turkey	32	6.0	1.76
Japan	68	-1.6	-0.24
Korea	24	1.3	1.02
Indonesia	103	22.7	2.00
Malaysia	9	2.9	2.74
Philippines	32	8.5	2.42
Thailand	37	3.0	0.80
China	765	61.7	0.78

* Russian Federation =78 million; ** Russian Federation = 0.360 million.

Source: International Labor Office, Economically Active population 1950-2010, Stat Working Papers n° 96-2.

Appendix 4. **Currency anchor**

The degree of nominal anchor is measured by standard deviations of monthly exchange rate changes (in logarithm). This volatility, computed against benchmark currency i, is called σ_i. The three benchmark currencies are dollar, yen and deutsche mark, the latter being the core of the EMS. The analysis of exchange rates, in changes and not in levels, makes it possible to account for crawling-peg regimes as well as nominal anchor regimes based on a currency or a basket. The relative volatility of the exchange rate is computed by dividing the relative volatility σ_i by total volatility against the three currencies:

$$\lambda_i = \frac{\sigma_i}{\left(\sigma_\$ + \sigma_y + \sigma_{DM}\right)}.$$

The currency considered should belong to the anchor zone i (dollar, mark or yen) if λ_i is below 0.25. If no λ_i is less than 0.25, it is possible to conclude that none of the three reference currencies was used as a nominal anchor (this does not exclude an anchor based on a currency basket).

Source: Bénassy-Quéré (1995) «Ni change fixe, ni change flexible», *La Lettre du CEPII No. 133*, March.

Appendix 5. **Aquino coefficient**

The Aquino coefficient is a similarity index measuring the structures of bilateral trade between two countries by products. It is computed as follows :

$$1 - 0.5 * \sum_k \left(\left| \frac{X_{i,j}^k}{X_{i,j}^\bullet} - \frac{X_{j,i}^k}{X_{j,i}^\bullet} \right| \right)$$

where k is the product, i and j the countries and $\bullet$ all countries or products.

The indicator takes a value between 0 and 1. A value of 0.48 means that 48% of bilateral trade is in the same branch. The value of the indicator is sensitive to the degree of classificatory detail. Data used for calculating the indicator are from the CHELEM database which breaks down its analyses into 71 categories of products.

Appendix 6. **Similarity of regional trade with extra-regional trade**

Each point on Figure 3 has for coordinates:

| South exports = North imports | South imports = North exports |

in abscissa :

$$SIM_i = 1 - 0.5 * \sum_k \left(\left| \frac{X^k_{i,j}}{X^{\bullet}_{i,j}} - \frac{X^k_{i,(\bullet-j)}}{X^{\bullet}_{i,(\bullet-j)}} \right| \right) \qquad SIM_i = 1 - 0.5 * \sum_k \left(\left| \frac{M^k_{i,j}}{M^{\bullet}_{i,j}} - \frac{M^k_{i,(\bullet-j)}}{M^{\bullet}_{i,(\bullet-j)}} \right| \right)$$

in ordinate :

$$SIM_j = 1 - 0.5 * \sum_k \left(\left| \frac{M^k_{j,i}}{M^{\bullet}_{j,i}} - \frac{M^k_{j,(\bullet-i)}}{M^{\bullet}_{i,(\bullet-i)}} \right| \right) \qquad SIM_j = 1 - 0.5 * \sum_k \left(\left| \frac{X^k_{j,i}}{X^{\bullet}_{j,i}} - \frac{X^k_{j,(\bullet-i)}}{X^{\bullet}_{i,(\bullet-i)}} \right| \right)$$

with i the south zone or country, j the corresponding north zone, k the product and $\bullet$ all countries or products. The regional flow is the same in abscissa and in ordinate:

$$\left(\frac{X^k_{i,j}}{X^{\bullet}_{i,j}} = \frac{M^k_{j,i}}{M^{\bullet}_{j,i}} \text{ and } \frac{M^k_{i,j}}{M^{\bullet}_{i,j}} = \frac{X^k_{j,i}}{X^{\bullet}_{j,i}} \right).$$

Appendix 7. **GDP and population growth (in percentages)**

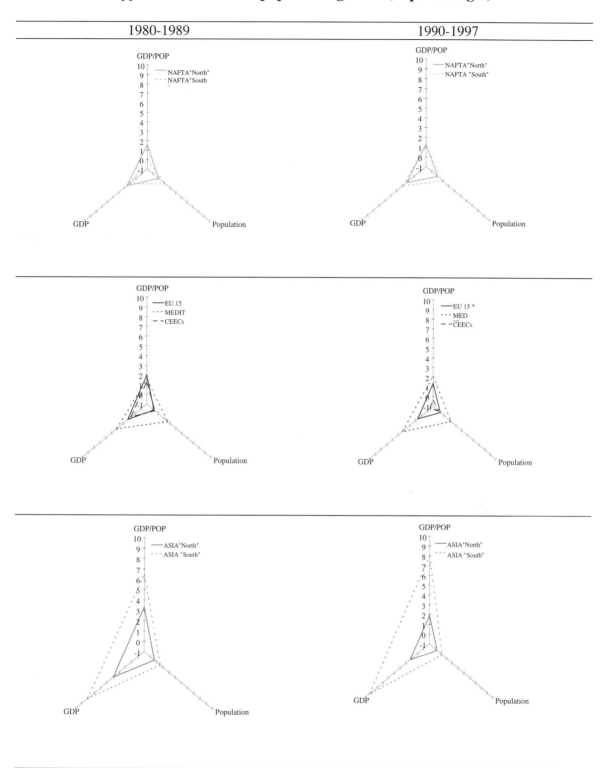

* For the European Union, growth rates are calculated for 1992-1997, after German reunification.

Source: Author's calculations from CHELEM database, CEPII.

Comments on the paper by
Isabelle Bensidoun and *Agnès Chevallier*

by
Yasushi Iguchi
Kwansei-Gakuin University, Japan

The authors' efforts to quantitatively indicate the characteristics of major groups of regional integration, especially those of the North-South relations, seem to be successful to a certain extent. However, the indicators adopted in the paper are not necessarily sufficient to make meaningful inter-regional comparisons and to offer a basis for discussions of regional development and international migration.

Indicators such as those concerning foreign direct investment, employment and labour force as well as labour mobility should be included in addition to the intra-industry-index, similarity with extra-regional trade and relative GDP per capita of "South" zones. This argument is justified due to the more complicated nature of de-facto regional integration compared to the primarily trade-related definitions in traditional economic theories and inter-national laws

The interpretation of the indicators should be made in a more cautious manner. For example, even when we talk about growing trade intensity in a region, there are some industrial sectors like computers, whose industrial location is targeting the world market rather than regional markets. The indicators of the narrowing income gaps between the "North" and the "South" in East Asia is misleading, as the income gap between the highest and the lowest local average income has been widening in the past decade in countries like Thailand, the Philippines and China. This may imply growing migration pressures, which differs from the implication drawn from lowering income gaps within the region.

Finally, although the paper should be of a technical nature, the authors could have stressed the need for more policy-oriented approaches in undertaking inter-regional comparisons, covering not only the North-American and European experiences, but also Asian experiences.

CAN ONE REALLY TALK OF THE GLOBALISATION OF MIGRATION FLOWS?

by
Georges Tapinos
Institut d'Études politiques (IEP) and Institut national d'Études démographiques (INED)
and
Daniel Delaunay
Institut français de Recherche en Coopération pour le Développement (ORSTOM)

1. Introduction

Do statistics on migration flows of the past three decades (1965-95) support the contention that there has been a globalisation of international migration? And what role does international migration play in economic globalisation?

Economists generally explain the globalisation process in terms of higher growth rates for foreign trade than for national products, sharp increases in capital movements (cross-flows of direct investment and short-term capital flows), internationalisation of production processes and, ultimately, economic integration of countries of the same region. The increasing importance of these traditional aspects of trade between nations is now interpreted as constituting a change in the nature of the international economic system. But beyond quantitative changes, the truly new development is the transformation of patterns of trade and productive systems. Krugman (1995) identifies four key elements: inter-branch trade, dispersion of production process across a number of sites, the emergence of economies highly oriented to international trade and the increase in the absolute and relative value of exports from new low-wage industrialised countries. For his part, Kébadjian (1998) makes a key distinction between internationalisation and globalisation – the former being a process by which the consolidation of national areas goes hand in hand with growth in international trade, while the latter is a process of breaking down national areas accompanied by greater international integration of productive systems.

What role does international migration play in these developments? The first difficulty is to define, measure and describe what is meant by the globalisation of migration. As an initial rough definition, it can be described as a rise in the number of immigrants: the absolute and relative stock of persons born outside their country of residence, and the appearance of new flows that indicate a diversification of destinations for sending countries and of the countries of origin of immigrants for receiving countries. But it is possible that the globalisation of migration, like the globalisation of trade in goods and services and capital movements, may be more a structural transformation of the process than a mere increase in flows. If true, four new structural indicators need examination: *i*) the fact that some countries are both emigration and immigration countries, *ii*) the existence of temporary labour migration that results in households with bases in two countries, *iii*) the fact that a small number of countries play a preponderant role in the global migration system and *iv*) the growing incentive to emigrate in new countries in economic transition. But while countries have implemented policies to promote trade and capital flows, they have also reinforced their control over migration movements.[1] After defining the scope and limitations of the statistical exercise (Section 2), the investigation will analyse the available data, which show that there was no trend towards the globalisation of migration movements in the period considered (Section 3).

The second difficulty is to show the links between migration trends and economic globalisation (Section 4). The analysis will first determine whether this lack of connection between migration and globalisation can be explained by temporary factors, given the short observation period. It will then examine the structural links between the two phenomena. In the case of migration, globalisation means two, and to some extent opposing, things. It may be viewed as the necessary complementarity between movements of persons and flows of capital and goods or, conversely, as an alternative to the international movement of workers. In the first case, globalisation would lead to the growth and diversification of migration flows, while in the second it would result in movements of goods and capital substituting migration, with the result that free trade would lessen the need for regional or international migration.

2.   Definitions and measurements

Any examination of international migration trends worldwide must deal with a series of statistical and methodological difficulties, namely, how should the phenomenon be defined and what is the scope of available statistics?

a)   *The definition of international migration*

The first difficulty is to identify the variable "international migration" – to isolate a specific category of movements among the many forms of mobility. The definition of international migration is based on two types of criteria: descriptive and analytical.

International migrants are defined as persons who cross a border, change their place of residence and have a foreign nationality at the time of entry in the country of immigration. All three of these criteria are necessary, but there are nevertheless cases in which these distinctions are not clear-cut. For example, political borders may separate homogeneous national or ethnic groups, as is frequently the case in Central America or Africa. In these cases, international migration cannot be analysed separately from internal mobility. Change of residence does not apply in the case of short-term labour migration in which other members of the household remain based in the home country. This applies to a significant proportion of international migration in Western Europe, Mexican workers in the United States and labour migration in the Gulf States. It is essential to bear in mind that migrants are both immigrants and foreigners when analysing the process by which they decide to emigrate, the socio-economic impact of migration and migration's role in globalisation. International immigrants are generally foreigners when they arrive in the host country, but there are frequent exceptions. For example, repatriated settlers from Algeria in France, *Aussiedler* in Germany and Pontine Greeks in Greece are immigrants but not foreigners. All foreigners, however, are not immigrants: this is the case of the children of immigrants who are born in the country of immigration but keep their nationality of origin. On the other hand, there are immigrants who have acquired the nationality of the host country through naturalisation or marriage.

---

1.   With the exception, to a certain extent, of the European Union, which allows the free intra-Community movement of EU nationals only, which will increase with the introduction of the single currency.

The importance of the distinction between the legal criterion of nationality (nationals/foreigners) and the demographic criterion for migrants (foreign born/native born) depends on the migration regime. The contrasting of two regimes will help clarify this distinction. The first is characteristic of countries that have an explicit immigration policy, often settlement countries such as the United States, Canada and Australia, which accept and often encourage the migration and settlement of foreigners. In these countries, a distinction is made between "foreign born" and "native born". On the other hand, there are labour immigration countries, such as the European countries, which have generally considered immigration as a temporary phenomenon, even though many immigrants ultimately settle in the country. In these countries, a distinction is made between foreigners and nationals, and these distinctions are reflected in migration statistics.

The investigation will retain three analytical criteria: reasons for emigrating, distance involved and length of stay. A distinction is traditionally made between migration for political and for economic reasons. There are cases in which this distinction is perfectly clear, but there are others in which the dividing line between political and economic factors is largely determined by the institutional and political context. For example, the country of immigration defines who qualifies for refugee status, and the United States long gave refugee status to Cubans, but not to Haitians. Likewise, when there are restrictions on the entry of workers, would-be immigrants have no choice but to file a request for asylum. This is what has taken place in Europe since borders were officially closed to immigration in 1973-74. The distinction between economic and political migrants only partly coincides with the distinction between freely chosen migration and involuntary migration. The distance of migration has also been introduced into the classification of migration, but it is necessary to determine what type of distance is involved. The criterion of physical distance used in the initial models must be "adjusted" to account for the means and costs of transport, and even the concept of cultural and ethnic "distance". The third criterion, that of the length of the stay or absence (actual or anticipated), is essential to the analysis of migration, but unfortunately the necessary data are generally lacking.

b)   *Measuring international migration*

The comparison of data of sending and receiving countries should theoretically make it possible to provide a double-entry accounting framework. This, however, is far from being the case, because the origin/destination matrix of international migration is very incomplete and thereby seriously limits the ability to analyse the globalisation of migration. It is also important to add that the different data recording methods used may measure flows or stocks, migrants or migration, gross or net migration, which further limits the possibility of making comparisons (see Table 1).

Statistics on stocks of immigrants and foreigners

The most complete and homogeneous measurement of international migration over the past thirty years worldwide is the data on immigrants and/or foreigners provided by censuses or population registers. These statistics are gathered in the database established by the United Nations Population Division, which provides estimates for identical dates (midway[2] between the most common census periods). For some countries, however, the interpolations or extrapolations are based on only one or two measurements, which are sometimes not consecutive; which means that the estimates are on the whole significantly more accurate at the beginning of the period (for 1965 and 1975).

---

2.   1 January 1965, 1975, 1985 and 1990.

The diversity of the sources used for this database gives rise to a number of difficulties. Three of them affect the ability to analyse the phenomenon under study.

–   The coverage is not homogeneous throughout the world, since all countries do not have the same number of censuses, and some (29 countries) only took a single census[3] during the period. A number of countries (including major countries, such as China and the former USSR) have no migration statistics whatsoever.[4] In general, information is fuller in developed countries, and also in Latin America.

–   Countries do not use an identical definition of international migration. In most cases (142 countries out of 216), place of birth is the defining factor, and foreign-born persons are counted. Nationality is used in 19% of countries that produce statistics on foreigners. This does not include naturalised immigrants, nationals born abroad and, above all, the children of foreigners born in the host country who keep their nationality of origin.

–   The case of refugees poses a problem: should they be included in the study of globalisation? This problem, however, is insoluble because refugees are recorded differently in different regions. Foreigners who have been granted the right of asylum are implicitly counted in censuses, making it impossible to distinguish them from other immigrants,[5] which in turn means that it is impossible to exclude them. Refugees in camps, on the other hand, particularly in Africa, do not seem to be taken into account. The Population Division found it preferable to add the statistics of the High Commissariat for Refugees (UNHCR) and the UNWRA[6] to the estimates for developing countries. This statistical option raises a dilemma: either the refugees assisted by the High Commissariat are taken into account, which is the more rigorous approach, but in doing so one introduces a bias into the interpretation of the "globalisation" of migration, or else they are excluded for developing countries only. This latter solution was retained.

Immigration flow statistics

Statistics on inflows of foreigners into host countries raise the same definitional problems; they also require a more sophisticated statistical system, which explains the low coverage in this regard. The statistics collected by OECD Continuous Reporting System on Migration, known under its French acronym SOPEMI, include more countries (14 rather than 8), while those of the Population Division of the United Nations cover a longer period (starting in the 1960s and the 1940s for some countries).

While the use of census data makes it possible to establish relatively consistent statistics on stocks, this is not the case for the estimate of inflows, which is based on a wide range of incompatible

---

3.   The estimates, therefore, assume that the relative size of their population remained stable during the period, unless well-known changes have taken place, as in Nigeria.

4.   They are mostly low-immigration communist countries. In these situations where statistics are totally lacking, the estimate is obtained by applying the following formula: $F = 0.345(P)/\exp(\log 10P-2)$ where P is the total population of the country and F is the international stock of migrants.

5.   In these countries, asylum seekers who obtain refugee status are obviously counted, but this is a flow statistic (annual entries under this status) which does not give information on the total number of refugees in a country.

6.   United Nations Relief and Works Agency for Palestinian Refugees in the Near East.

sources, such as population registers,[7] statistics on residence or work permits issued and migration data collected at borders. This diversity is made even more complex by the fact that different criteria are used to distinguish immigrants from ordinary visitors. In countries of settlement immigration, statistics distinguish between immigrants and non-immigrants at the time of entry. But most OECD countries grant an initial entry for a limited duration in the form of a permit that is renewable after an extensive stay in the country. There are numerous exceptions to both these systems, such as temporary entry, granted to seasonal workers or to staff of subsidiaries, to facilitate transfers and also to asylum seekers. When a temporary residence permit is the norm, some categories qualify for permanent residence, such as refugees admitted under quotas and certain minorities and family members of permanent residents. European nationals are also a special case, for they have the right to move freely, and are not recorded in residence permit registers unless they file a request to be included.

Some countries adopt specific statistical treatment for certain groups of foreigners. *Foreigners in irregular situations* are obviously not counted, except at the time of regularisation procedures, which have been implemented only by a few countries. Registering large numbers of them at once under such a procedure introduces a bias into time series; the same is true of family reunifications, which occur soon afterwards. *Refugees and asylum seekers* are not uniformly recorded. In some countries, they are registered in the annual entry statistics at the time of their arrival, while in others they are recorded when their application is accepted. Refugees could be counted separately in the flow statistics of developed countries, but this would be in contradiction with the information made available by statistics on stocks.

Emigration statistics by stocks and flows

Emigration statistics, which measure outflows or estimates of expatriate populations, are generally very incomplete if not non-existent. Countries that maintain a population register should theoretically be able to measure outflows, but the double registration system used to record internal mobility is lacking and, in addition, the country of destination is unknown. It is therefore necessary to use the data collected by those countries of destination that record the nationality or place of birth of immigrants. To these reservations must be added the element of uncertainty about nationality when it is declared by those concerned, as is the case in a census, particularly for individuals who have acquired the nationality of the country or for the children of immigrants born there.

SOPEMI databases provide the countries of origin for immigrants in some OECD or EU countries. But the statistics they contain only cover part of the 1980s, through the middle of the present decade. The origin of immigrants to the United States, however, is known for the entire history of modern international migration. The investigation has been able to reconstitute this information since 1850 from census samples (Ruggles and Sobek *et al.*, 1997). A portion of *emigration flows* can also be recovered through the administrative statistics on inflows in selected OECD host countries, including the United States. The procedures used to collect these statistics – issuance of immigration visas or work or residence permits – ensure that the declarations of nationality or place of birth are more reliable, though they are rarely exhaustive.

The nature of available data makes it difficult to determine whether there has been a globalisation of migration. To this must be added the lack of knowledge of the statistical magnitude of illegal migration and the absence of data on stocks after 1990. It would be advisable to review some of the choices taken by concern for the coherence required when making international comparisons. In

---

7.   Most of the OECD countries contributing to SOPEMI do not have a population register: Australia, Canada, Mexico and the United States outside Europe, and France, Greece, Ireland, Portugal, the United Kingdom and Turkey.

the United States for example, temporary workers are registered separately from immigrants and are therefore excluded from our analysis despite a regular and large growth in their numbers over the period under review.[8] A relative increasing importance of labour mobility could well be a structural indicator of a globalisation process. What is more, this study was not able to cover all migration systems at this stage, in particular those of the Arab world, West Africa and the Pacific, due to lack of comparable data. A more detailed analysis over a longer period can only be made for the United States, which has census samples dating back to 1850.[9]

3.   Has there been a globalisation of international migration?

a)   An overview of international migration worldwide

An overview of international migration is provided in two maps (see Map 1 and Map 2) illustrating the migration statistics analysed. The first map, based on data of the United Nations Population Division (UN, 1995), shows the stock of foreign or immigrant population worldwide in 1990. Absolute stocks are represented by squares proportional in size to the foreign population; relative proportions are calculated in relation to the native population of the host country, which explains why some figures are higher than 100%. This, incidentally, makes it possible to point out countries that do not have reliable statistics on migration flows – mainly former communist bloc countries. The overview shows the high level of specialisation of some countries, ultimately few in number, that account for a large majority of migrants. While the second map uses flow statistics, measured at the time of entry, of several countries selected by SOPEMI, it shows the countries of origin of these flows. Proportions of emigrants are calculated in relation to the initial total population (native and foreign). Absolute stocks are illustrated by symbols. This map provides a partial measurement of emigration flows to some developed countries around 1992 and shows that emigration countries are located in proximity to Europe, the United States, Japan and Australia. It does not however show internal movements within Africa, Latin America and much of Asia. Its main advantage is that it presents the flow statistics used in this work.

b)   Has global mobility increased?

Trends by stocks of immigrants

Have the stock and proportion of immigrants or foreigners risen? Between 1965 and 1990, the stock of immigrants increased from 47 to 57 million in developing countries and from 30.2 to 54 million in developed countries.[10] This represents a very slight decrease in terms of the percentage of the total population for the developing countries (1.51% compared to 1.76%) and a significant increase for developed countries (5.89% compared with 3.94%) (see Table 2). Europe has become the region

---

8.   In 1994, temporary workers numbered 185 988 following a steady increase since 1981. They represent nearly one-quarter of the immigrant population, but, as they are not deemed to settle, it is supposed that their incidence on the growth of stocks is minor.

9.   An initial use of these data to place the contemporary phase of globalisation in a historical context has not been presented here because it is impossible to account for the other countries.

10.   Unless otherwise stated, the data in this paragraph are taken from the international migration data set of the Population Division of the United Nations, which gives an estimate of the number of immigrants or foreigners in each country for the middle of the last three decades (last updated in 1990).

with the largest stock and the highest proportional increase (from 3.3% in 1965 to over 5% in 1990), while North America and naturally Australia and New Zealand remained the regions of the world with the largest proportion of foreign-born residents. The relative proportion of immigrants in 1990 was almost exactly the same as 25 years earlier (2.28%) after a substantial drop in 1975. These figures include refugees in developing countries,[11] a stock that has grown sharply; the 1.4 million refugees counted in 1965 have increased ten-fold. These involuntary movements tend to be unstable, and are sometimes accompanied by return movements as soon as the conflict that caused them subsides or is resolved. Since these movements are not directly related to the global economic system, they can justifiably be excluded from comparison. In this case, the relative proportion of migrants worldwide seems to have fallen only very slightly in 1990. The drop would have been even greater if it had been possible to isolate refugees in developed countries, but this figure is unknown. In interpreting these downward trends, one must also consider two factors: the fact that some immigrants have acquired the nationality of host countries in those countries where the estimate is based on the criterion of nationality, and the varying degree to which illegal immigrants are included in statistics. That these two kinds of data tend to offset each other may lead to the conclusion that there has been no significant rise in international migration, at least in terms of stocks over the entire period.

This general conclusion does not, of course, hold true for all countries. What then are the geographical patterns of these trends between 1965 and 1990? Map 3 indicates the absolute variations in the stock of immigrants or foreigners between 1965 and 1990, not including refugees counted in developing countries. It shows the main regional poles of migration: North America, Australia, Western Europe, the oil-producing countries of the Middle East and the Ivory Coast. Although it reveals that one country is predominant within a migration system (such as the United States or Germany), it also suggests that there is greater interaction among countries in the same region. The second conclusion that can be drawn from these geographical patterns is the stability of the stock of immigrants worldwide observed earlier, which is concentrated in countries that exerted a strong force of attraction during the prosperity of the post-war period and above all the 1970s. Correlative variations between the stock of international migrants and economic indicators confirm this, as does the key impact of the size of existing immigrant populations, which leads to the arrival of additional migrants. This inertia, which is due to a number of factors (see below), is a decisive component of the stability of migration flows.

Trends in terms of flows

Is this stationary trend, deduced from the analysis of stocks, confirmed by statistics on flows?

The trend of inflows in fourteen countries analysed by SOPEMI, on the contrary, shows a significant rise, but with strong fluctuations (see Chart 1). Between 1980 and 1990, inflows rose by approximately 75%, following a low point in 1983 when inflows of foreigners or immigrants were only three-quarters of the 1980 total. Between this low (1983) and the high of the series (1991), the flow increased by a factor of 2.7; but, after subsequently dropping by the same magnitude in 1995,[12] it returned to a level only 20% higher than that in 1980. No generalisations may be drawn from the analysis of this non-representative subset (but which nevertheless encompasses 45% of immigrants worldwide) over a period of only 10 years, during which no regular trend is apparent. The unusual nature of these statistics is clear in Table 3, which shows the trend of both the stock of immigrants (for 1980-90) and mobility as measured by inflows of foreigners. For this group of countries, contrary to

---

11.　Except for developing countries that count them in the "asylum seekers" category.

12.　A year for which statistics are lacking for Denmark.

what is observed for the world as a whole, the number of foreigners is rising constantly and steadily. The impression of a more regular progression is mainly due to the ten-year interval of censuses or revised statistics on stocks.[13]

A more detailed comparison of stocks and flows, though for a more limited number of countries, is possible by using UN statistics containing longer series. The comparison of variations in the stock of foreigners with total inflows during two periods (1975-85 and 1985-89) is shown in Table 4. Minor discrepancies are to be expected due to the nature of the statistics collected from different countries,[14] but the main discrepancy arises as a result of the more fundamental difference between migrants and migration. High mobility does not necessarily mean that an equivalent number of migrants settle in the host country, if only because some return to their country of origin or because there are substantial movements towards other destinations. The comparison reveals significant differences between countries and clearly shows the distinction between two migration systems. In the United States, the increase in the stock of foreign-born persons almost matches the total number of immigrants registered upon entry, and the same is true of Australia. The indicator is higher for Canada which, to some extent, acts as an entry point to the United States. In Europe, however, the ratio between inflows and variations of stocks is higher, as a result of the migration system.[15] There is a slight increase in the ratio of inflows to stocks from one period to the next (from 1.77 to 1.84). This, however, is not significant given the inaccuracy of these measurements.

c)   *Has there been a diversification of international mobility?*

Having observed that the proportion of immigrants worldwide has remained stable, it is important to determine whether there has not been a change in their distribution. A greater diversification of migratory movements can be interpreted as a sign of globalisation of migration; more countries have become either emigration or host countries. But in addition to measurement difficulties that arise when evaluating trends, the problem of choosing and interpreting the dispersion index also comes to the fore. In fact, four types of change are conceivable, depending on whether one views the problem from the standpoint of countries of destination or countries of origin or an increase or decrease in the number of countries. When both emigration and immigration countries are more evenly distributed or more numerous, the global expansion of migration becomes evident. On the other hand, if the number of countries has fallen or if flows have become concentrated on a few countries, this would clearly mean that the opposite is true. But a concentration of outflows (or a reduction in the number of sending countries) combined with a dispersion of inflows (or an increase in the number of receiving countries) does not allow for a clear diagnosis. The same is true for the "symmetrical" situation – a dispersion of host countries and a concentration of sending countries.

The criterion for the number of countries participating in international migration also poses difficulties, since some countries are listed simply because of demographic growth and because more detailed statistics suddenly take this into account. What is more, the number of immigrants in countries at the low end of the distribution is negligible but virtually all countries are represented. This

---

13.   At least for some of the countries that do not maintain population registers on which to base these estimates; but the Population Division has converted more frequent measurements to five or ten-year periods.

14.   Based on place of birth or nationality, using population registers or censuses, according to criteria for differentiating between inflows of immigrants and tourists, and lastly because of gaps specific to each source.

15.   With the single exception of the Netherlands, probably because of their population register system, which measures inflows better, with poor coverage of outflows.

is why a diagnosis based on dispersion is more rigorous. It uses the relative cumulated distribution by rank (a classification based on the stock of migrants or migration) which does not take geographical location into account. A curve tending to the asymptotes indicates a concentration of immigrants in certain countries, while a distribution converging to the diagonal shows a trend towards a more even distribution.

The distribution of migrants among host countries was determined based on the trend of the stock of immigrants between 1965 and 1990 (UN data) and on the distribution of inflows into certain countries based on flow statistics (SOPEMI, 1980-95 and/or UN, 1960-95 data). Two sources were used for the distribution of nationalities or the origin of migrants: data on the origin of immigrants in the United States between 1965 and 1990, and data on the country of origin of flows towards the countries selected by SOPEMI between 1980 and 1995.

The distribution of migrants among host countries

Statistics on stocks suggest that migrants are very unevenly distributed among host countries. In 1990, the United States alone had 18.7% of the total worldwide immigrant or foreign population. The first seven countries account for half of the total of foreigners, and 80% are concentrated in the first 27 countries.

What was the trend in distribution between 1965 and 1990? First of all, it changed relatively little. The changes are so slight that the lines of the different curves in the graph are hardly distinguishable. To try to separate them using traditional indicators seems an even less promising endeavour since these curves intersect a number of times at the beginning of the distribution. To show this trend more clearly, Chart 2 shows the deviations between the cumulated distributions at each date compared to 1965. Positive values show a concentration in countries that precede (which are the largest, because the accumulation starts with the largest contributions), while negative values show a redistribution in countries that follow. Overall, a trend towards a more even dispersion emerges that points to a "globalisation" of international migration. This observation must however be tempered by three complementary observations that limit its significance.

– First, the change is irregular. The United States' contribution goes up by more than 5 points, but that of countries immediately following decreases, while the contribution of the next group of countries rises so that, by the tenth-ranked country, the leeway has been accounted for, leading to a further intersection of the cumulated curves. This trend towards a more even distribution is subsequently confirmed, but concerns those countries that make only a small contribution to migration, accounting for approximately one-third of total immigrants. This means that for two-thirds of immigrants, who emigrate to the top-ten countries, it is impossible to identify a trend towards or away from globalisation.

– The pattern of changes observed over the period is virtually set during the first decade, from 1965 to 1975. This trend continues over the next fifteen years, but remains very slight. The mid-1970s were a decisive period when some countries implemented barriers to immigrant entry and the economic situation in virtually all countries was unfavourable to the use of immigrant labour.

– The trend towards a greater dispersion of immigrants seems to be more pronounced when including refugees counted in developing countries. But this trend cannot be verified in developed countries (see above).

Distribution trends based on flow statistics can be analysed for a small number of countries only (those selected for SOPEMI statistics) and for a shorter period of time than for stocks (see Chart 3). This list does not include all the leading countries in terms of the distribution of immigrant stocks (India and Pakistan are absent). But the three main countries in terms of inflows at each date are still the United States, Germany and Japan. Only afterwards does the classification change. This series has the advantage of covering the years subsequent to 1990, when major changes in the volume of flows occurred. It is precisely as of this date that the distribution begins to change, but towards a higher concentration in the leading countries. This recent trend invalidates, for a short period, the hypothesis that a more even distribution of international mobility and thus of globalisation are occurring.

The distribution of migrants by nationality or country of origin

To address the question of the dispersion of nationalities or countries of origin, it is first necessary to determine whether a broadening of the geographical range of inflows to immigration countries has taken place. A situation of complete globalisation would mean, for example, that all countries would participate in globalisation in proportion to their demographic size (or to another criterion), though a migratory "specialisation" on the part of some countries will lead to an unequal distribution. But in the case of emigration, the difficulty arises from the lack of information on outflows or departure stocks. It is therefore necessary to reconstitute the origin of departures in several developed OECD receiving countries. The result is an incomplete and probably one-sided picture of the dispersion of emigration countries.

A useful distinction must initially be made between developed countries and others. Statistics on immigration countries show that there has been a greater increase in the number of emigrants from the Third World than from developed countries. This is particularly true for settlement countries as shown in Table 5.

Since SOPEMI data are considerably less accurate for sending countries, the eight countries included in UN data during 1965-90 will be analysed.[16] A distinction will be made between settlement countries (Australia, Canada and the United States) and European countries (Belgium, Germany, Sweden, the Netherlands and the United Kingdom) (see Chart 4 and Chart 5).

Inflows into the first group of countries follow a trend that confirms the previous observations about them, including the growing participation of lower-ranking regions – a broader global distribution of flows. But this trend soon stops, during the 1970s. The same occurs in European countries somewhat later, since the cumulated frequencies only stabilise around 1975. This seems to confirm the slowdown in the trend towards a more even global distribution of flows.

In light of the caution required, as a result of the lack of precision of measurements and definitions, how should these new statistics be interpreted? From the only "global" perspective possible (the stock of foreigners), it is true that the population of immigrants is distributed more evenly, although its relative size is diminishing. But this conclusion does not hold true for the leading countries, including the foremost among them, the United States, which gained five percentage points of the total. This is primarily due to the attraction exerted by established migrants, particularly with regard to family reunification. Inflow movements, which are known for each year for some countries, give a picture of migration trends "in real time". Among the developed countries for which flow statistics are known, there is a significant concentration of immigrants in the leading countries (United

---

16. Before and after these dates, some receiving countries did not provided details on flows for all regions of origin.

States, Germany and Japan). Immigrants once came from a broad range of countries, which initiated a movement of globalisation that stabilised in the 1970s. Since then, the profile of flows by nationality of origin has remained stationary.

In the final analysis, one can conclude without hesitation that the globalisation of international migration is not borne out by the statistics, even though the comparison of stocks and flows may leave some doubt in this regard. This investigation has shown that the divergence between the two trends was explained by the different capacity to retain immigrant inflows. On the one hand, there are European countries that retain a moderate proportion of the flows of immigrants that cross their borders and, on the other, there are settlement countries (United States, Canada, Australia) that retain virtually all the immigrants who enter.

The world map of the variations of stock that traces the major regional migration systems is particularly interesting in the light of this significant imbalance in flow and stock trends, for it shows that immigrants now seem attracted to regions rather than specific countries. A country that is a strong pole of attraction for migration has an impact on its neighbours, which apparently receive larger inflows.

4. Migration, regionalisation and globalisation

The descriptive approach followed thus far, based on available statistics, has demonstrated that the claims about the globalisation of international migration are unfounded. Migration processes in the past three decades have not witnessed the same level of growth as trade in goods and services and capital flows. The fact that migration seems to be an exception to the process of economic globalisation can be explained in two ways: either the observation period is too short for the demographic, economic and political contexts to have produced their full effect, or the diverse and opposing effects of the interaction between migration and globalisation make it impossible to identify a clear-cut trend.

a) Long-term trends and temporary effects

To what extent should changes in the determining factors of international migration between 1965 and 1995 be considered temporary? Can the absence of the globalisation of migration be explained by the fact that the observation period is too short? Four series of factors can explain the stationary trend observed in international migration: *i*) the effect of inertia stemming from the stock of immigrants and the dynamics of the migration process; *ii*) the differential trend of demographic indicators depending on the phase of transition; *iii*) possible diverging economic trends between developed countries and countries in the initial stages of their economic transition; and *iv*) the impact of migration policies.

The major immigration countries have a large and long-established foreign population. A close relationship exists between the total stock and the increase in the number of immigrants or foreigners, which reflects the inertia of flows created by foreigners' fellow countrymen already established in the host country. The analysis of immigrant flows to the United States by country of origin shows that there is a strong statistical correlation between flows and stocks of foreigners of the same origin (Yang, 1995 for 1982-86; Kritz, 1996 for 1989-93). Channels of migration contribute to this inertia, which is specific to the dynamics of the migration process, but an even more important factor is the right of residence associated with family reunification, or the birth of foreign children in countries where *jus solis* does not prevail. Throughout the period under consideration, the relative share of subsequent family migration rose. If labour flows could be isolated, it is probable that the slowdown of migration after the mid-1970s would be even more visible.

The various regions of the world are in different phases of demographic transition. The end of the transition period is marked by a convergence of demographic indicators, which is the case in virtually all European countries. On the other hand, a greater dispersion of fertility and mortality indicators is observed both at the national and international level at the beginning of the transition period. This leads to differentials in demographic growth that worsen the imbalances and increase the probability of emigration; this is the case, *inter alia*, in Asia, Central and South America and to a lesser extent Africa. The political instability and armed conflicts that have marked the history of many countries in recent decades also increase the likelihood of emigration. But the fact remains that these factors, although they may increase or decrease the likelihood of migration, are rarely the determining causes of international mobility.

The decisive variables are more of an economic nature. The main factors behind international migration are the differentials of anticipated income and the cost of travel (and particularly of transport), and, on the part of receiving countries, firms' demand for labour. Here again, there is a difference between the most advanced countries and developing countries, most of which have begun a process of transition and structural adjustment. In advanced countries, in which economic trends are converging, income differentials and thus the incentive to emigrate have declined sharply. However, changes due to economic transition and adjustment policies have increased the incentive to emigrate; one thinks in particular of cuts in public employment, the widening income gap, growing poverty and the difference between social protection systems. But these are effects observed in the short term, which again raises the question of long-term trends. It is also important to point out that, with the exception of the Southern European countries whose economies opened up at the beginning of the 1960s, the integration of most emigration countries into the international economy came late. Two periods of greater openness can be distinguished according to Sachs and Warner (1995): the second half of the 1980s for developing countries (Morocco, Tunisia, Turkey and Mexico among others) and the 1990s for the countries of the former Soviet bloc. In this situation, it is hardly possible to observe the impact of the globalisation of trade and production on migration with the somewhat outdated data available.[17]

Economic policies have played a key role in economic globalisation, whether through the establishment of international institutions, such as the WTO, or through privatisation, trade liberalisation and capital flow policies. International migration is an exception in this regard, for the attempt to create a worldwide institutional structure for immigration has never gone beyond statements of intention and, ultimately, many major immigration countries have tightened restrictions on the admission of immigrants. These often draconian policies have discouraged immigrants from returning home and have thus contributed to stabilising the foreign population, and even to increasing it via illegal entry and asylum seekers. The exception to this rule is the establishment of areas of free movement of persons, of which the European Union is the best example. The supposed impact on mobility is less clear-cut in this case, in as much as borders were only opened after the opening up of trade.

b)   *Migration, development and globalisation*

Although a genuine globalisation of international migration has not taken place in the period considered, the question of the interrelation between migration and continuing economic globalisation

---

17.   The statistics on stocks provided by censuses are only updated each decade, and those on flows are too incomplete.

remains. To what extent is migration a part of the phenomenon of globalisation? To what extent does globalisation affect mobility?

International migration is now taking place in the context of the globalisation of economies, and must therefore be analysed from an international perspective, emphasising the interdependence of sending and host countries, as opposed to the traditional approach that focused on these countries' respective impact on each other. What is more, the economic, political and social aspects of migration are now seldom analysed as separate factors, whether to explain the reasons for emigration or its impact on the societies concerned. The debate on migration has become inseparable from the issue of human rights, the political organisation and economic development of the country of origin, and the national cohesion and future of the welfare state in host societies.

Free trade is again being viewed as a substitute for international migration, but the significance of this alternative has changed completely. Free trade, accompanied by domestic factor mobility, was originally presented as a more realistic path to specialisation than international migration; but it is now used to prevent migration – illegal migration in the United States, and all forms of labour migration in Europe. It is in this context that, in both these regions, the development of emigration countries is presented as the alternative to migration. It is not the first time such an approach has been proposed. In the United States, in 1964, when the temporary labour recruitment programme (the *bracero* programme) begun in 1942 was ended, the fear of a rise in Mexican migration led to the introduction of a preferential customs system that made it possible for firms established on the Mexican side of the border (*maquiladoras*) to import parts and export goods duty free. This system had mixed results, for although it had a major impact on industrial development and job creation in the regions concerned, it had scant positive linkage effects on the national economy and, most importantly, from this paper's standpoint, it failed to reduce the emigration of Mexicans significantly. Following regularisation legislation in 1986, a congressional commission responsible for monitoring the implementation of the Act and proposing measures to reduce illegal immigration reached the conclusion that the economic development of the country of origin, promoted through commercial and financial openness, was the only realistic option in the long term. The free-trade agreement between Mexico and the United States, which does not address migration issues, reflects this approach.

In Europe, when borders began to close to immigration in 1973-74, policy makers sought to replace migration with policies aiming to promote investment in the countries of origin, to encourage European firms, especially those that employed migrant workers, to create production units in the countries of origin and advocate the return of migrant workers. This "new international division of labour" has not lived up to its promise and the situation is quite different now. A number of factors suggest that the alternative to migration should now be considered more realistically. First, it is necessary to move beyond the misguided policy that made labour-importing firms and migrants themselves responsible for adjustment. Second, the closing of borders to the immigration of workers, which initially seemed like a temporary measure made necessary by the energy crisis, has become a permanent feature of the migration system of EU countries. Last and most importantly, although the "new division of labour" initially seemed like an attempt on the part of developed countries to deflect southern countries' criticism of the unilateral closing of borders, the recent version of the alternative to migration fits into sending countries' new development strategy, which is moving away from self-reliant development and import substitution. Structural adjustment programmes, accompanied by policies of privatisation, commercial openness and liberalisation of capital movements, have led to free-trade agreements between the European Union and Tunisia, Turkey and Morocco. However, alongside these positive factors, a new concern has arisen, especially in southern and eastern Mediterranean countries, to the effect that free-trade agreements represent in some respects the end of the special relationships between these countries and the European Union. The enlargement of the European Union, the agreements with other Mediterranean countries and the countries of Central

Europe, the signing of the GATT agreements and the dismantling of the Multifibre Arrangement have eliminated the specific advantages that the previous agreements with the EEC had granted to these countries.

The fact remains that, with regard to international migration, the process of convergence predicted by international trade theory is not entirely convincing. In the case of regional integration, the trend towards factor-price equalisation, which reduces the propensity for mobility between partner countries, also acts as a greater incentive for emigration from third countries, as the European experience has shown. But above all, the level of equalisation and the time required to achieve it cannot be inferred from a model based on comparative statistics. It is precisely the duration of the process that is a key factor when potential migrants choose between the hope for a lasting, but future improvement of their standard of living through free trade, and an immediate, but perhaps only temporary improvement if they decide to emigrate. There is a fundamental difference between these two choices if the political and economic stability of the country of origin is uncertain. To emigrate is to take matters into one's own hands, and to stay is to trust in the government or market.

The trend towards factor-price equalisation may in the long term reduce the incentive to emigrate. In the meantime – which might be several decades – the structural changes in the economy, associated with the initial phases of development, are expected to increase the propensity to emigrate. The development process needs and also generates the sectoral and spatial mobility of the population. As the population shifts to the secondary sector and to construction in particular, incomes rise, making it easier to finance the cost of migration. Employment also becomes more vulnerable to fluctuations in activity, which in turn encourages emigration. At the same time, higher levels of education reduce the cultural distance. As long as developed countries display characteristics that attract immigrants, such as an active settlement policy along the US model or labour demand linked to the segmentation of the labour market (as seems to be the case in Europe, especially in southern countries), it is likely that migration flows will continue even if there is a rise in per capita production in the regions of origin.

5.   Conclusion

A paradoxical relationship, therefore, exists between migration and globalisation. On the one hand, migratory and economic policies associated with globalisation are explicitly or implicitly aimed at preventing mobility while, on the other, the very market mechanisms these policies try to re-establish are just as likely to increase rather than reduce migration flows. If the current period is viewed from a long-term perspective, the conclusion is clear. Until the First World War, international migration played a key role in the integration of economies on both sides of the Atlantic. After the Second World War, migration of workers contributed to economic and social integration between countries in the South and North, in particular in the European (Europe, Maghreb and Turkey) and North American (United States, Canada, Mexico and Central America) areas. During both these periods, labour went hand in hand with capital mobility, and migration was a key factor in the globalisation of economies. International migration now seems to be excluded from the new process of globalisation. This exclusion constitutes the single greatest difference distinguishing the new trends of the world economy from the two previous major historical periods of globalisation. The restrictive vision of "globalisation" without human mobility raises a three-fold question on the ethics, political realism and economic effectiveness, and long-term sustainability of this kind of global development strategy.

BIBLIOGRAPHY

FAINI, R., GRETHER, J.M. and de MELO, J. (1997)
"Globalisation and migratory pressures from developing countries: a simulation analysis", *Trade and Factor Mobility*, a CEPR Conference, Venice.

GÄCHTER, A. (1995)
Migration Potential and World Economic Development. An Exploration, Studie im Auftrag des Bundesministeriums für Wissenschaft, Forshung und Kunst (BMWFK), September.

KEBADJIAN, G. (1998)
"Analyse économique et mondialisation : cinq débats", Report for the *Groupement économie mondiale et développement* (GEMDEV), Université Paris I.

KRITZ, M. (1996)
"Population growth and international migration. Is there a link?", *Migration Policy in Global Perspective Series*, Occasional Paper No. 1, The International Centre for Migration, Ethnicity and Citizenship, New York, N.Y.

KRUGMAN, P. (1995)
"Growing world trade: causes and consequences", *Brookings Papers on Economic Activity*, No. 1, Brookings Institution, Washington, D.C.

OECD (1995, 1996, 1997)
Trends in International Migration, Annual Reports, OECD, Paris.

OECD (1997)
International Migration Statistics, OECD, Paris.

RUGGLES, S., SOBEK, M. *et al.* (1997),
Integrated Public Use Microdata Series : Version 2.0 (http://www.ipums.umn.edu.), Minneapolis Historical Census Projects, University of Minnesota.

SACHS, J.D. and WARNER, A. (1995)
"Economic reform and the process of global integration", Brookings Papers on Economic Activity, No. 1, Brookings Institution, Washington, D.C.

TAPINOS, G. (1994)
"Migrations internationales et développement", *Bulletin démographique des Nations Unies*, No. 36, New York.

TAPINOS, G. (1997)
"Migration trade and development. The European Union and the Maghreb countries", in R. King, G. Lazaridis and C. Tsardanidis (eds.), *Eldorado or Fortress? Migration in Southern Europe*, MacMillan, London.

UNHCR (1998)

    The State of the World's Refugees 1997-98. A Humanitarian Agenda, Oxford University Press, New York, N.Y.

UNITED NATIONS (1995)

    Trends in Total Migrant Stock, Revision 2, Database maintained by the Population Division of the Department for Economic and Social Information and Policy Analysis, New York, N.Y.

YANG, P. Q. (1995)

    Post-1965 Immigration to the United States: Structural Determinants, Praeger, Westport, Connecticut.

ZLOTNIK, H. (1991)

    "South-North migration since 1960: the view from the North", *Bulletin démographique des Nations Unies*, No. 31/32, New York, N.Y.

ZLOTNIK, H. (1997)

    "Population growth and international migration", *Conference on International Migration at the Century's End: Trends and Issues*, IUSSP/UIESP, Barcelona.

Map 1 Stocks of immigrants or foreigners (1990)

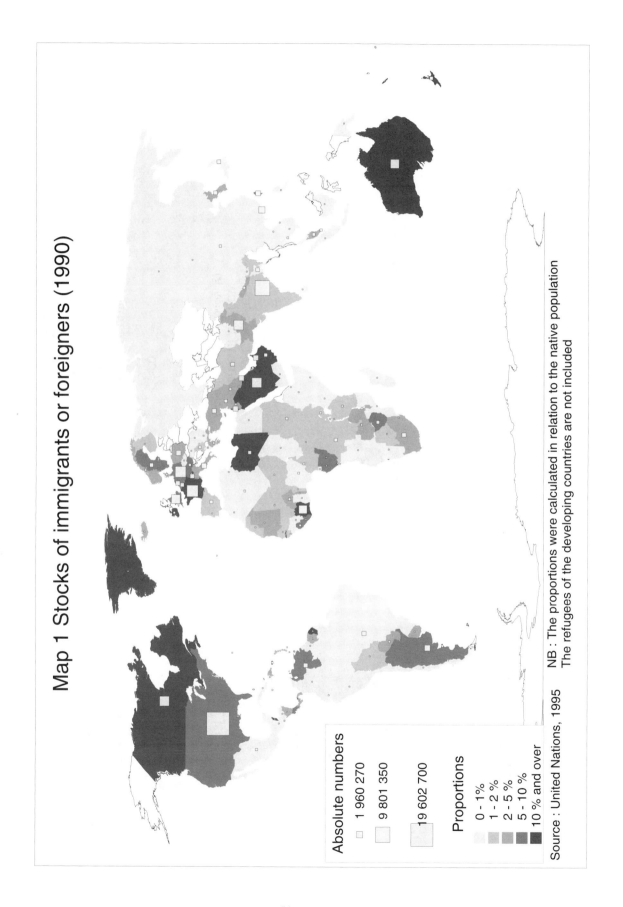

Absolute numbers

1 960 270

9 801 350

19 602 700

Proportions

0 - 1 %
1 - 2 %
2 - 5 %
5 - 10 %
10 % and over

Source : United Nations, 1995

NB : The proportions were calculated in relation to the native population
The refugees of the developing countries are not included

51

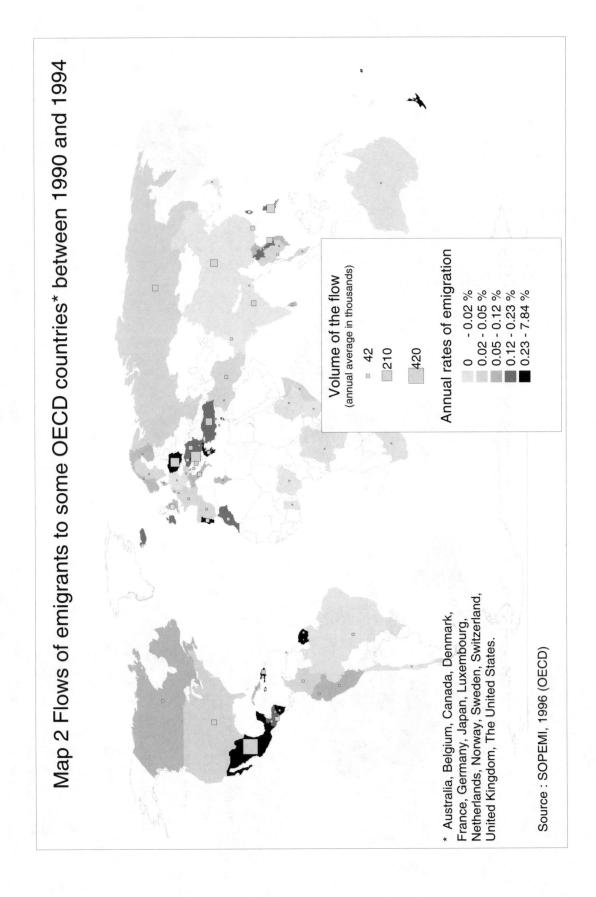

Map 2 Flows of emigrants to some OECD countries* between 1990 and 1994

Volume of the flow
(annual average in thousands)

- 42
- 210
- 420

Annual rates of emigration

- 0 - 0.02 %
- 0.02 - 0.05 %
- 0.05 - 0.12 %
- 0.12 - 0.23 %
- 0.23 - 7.84 %

* Australia, Belgium, Canada, Denmark,
France, Germany, Japan, Luxembourg,
Netherlands, Norway, Sweden, Switzerland,
United Kingdom, The United States.

Source : SOPEMI, 1996 (OECD)

Map 3 Change in stocks of foreigners or immigrants between 1965 and 1990

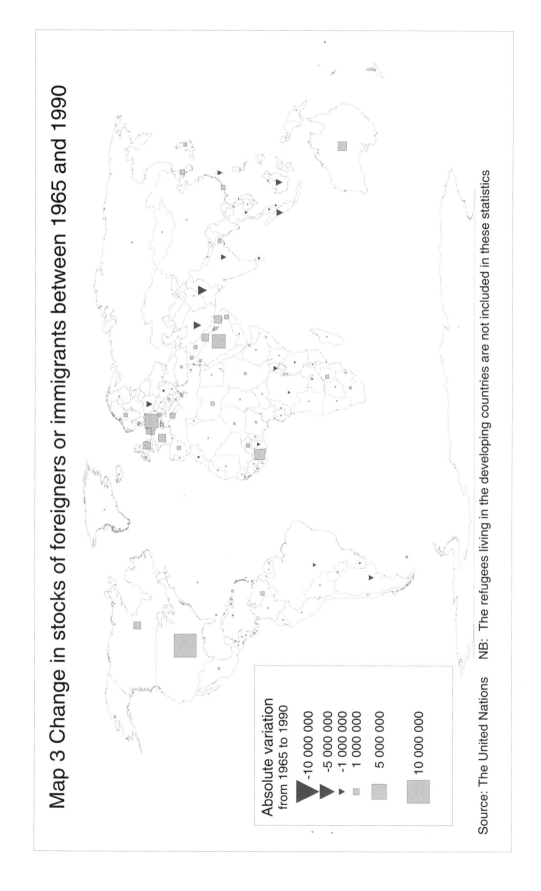

Absolute variation
from 1965 to 1990

-10 000 000
-5 000 000
-1 000 000
1 000 000
5 000 000
10 000 000

Source: The United Nations   NB: The refugees living in the developing countries are not included in these statistics

53

Table 1. **Migration statistics examined in this study**

	Flows	*Stocks*
Immigration	▪ Entries in fourteen selected OECD countries[1] 1980-1995 (SOPEMI,[2] 1996) ▪ Entries in eight western countries 1946-1995 (UN)[3]	▪ *Immigrants* in countries of the world in 1965, 1975, 1985, 1990 (UN)
Emigration	▪ According to the origin of the entries in selected countries[3] from 1946 to 1995 (ONU) ▪ According to the origin of the entries in certain OECD countries[1] from 1980 to 1995 (SOPEMI,[2] 1996)	▪ According to the country of origin of the immigrants in the United States from 1950 to 1990 (Ruggles, Sobek *et. al*, 1997) ▪ According to the country of origin of the immigrants in certain[1] OECD Member countries around 1982 and 1990 (SOPEMI,[2] 1996)

1. Australia, Belgium, Canada, Denmark, France, Germany, Japan, Luxembourg, Netherlands, Norway, Sweden, Switzerland, United Kingdom, United States.
2. SOPEMI: Continuous Reporting System on Migration (OECD, 1997).
3. Germany, Belgium, United States, Canada, Sweden, Australia, United Kingdom, Netherlands.

Table 2. **Relative variations (%) in the recorded foreign population**

Years	1965	1975	1985	1990
Proportion of the foreign population, refugees included	2.27	2.08	2.18	2.28
Proportion of the foreign population , not including refugees from developing countries	2.21	2.03	2.03	2.00

Source : International migration data set, United Nations.

Table 3. **Variations in stocks and flows (SOPEMI countries)**

Year	Annual entries	Number of foreigners		
	Absolute	Absolute	Relative	
			A[1]	B[2]
1965		24 661 454	4.68	4.91
1975		33 680 054	5.56	5.88
1980	2 013 088			
1985	1 593 992	43 275 202	6.62	7.09
1990	3 420 124	48 852 228	7.24	7.80
1995	2 415 278			

1. A = as percentage of the total population.
2. B = as percentage of the native population.

Sources: UN, Population Division (for the stocks of immigrants and foreigners), 1996; SOPEMI (OECD, 1996).

Table 4. **Comparisons of the stocks and flows of foreigners**

	Variations of the number of foreigners		Sum of the entries of foreigners		Ratio between flows and stocks	
	1975-1984	**1985-1989**	**1975-1984**	**1985-1989**	**1975-1984**	**1985-1989**
United States	5 015 580	3 058 650	5 133 948	3 507 182	1.02	1.15
Australia	720 018	519 565	814 567	615 752	1.13	1.19
Canada	401 325	374 320	1 220 911	689 549	3.04	1.84
Belgium	124 016	11 176	530 666	248 404	4.28	22.23
Netherlands	432 533	389 705	884 949	452 836	2.05	1.16
Sweden	79 423	114 144	315 911	202 442	3.98	1.77
Germany	1 297 190	558 040	4 236 193	2 768 224	3.27	4.96
United Kingdom	391 255	209 438	1 864 600	1 160 600	4.77	5.54

Sources: United Nations (1995) and OECD.

Table 5. **Developing countries' share of inflows into selected settlement countries**

Period	United States	Canada	Australia
End of the 1960s	40 %	12 %	8 %
End of the 1980s	90 %	70 %	50 %

Source : Zlotnik (1991).

Chart 1. **Change in stocks and inflows of foreigners in some OECD countries**

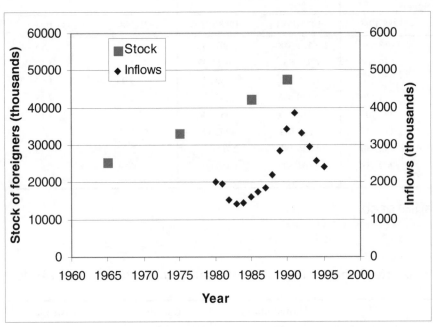

Note: See the countries included in the Statistical Annex of *Trends in International Migration*.
Sources: Stocks: UN, Population Directorate, 1996; Flows: *Trends in International Migration*, (OECD, 1997).

Chart 2. **Change in cumulated contributions of foreign population in each country, (presentation by rank)**

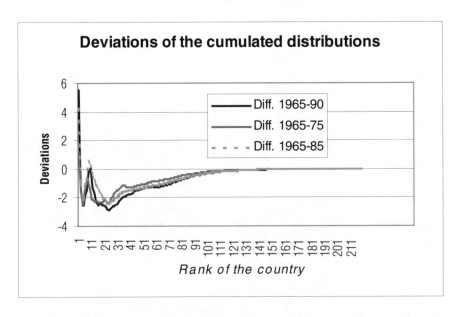

Note: See the countries included in the Statistical Annex of *Trends in International Migration*.
Sources: Stocks: UN, Population Directorate, 1996; Flows: *Trends in International Migration*, (OECD, 1997).

Chart 3. **Cumulated distributions of flows to some OECD countries**

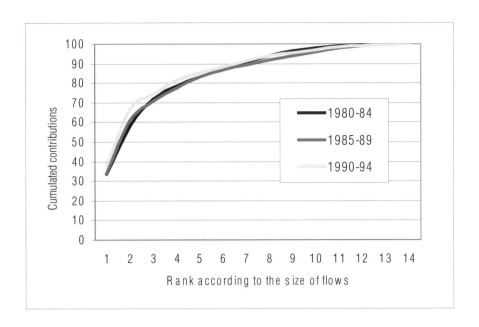

Note: See the countries included in the Statistical Annex of *Trends in International Migration.*

Sources: Stocks: UN, Population Directorate, 1996; Flows: *Trends in International Migration,* (OECD, 1997).

Chart 4. **Change in inflows to the United States, Canada and Australia, 1965-1990**

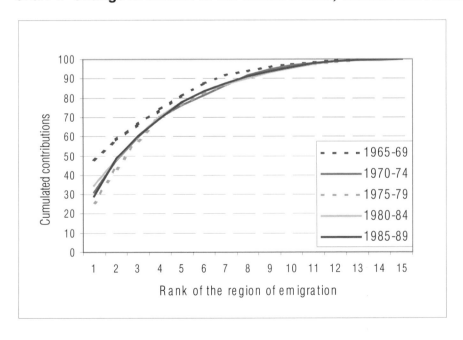

Source: Trends in International Migration (OECD, 1997).

Chart 5. Change in inflows to Sweden, Belgium, the UK, Germany and the Netherlands, 1965-1990

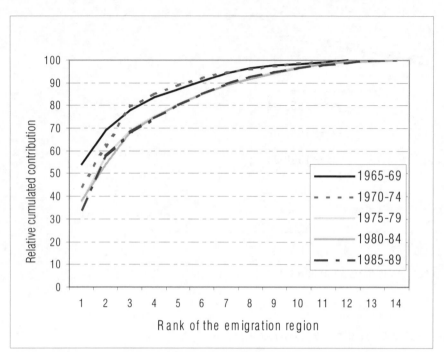

Source: Trends in International Migration (OECD, 1997).

REGIONAL INTEGRATION AND MIGRATION FLOWS:
A CRITICAL REVIEW OF RECENT LITERATURE

by
Laurence Assous
Consultant to the OECD at the time the paper was written

Introduction

Although trade may be a substitute to factor movements, in particular to labour migration, the mechanisms at work are complex and can not be reduced to a one-to-one relation. A basic free-trade agreement does not suffice to durably reduce migration flows destined to a regional pole. Analyses must obviously account for the degree of regional integration, variable according to the nature of the agreements establishing trade relations between countries. This study will consider this question in the light of recent literature using two approaches. It will draw first of all pertinent lessons from international trade theory and from recent developments. The second section will seek to go beyond the purely economic aspects to take into account factors that determine the decision to emigrate which are more of a micro-economic and sociological order.

1. Impact of regional integration on the size of migration flows – review of recent economic literature

a) *Quantitative impact of trade liberalisation on migration*

The basis of the classical theory of international trade is that countries tend to produce relatively more of those goods which make intensive use of their major abundant resources. Within the framework of this theory, trade and migration are substitutes. Thus, a country where labour is abundant (and therefore relatively cheap) has the option to export both labour-intensive goods or labour. According to the neo-classical theory of international trade, in particular the analyses of Mundell (1957) and the Heckscher-Ohlin-Samuelson (HOS) factor price equalisation theorem (see Jones, 1956), the opening of trade links between countries with similar factor endowments and production functions reduces the disparities in factor prices and diminishes the propensity of individuals to move within the zone. However, while economic theory provides the principal argument, the specifications of the model suggest that convergence will occur only in the very long term.

The question of whether trade and migration are complements or substitutes has been the focus of numerous studies, the results of which differ markedly according to the hypotheses selected. According to some authors free trade could lead to a reduction in migration flows. For others, it could have no visible effect on migration or it could bring about an increase of these flows (disruptive effect) by having a negative effect on small and medium-size industries and by accelerating the drift from the rural to urban areas.

An empirical study by Abowd and Freeman (1991) shows that, whatever the sector, the share of foreign workers in the United States is positively correlated with the import penetration ratio and negatively correlated with the export/output ratio. This suggests a substitutability relationship. In sectors such as textile and clothing, which have long enjoyed considerable levels of protection, the share of immigrant labour reaches 10.4%. Straubhaar (1988) shows that during the period 1958-80, while the intra-EC-trade share of total EC-trade increased by 0.8% a year, the intra-EC-migration share of total EC-migration flows decreased at an annual rate of 1.3%. In the EU, today, only 2% of workers in national labour markets are foreign. Molle (1994) concluded from this evidence that goods and capital movements have been largely substitutes for labour movements.

According to Faini and Venturini (1993), empirical results show that protectionist policies in industrialised countries have a twofold impact on migration flows: *i*) by fostering growth in low-skilled labour-intensive sectors, they increase the demand for foreign workers, thereby strengthening one of the pull factors of migration; and *ii*) by discouraging the expansion of labour-intensive exports in developing countries, they reinforce one of the push factors of migration. Their conclusion is that "by pursuing more liberal trade policies, industrialised countries may contribute to significantly reducing migration pressures".

Using a standard one-good macro-economic model, Faini and De Melo (1994) find that trade liberalisation has a substantial effect on the propensity to migrate. According to them, the effect of trade liberalisation comes mostly through its impact on the real exchange rate. Depreciation boosts exports and, as a result, labour demand.

All these arguments seem to support the view that trade and migration are substitutable. In most cases, however, model specifications suggest that a reduction in migration flows is not likely to happen in the short run. It is, in fact, far from certain that a reduction in migration flows would take place in every case. Between countries with similar levels of technological endowment (for example, EU members), the substitutability relationship between trade and migration seems to hold. However, to ensure this relationship between industrialised and less-advanced countries, large compensatory measures are necessary. Moreover, the substitutability relationship between international trade and factor movements does not hold if certain hypotheses concerning production functions and market structure are dropped. According to Markusen (1983), the introduction of scale economies or technological differences brings out the complementarity between international trade and migration. By adding certain characteristics (such financial constraints to migration) to the HOS model, one obtains complementarity between trade, aid and co-operation, on the one hand, and migration on the other.[1]

The model by Cogneau *et al.* (1998) shows that the impact on migration flows of the first stage of regional integration (only trade liberalisation) is negligible. However, an institutionally deeper regional integration, with massive financial transfers directed towards externality producing public expenditure (infrastructure, investment in human capital, and so forth), could significantly reduce the propensity to emigrate.

Mouhoud (1998) also defends the view that free trade by itself does not constitute a substitute for labour mobility. Only under certain conditions will regional integration promote the catching-up of poor countries. The degree of integration plays a significant role in the exploitation of externalities linked to regional integration. The higher the degree of integration, the more

---

1. In his 1994 paper, Schiff shows using a HOS model that the introduction of migration costs and financial constraints generates complementarity between trade and migration.

multinational corporations (MNCs) are likely to invest in the newly associated countries. Foreign direct investment (FDI) is crucial in this development dynamic. The greater the FDI and the knowledge imported, the greater the positive impact of regional integration on economic growth and employment creation. If the "signal" sent to the MNCs is not strong enough, it will not lead to the creation of a sufficient number of jobs.

In countries with rapidly growing populations, such as the Maghreb countries and Mexico, there is little chance that the propensity to migrate will be reduced before 2020. Giubilaro (1997) explains that "to cope with the additional supply alone, the Maghreb countries as a whole would have to create about 10 million jobs during the 1995–2010 period". This figure more or less corresponds to the total employed population in the Maghreb countries in 1982. This objective seems therefore difficult to attain. And so, according to Giubilaro, "in the absence of measures designed to promote employment creation in the Maghreb countries, migration potential will increase rapidly". By contrast, countries that have gone through the demographic transition stage (this applies to the CEECs) are not experiencing this kind of problem. In this case, a regional integration agreement can more easily contribute to reducing the propensity to emigrate. Demography is far from being the only factor influencing migration flows; it nevertheless plays an important role.

International trade liberalisation might provoke an acceleration in migration flows

With regard to trade and migration flows between countries at different levels of development, empirical work tends to point to a relationship of complementarity rather than substitution. This means that regional integration, even in the best of cases, would have no impact on migration flows; it would not entail a significant decrease in emigration.[2] There are also many authors who argue that international trade liberalisation might provoke an increase in migration flows. These researchers believe that regional integration agreements, which go no further than free trade, and in certain cases even high level integration, cannot lead (at least over the short to medium term) to a decrease in migration flows. On the contrary, they might even increase. This would be due mainly to disruptive effects. Indeed, even development aid directed at investment in human capital may paradoxically stimulate migration if, for example, the skills acquired by the potential emigrant are those sought after in rich countries (Martin, 1994).

It is important to underline that development aid, as it improves living standards, has roughly the same effects as a movement towards free trade. If trade and migration are likely to be substitutes, development aid will tend to enhance this effect (Schiff, 1994). Such aid is intended to help narrow income disparities between countries by accelerating economic growth. But this will only be true if development aid is directed towards activities likely to favour job creation and towards investment in human capital (education, health) (see Tapinos, 1998). Transfers, moreover, must be considerable to allow countries to "catch-up". However, official development assistance is both very limited in quantity and regularly decreasing.

Trade liberalisation and structural adjustment programmes can also be very disruptive. Budgetary measures (increases in indirect taxes) and monetary measures (devaluation) that accompany the lowering of trade barriers significantly reduce the positive effects of improved factor allocation (Cogneau and Tapinos, 1995). If no accompanying measures are implemented to counterbalance these

---

2. Among others, three papers support this viewpoint: "Free trade cannot constitute an alternative to migration flows" (Alba *et al.*, 1998; Cogneau and Tapinos, 1995). "Trade and migration are most often complements, not substitutes" (Richards, 1994).

disruptive effects, free trade can lead to a cumulative process of regional divergence.[3] The lowering of import duties exposes agriculture and industry to international competition, often reducing employment and wages.[4] Rapid economic development can also destabilise the old social and economic orders, rupturing traditional social networks; rural-to-urban migration is thereby encouraged. Once uprooted from rural communities, certain migrants might envisage emigration to another country as a logical next step (Stalker, 1997).

The disruptive effect of development means that during the first phase of development, emigration tends to increase rather than diminish and then, in a second phase, to decline slowly as per capita GDP rises. This can be expressed graphically as a "migration hump". Indeed, many authors assert that migration and trade are complementary in the short run and substitutable in the long run. According to Martin (1993), large-scale emigration from Mexico to the United States would continue in the 1990s and, because of Mexican economic reforms and NAFTA, a "migration hump" would be likely. However, if considered over a number of decades, migration will be less with the FTA than without the FTA. Examining the issue within a broader framework, Russell and Teitelbaum (1992) reached a similar conclusion.

The existence of imperfect capital markets also represents a real problem for a large number of developing countries. Most people in developing countries can borrow money only at prohibitive rates. In fact, migration costs are quite high since they include transportation costs, investment in information, payments to various intermediaries (in the case of illegal migration) and living expenses in the destination country until a job is found. Many unskilled would-be migrants, therefore, are unable to finance their migration costs out of their low-wage income (Schiff, 1994). Trade liberalisation and foreign aid may, in a first phase, favour emigration by increasing income from labour and thereby relaxing the financial constraint. The lower the labour income and the higher the costs of migration, the more likely will trade liberalisation and development aid lead to increased emigration in the short term.

b)   *Qualitative impact of trade liberalisation on migration*

The study of the differential impact of trade liberalisation on the skill composition of the labour force is the subject of a contribution by Lopez and Schiff (1995). To a standard HOS model, they add four factors: labour skill levels, international labour mobility, migration costs and financing constraints. They examine two scenarios. The results obtained show that, in a country with a stable population (a CEEC, for instance), opening up the economy raises the emigration flow of unskilled workers, while the emigration of skilled workers remains unaffected. Therefore, on average, the population's skill level rises. Alternatively, in a country where population growth will sufficiently replace the migrants (developing countries with rapidly growing populations), trade liberalisation will

---

3.   In traditional exogenous growth models, factor mobility is found to promote convergence of economies. But certain empirical tests seem to support the hypothesis that economies with different technological endowments tend to diverge. Moreover, more recent research on growth theory, which takes into account increasing returns to scale and, contrary to the traditional models, considers technical progress as endogenous, finds that factor mobility leads to a cumulative process of regional divergence.

4.   "In a number of developing countries, the most protected sectors are labour-intensive smallholder agricultural sectors. Notable cases are the wheat sector in Morocco and the maize sector in Mexico, where protection has been used to support the rural poor. In those cases, trade liberalisation may result in a decrease in the demand for labour and a fall in the wage rate" (Schiff, 1996*a*).

increase emigration of the unskilled and decrease emigration of the skilled, which translates into a continuous improvement in the average skill level of the population.[5]

Finally, Walz and Wellisch (1998) showed that if governments institute redistribution policies when a free zone is extended to a common market, workers move from countries with a large number of unskilled workers to countries with a small number, on purely financial grounds.

In short, a basic free trade agreement does not generally entail a reduction in migration flows. Trade and migration are most often complements rather than substitutes. Moreover, trade liberalisation alone is likely to produce disruptive effects and increase the propensity to emigrate, at least over the medium term. In fact, the deeper the planned degree of regional integration, the more likely the incentives to migrate will diminish quickly. Regional integration is more efficient than a basic free trade agreement as the "signal" sent to foreign investors is much stronger and the financial transfers much higher. But it is mainly via FDI that regional integration is more likely to create employment and reduce "migration potential".

2.   Reasons for migrating: critical approach of economic literature

In a seminal contribution, Harris and Todaro (1970) developed a model where the probability of finding a job combined with the size of the wage gap determines the rate of migration. Empirical evidence from developing countries generally confirms that one of the crucial determinants of migration is the prospect of earning more money. But this is not the only reason. Recent work, by Stark (1991) for example, shows that even if migration is an individual act, the decision to emigrate might be taken by the family or the household. According to this portfolio investment theory, families spread their human capital over geographically dispersed and structurally different markets in order to reduce risk. Remittances from migrants to their families reinforce mutual interdependence and operate as an insurance against uncertain income flows.

Moreover, the discrepancies between income and unemployment levels need not recede in order for migration to cease. The EEC experience, with relatively low intra-regional migration from the poorest countries to the richest countries – despite the greater freedom with which EU citizens may now move within the zone – shows, that in the presence of a stable and democratic political system, migration can only be stimulated by a very wide economic gap. Thus it is evident that wage discrepancies are not the only factors playing a role.

a)   The importance of social capital

Coleman (1987) first introduced the concept of social capital. Several authors, including Platteau (1994) and Putman (1993), have since made interesting contributions to this topic. Putman defined social capital as "trust, norms and networks" that facilitate social co-ordination and co-operation for the mutual benefit of society members. These variables are difficult to estimate, but Molle and Van Mourik (1989) found that they significantly restrain migration within Europe. The authors (1988) also found that the impact of the removal of barriers to labour mobility has been negligible within the EEC. They argue that this lack of inter-penetration is mainly due to cultural barriers. This ties in with the point of view expressed by Faini and Venturini (1993) who state that cultural, social and linguistic differences may at least partly account for the much lower labour mobility in Europe than in the United States.

---

5.   These results are in contradiction with Baldwin and Venables (1994), Faini (1996) and Alba *et al.* (1998).

The fear of housing problems in the receiving area, assimilation difficulties and racism, are factors that can also dissuade someone from emigrating. According to Schiff (1996b), considering that such barriers play a significant part in intra-European migration, it appears reasonable to suppose that these barriers are likely to play an important role in South-North migration.

Among the sociological factors contributing to the emigration decision process, chain migration also plays an important role. Friends and relatives already living abroad may stimulate potential migrants. Their contacts can provide them with information and ensure them a place to stay when they arrive.[6] According to Stalker (1995), these human chains often start with one person. It is enough that an immigrant becomes a union representative for him to draw many other people from the same town. Schiff (1996b) also stressed that "immigrants from a given country tend to cluster in specific cities and neighbourhoods in order to benefit from the common social capital".[7] Besides, the networking aspect of migration also means that MNCs may serve to facilitate migration. In this manner, the Mexican employees of a MNC establish contacts with their American colleagues who might help them obtain a work permit (Bhagwati, 1991a).

Even if studies on the impact of social capital on migration are limited in number, these examples are enough to demonstrate the important role it plays in the emigration decision process. Social capital is therefore an important factor, which should be introduced to migration models.

b)   The importance of the demand side

Push factors relative to labour supply in sending countries are more often accounted for in models than pull factors relative to the demand-side in host countries.

According to Martin (1993), "despite trade barriers and differences in wages and job opportunities, most people do not migrate. Migration is extraordinary; for this reason, most of today's unwanted migrations began with industrial country programs that recruited workers from what became an emigration country". In his study of migration to Germany, Bhagwati (1984) showed that the *Gastarbeiter* system was determined by internal demand considerations, rather than by the interaction of supply and demand. Straubhaar (1988) also argues that migration flows are mainly demand driven.

In the 1960s and in the first half of the 1970s, a period of high growth, pull factors obviously predominated. Today, with the slow-down of economic growth, notably in Europe, one observes a decrease in the demand for foreign labour. Dual labour theories, however, explain how certain industries become structurally dependent on migration, entailing a permanent need for immigrant workers. According to this theory, there will always exist a demand for labour willing to work in difficult and precarious conditions. Industrial economies can neither eliminate nor make attractive these unskilled activities to native workers (Piore, 1979). Finally and to conclude, Saith (1997) states that "in determining the actual flows of migrants between rich and poor countries, it is the demand and not the supply side factors which dominate the magnitude of flows".

When analysing "push" and "pull" factors, it is important to make the distinction between the overused expression "migration pressure" and the concept of "propensity to migrate". The first

---

6.   Moreover, the steep drop in the costs of transport, as well as in the charges for long-distance calls and the development of Internet access facilitates the circulation of information and reduces the emotional distance between one country and another.

7.   Chinatown in San Francisco, Little Italy in New York and Little Havana in Miami are as many proofs of this assertion.

term is generally defined as "an excess labour supply in the presence of a negative per capita income differential" (Bruni and Venturini, 1991). If taken literally, it would apply to most of developing countries and, as Saith (1997) underlines, "these criteria will lead to the bizarre conclusion that the vast majority of people in China and India are hankering to leave their country". The expression "migration pressure" does not sufficiently take into account the individual decision-making capacity of potential migrants. The concept of "propensity to migrate" is of greater relevance, as it corresponds "to the relation between effective migration flows and migration potential"(Giubilaro, 1997).

While pull factors are essential in determining migration flows, it should nevertheless be admitted that push and pull factors can be complementary. In the case of Mexico-to-US migration, it is a continued demand-pull from the American market allied to a sizeable supply which generates the migration flows. But "an approach which does not take into account the dominance of the demand-determined causes is of limited value in explaining the causes of legal international labour migration" (Straubhaar, 1993).

c)   Critique of some results

Forecasting exercises, like those of CGE and theoretical models, often overemphasise the supply aspect to the detriment of the demand aspect in the determination of the decision to emigrate.[8] For example, Lopez and Schiff (1995), in their model analysing the impact of trade liberalisation on the skill composition of the labour force, accord excessive importance to demographic factors. They do not at all take into consideration the demand-pull factors in the developed countries, which leads to results that do not fit the facts (Alba et al., 1998). The works of Faini and De Melo (1994) and Panagariya (1992) are subject to the same criticism. What is more, these models do not include social capital in the migrant's utility function. In this way, Faini and De Melo (1994) found, using a macroeconomic model, that real currency depreciation leads to lower migrations. According to them, trade liberalisation boosts exports and "as a result, labour demand". This link is rather questionable. They also completely ignored, among other things, the disruptive effects of trade liberalisation.

It should be acknowledged, however, that some authors have presented studies that take into account not only the demand-induced side of migration,[9] but also the importance of social networks.[10] Unfortunately the inclusion of these variables in mathematical models has met with insuperable technical difficulties. Not all authors are alarmist concerning the previsions of future migration flows. Giubilaro (1997) shows, for example, that whereas the "migration potential" for Maghreb and Turkey may increase considerably over the next 15 years, the propensity to migrate will decline for all countries. This analysis demonstrates that there is nothing alarming about the situation: "contrary to what was feared by European countries, which consider that emigration (legal and illegal) depends first and foremost on push factors in the country of departure, the decline in propensity to migrate shows that the variation in the inclination of workers to emigrate reflects above all the need for immigrant workers in foreign labour markets" (Giubilaro, 1997).

Although CGE models are extremely useful at shedding light on the complex interactions between economic variables, they possess the disadvantage of being very sensitive to the parameters and hypotheses selected. According to Sobarzo-Fimbres (1998), the sensitivity of these models to variations in specification may even lead to conflicting conclusions. Moreover, CGE models are

---

8.   Refer to critique of Baldwin and Venables (1994) and Alba et al. (1998) among others.

9.   Saith (1997) and Stalker (1997), for example.

10.   Bliss (1994), Faini and Venturini (1993), Molle and Van Mourik (1988 and 1989), Schiff (1996a and 1996b), Tuiran et al. (1998).

mostly static; a fully dynamic model would be needed to set out the possible adjustment paths of developing economies.

The model of Cogneau and Tapinos (1995) is dynamic, but migration is not endogenised. In fact, it is only by studying the impact of trade liberalisation on the economy that the authors draw conclusions regarding migrations. They argue that trade liberalisation cannot be an alternative to migration flows – a deduction made simply by examining the economic situation. The 1998 CGE model of Cogneau, Dumont and Izzo is static, but apparently for the first time the authors have endogenised migration and FDI. They studied the impact of five different scenarios on people's welfare (not on economic growth), which explains why the model is static. Moreover, the simulations are not restricted to free trade agreements. Five different levels of regional integration are studied and the final one simulates an advanced form of economic integration. The risk premium diminishes with the degree of regional integration. In this model, however, social capital is not included in the migrant's utility function, since the migration decision is entirely motivated by wage differentials.

Other predictions have been made by Layard *et al.* (1992), though they are more alarmist than realistic. They are based simply on extrapolations of previous situations, for example, when between 1950 and 1970, nearly 3% of the population of South Europe emigrated to West or North Europe, or when, more recently in the 1970s, Mexicans emigrated to the United States.

Straubhaar (1988) refutes this approach and explains that, with regard to the formation of the Common Labour Market, contrary to host country fears, it did not induce a strong movement of workers migrating from low-income to high-income countries. It is interesting to note that, in 1984, Straubhaar wrote a paper about the accession of Spain and Portugal to the EC where he asserted that these countries would produce a migration potential of 1.5-1.6 million workers.

These critiques do not put into question the interest or conclusions of these models, but rather show their limits. CGE models should just not be considered as forecasts. They should also be viewed as an additional tool for policy makers.

Conclusion

Links between migration and regional integration are complex. Even if regional integration does lead to a decrease in migration flows, it may not necessarily be for the reasons established by standard trade theory. Other factors could include: *i*) a reduction in the demand for foreign labour; *ii*) the existence of significant cultural barriers to assimilation which discourage many potential migrants; and *iii*) a stable political situation and effective economic management in sending countries which, even if the economy has not yet generated much employment, could instil confidence in its citizens by offering them the hope of a rapid improvement in their living standards.

Merely opening up the economy is unlikely to lead, at least not in the short term, to a reduction in migration flows. Indeed, by itself, free trade is not a credible alternative to migration flows. During an initial period, one might observe an increase in migration flows. On the other hand, a more profound regional integration agreement, such as that of the European Union, is more likely to lead to a brisk drop in emigration incentives. Nevertheless, the demographic situation in the country of origin or the existence of an emigration tradition towards a particular country are also important factors. For this reason, it would be preferable to differentiate the situations according to the region examined.

It is clearly necessary to distinguish between short- and long-term effects. In the short to medium term, trade liberalisation (accompanied by economic reforms and a strengthening of regional economic co-operation) could lead to an increase in migration flows. In the long term, however, these measures, by reducing economic disparities and wage differences between the two groups of countries, will diminish the propensity to emigrate.

BIBLIOGRAPHY

ABOWD, J.M. and FREEMAN, R.B. (1991)
  Immigration, Trade, and the Labor Market, University of Chicago Press.

ALBA, F., GARSON, J. P. and MOUHOUD, E. M. (1998)
  "Migration policies in a free trade area: the issue of convergence with the economic integration process", *Migration, Free Trade and Regional Integration in North America*, OECD, Paris.

BALDWIN, R. and VENABLES, A. J. (1994)
  "International migration, capital mobility and transitional dynamics", *Economica*, Vol. 61, pp. 285-300.

BARROS, L. and GARSON, J. P. (1998)
  "Migrations et intégration régionale : l'Union européenne face aux pays tiers du Bassin méditerranéen", *Migration, libre-échange et intégration régionale dans le Bassin méditerranéen*, OECD, Paris.

BHAGWATI, J.N. (1976)
  "The brain drain and taxation: theory and empirical analysis", Amsterdam, North Holland.

BHAGWATI, J.N. (1984)
  "The West German *gastarbeiter* system of immigration", *European Economic Review*, Vol. 26, pp. 277-294.

BHAGWATI, J.N. (1991*a*)
  "Investing abroad", *Political Economy and International Economics*, MIT Press, Cambridge, MA.

BHAGWATI, J.N. (1991*b*)
  "Free traders and free immigrationists: strangers or friends", Working Paper No. 20, April, Russell Sage Foundation, New York.

BLISS, C. (1994)
  "Trade blocks and migration", *Economic Theory and Policy for Trading Blocks*, Chapter 5, Manchester University Press.

BÖHNING, W. R. and SCHLOETER-PAREDES, M. L. (eds.) (1994)
  Aid in Place of Migration, International Labour Organisation (ILO), Geneva.

BORJAS, G. J. (1990)
  Friends or Strangers: The Impact of Immigrants on the US Economy, Basic Books, New York.

BORJAS, G. J. and FREEMAN, R. B. (1992)
"Introduction and summary", in G. J. Borjas and R. B. Freeman (eds.), *Immigration and the Work Force. Economic Consequences for the United States and Source Areas*, University of Chicago Press, Chicago.

BRUNI, M. and VENTURINI, A. (1991)
"Pressure to migrate and propensity to emigrate: the case of the Mediterranean Basin", paper prepared for the Conference of the ESPE, Pisa, Italy, 6-8 June.

CASHIN, P. and SAHAY, R. (1996)
"Internal migration, center-state grants, and economic growth in the States of India", IMF Staff Papers No. 1, pp. 123-171.

COGNEAU, D. and TAPINOS, G. (1995)
"Libre-échange, répartition du revenu et migrations au Maroc", *Revue d'économie du développement*, No. 1.

COGNEAU, D., DUMONT, J. C. and IZZO, P. (1998)
"Enseignements d'un modèle d'équilibre général calculable", *Migrations, libre-échange et intégration régionale dans le Bassin méditerranéen*, OECD, Paris.

COLEMAN, J. S. (1987)
"Norms as social capital", in G. Radnitzky and P. Berholz (eds.), *Economic Imperialism. The Economic Method Applied Outside the Field of Economics*, Paragon, New York, pp. 133-153.

DE MELO, J. and PANAGARIYA, A. (eds.) (1993)
New Dimensions in Regional Integration, Cambridge, MA.

FAINI, R.J. (1996)
"Increasing returns, migrations and convergence", *Journal of Development Economics*, Vol. 49, pp. 121-136.

FAINI, R. J. and de MELO (1994)
"Trade policy, employment and migration: some simulation results from Morocco", OECD Workshop on Employment and Migration, 11-13 July.

FAINI, R. J. and VENTURINI, A. (1993)
"Trade, aid and migration: some basic policy issues", *European Economic Review*, Vol. 37, pp. 435-442.

GHATAK, S., LEVINE, P. and WHEATLEY-PRICE, S. (1996)
"Migration theories and evidence: an assessment", *Journal of Economic Survey*, Vol. 10, June, pp. 165-198.

GIUBILARO, D. (1997)
"Migration from the Maghreb and migration pressures", ILO International Migration Papers No. 15.

GRIFFIN, K. (1989)
Alternative Strategies for Economic Development, Macmillan, London.

HARRIS, J. R. and TODARO, M. P. (1970)
"Migration, unemployment and development: a two-sector analysis", *American Economic Review*, Vol. 60, pp. 126-142.

HIEMENTZ, U. and SCHATZ, K.V. (1979)
"Trade in place of migration", ILO, Geneva.

INTERNATIONAL LABOUR OFFICE – ILO (1992)
"ODA as a means to reduce economic and social emigration pressure", paper for Joint ILO-UNHCR Meeting on International Aid as a Means to Reduce the Need for Emigration: Informal Summary Record, Geneva.

JONES, R.W. (1956)
"Factor proportions and the Heckscher-Ohlin theorem", *Review of Economic Studies* 24, pp. 1-10.

KRUGMAN, P. (1991)
Rethinking International Trade, MIT Press, Cambridge, MA.

LAYARD, R., BLANCHARD, O., DORNBUSH, R. and KRUGMAN, P. (1992)
East-West Migration. The Alternatives, MIT Press, Cambridge, MA.

LOPEZ, R. and SCHIFF, M. (1995)
"Migration and the skill composition of the labor force: the impact of trade liberalization in LDCs", World Bank Policy Research Paper No. 1493, August.

MACMILLEN, M. (1982)
"The economic effects of international migration: a survey", *Journal of Common Market Studies*, Vol. 20, pp. 245-267.

MARKUSEN, J. R. (1983)
"Factor movements and commodity trade as complements", *Journal of International Economics*, Vol. 14, pp. 341-356.

MARKUSEN, J. R. (1995)
"The boundaries of multinational enterprises and the theory of international trade", *Journal of Economic Perspectives*, Vol. 9, No. 2, Spring, pp. 169-189.

MARTIN, P. L. (1993)
Trade and Migration: NAFTA and Agriculture, Institute for International Economics, Washington, D.C.

MARTIN, P. L. (1994)
"Epilogue: Reducing emigration pressure. What role can foreign aid play", in W. R. Böhning. and M. L. Schloeter-Paredes (eds.), *Aid in Place of Migration*, ILO, Geneva.

MOLLE, W. (1994)
The Economics of European Integration: Theory, Practice, Policy, Aldershot, Dartmouth Publishing Company, Chapter 9.

MOLLE, W. and VAN MOURIK, A. (1988)
"International movements of labour under conditions of economic integration: the case of Western Europe", *Journal of Common Market Studies*, Vol. 26, No. 3, pp. 317-339.

MOLLE, W. and VAN MOURIK, A. (1989)
"A static explanatory model of international labour migration in Western Europe", in I. Gordon and A. P. Thirlwall (eds.), *European Factor Mobility: Trends and Consequences*, MacMillan, London.

MOUHOUD, E. M. (1997)
"The links between migration, free trade and regional integration: specific characteristics of the CEECs", *Migration, Free Trade and Regional Integration in Central and Eastern Europe*, OECD, Paris.

MOUHOUD, E. M. (1998)
"Investissements directs étrangers, migrations et intégration régionale", *Migration, libre-échange et intégration régionale dans le Bassin méditerranéen*, OECD, Paris.

MUNDELL, R. (1957)
"International trade and factor mobility", *American Economic Review*, Vol. 64, December, pp. 321-335.

OECD (1994*a*)
Migration and Development. New Partnerships for Co-operation, Paris.

OECD (1994*b*)
"New orientation for social policy", *OECD Social Policy Studies* No. 12.

OECD (1995)
Economic Outlook, December, Paris.

OJEDA, R. H. (1998)
"Economic effects on NAFTA: employment and migration modelling results", *Migration, Free Trade and Regional Integration in North America*, OECD, Paris.

PANAGARIYA, A. (1992)
"Factor mobility, trade and welfare. A North-South analysis with economies of scale", *Journal of Development Economics*, Vol. 39, pp. 229-245.

PIORE, M. J. (1979)
Birds of Passage: Migrant Labour and Industrial Societies, Cambridge University Press, Cambridge, MA.

PLATTEAU, J. P. (1994)
"Behind the market stage where real societies exist – Part II: The role of moral norms", *Journal of Development Studies*, Vol. 30, No. 4, pp. 753-817.

PUTMAN, R.D. (1993)
Making Democracy Work – Civic Traditions in Modern Italy, Princeton University Press, Princeton.

RAUCH, J. E. (1991)
"Reconciling the pattern of trade with the pattern of migration", *American Economic Review*, Vol. 81, pp. 775-796.

RICHARDS, A. (1994)
"Trade liberalisation and migration flows: some evidence from developing countries", *Migration and Development. New Partnerships for Co-operation*, OECD, Paris.

RUSSELL, S.S. and TEITELBAUM, M.S. (1992)
"International migration and international trade", World Bank Discussion Paper No. 160, World Bank, Washington, D.C.

SAITH, A. (1997)
"Emigration pressures and structural change. Case study of the Philippines", International Migration Papers No. 19, ILO, Geneva.

SAMANIEGO, N. (1998)
"Globalisation, economic growth and the labour market in North America", *Migration, Free Trade and Regional Integration in North America,* OECD, Paris.

SCHIFF, M. (1994)
"How trade, aid, and remittances affect international migration", World Bank Policy Research Paper No. 1376, November, World Bank, Washington, D.C.

SCHIFF, M. (1996*a*)
"South-North migration and trade: a survey", World Bank Policy Research Paper No. 696, December, World Bank, Washington, D.C.

SCHIFF, M. (1996*b*)
"Social capital, trade and optimal migration policy", mimeo, International Trade Division, IEC, World Bank, Washington, D.C.

SIMON, J.L. (1989)
The Economic Consequences of Immigration, Basil Blackwell, Cambridge, MA.

SOBARZO-FIMBRES, H. (1998)
"Applied general equilibrium models: the Mexican experience of NAFTA", *Migration, Free Trade and Regional Integration in North America*, OECD, Paris.

STALKER, P. (1995)
The Work of Strangers: A Survey of International Labour Migration, ILO, Geneva.

STALKER, P. (1997)
"Global nations. The impact of globalization on international migration", International Migration Papers No. 17, ILO, Geneva.

STARK, O. (1991)
The Migration of Labor, Basil Blackwell, Cambridge, MA.

STRAUBHAAR, T. (1984)

"The accession of Spain and Portugal to the EC from the aspect of the free movement of labour in an enlarged Common Labour Market", *International Migration Quarterly*, Vol. 22, pp. 228-238.

STRAUBHAAR, T. (1988)

"International labour migration within a Common Market: Some aspects of EC experience", *Journal of Common Market Studies*, Vol. 27, No. 1, pp. 45-62.

STRAUBHAAR, T. (1993)

"Migration pressure", *International Migration Quarterly*, Vol. 31, No. 1, pp. 5-38.

TAPINOS, G. (1991)

"Development assistance strategies and emigration pressure in Europe and Africa", in S. Diaz-Briquets and S. Weintraub (eds.), *The Effects of Receiving Country Policies on Migration Flows*, Westview Press, San Francisco, Oxford, Vol. 6, pp. 258-274.

TAPINOS, G. (1994*a*)

"Regional economic integration and its effects on employment and migration", *Migration and Development. New Partnerships for Co-operation*, OECD, Paris.

TAPINOS, G. (1994*b*)

"The macroeconomic impact of immigration review of the literature published since the mid-1970s", *Trends in International Migration*, Annual Report 1993, OECD, Paris.

TAPINOS, G. (1997)

"The need to better identify the links between migration, free trade and regional integration and to pursue new thinking on these issues", *Migration, Free Trade and Regional Integration in Central and Eastern Europe*, OECD, Paris.

TAPINOS, G. (1998)

"La Libéralisation des échanges et ses effets sur l'économie, l'emploi et les migrations dans le Bassin méditerranéen", *Migration, libre-échange et intégration régionale dans le Bassin méditerranéen*, OECD, Paris.

TUIRAN, R., PARTIDA, V. and AVILA, J. L. (1998)

"The impact of demographic trends and economic forecasts on the labour market and migration", paper for the OECD Conference on Migration, Free Trade and Regional Integration in North America, Mexico, January.

WALZ, U. and WELLISCH, D. (1998)

"Why do rich countries prefer free trade over free migration? The role of the modern welfare state", *European Economic Review*, Vol. 42, pp. 1595-1612.

WINTERS, A. (1993)

"The European community", in J. de Melo and A. Panagariya (eds.), *New Dimensions in Regional Integration*, University Press, Cambridge, MA.

ZIMMERMAN, K. F. (1995)

"Tackling the European migration problem", *Journal of Economic Perspectives*, Vol. 9, No. 2, pp. 45-62.

PART II

ECONOMIC GROWTH, DIRECT INVESTMENT AND MIGRATION

REGIONAL INTEGRATION, MIGRATION, GROWTH AND DIRECT INVESTMENT: A READING OF THE ECONOMIC LITERATURE

by
Denis Cogneau
DIAL-ORSTOM Paris[1]
Jean-Christophe Dumont
DIAL, Paris[2]
and
El-Mouhoub Mouhoud
CEDI-Paris XIII[3]

Standard international trade theory concludes that substitution is possible between trade in goods and services and flows of factors, labour or capital. It thereby posits the ability of trade liberalisation policies to help slow down migration flows between North and South. At the same time, it infers a reduction in capital flows and a build-up in specialisation in line with comparative advantages, on the basis of existing factorial assets. In most of concrete examples, essays in applied modelisation have shown that the degree of substitution – always in terms of the standard assumptions – between flows of goods and flows of workers cannot be very substantial. It is therefore necessary to put standard theory aside to understand how free-trade policies and regional integration might strongly inflect arguments that normally lead to a decision to emigrate. Such a change has to be sought in the dynamic effects of these policies, that is, in their growth effects rather than in their step effects (efficiency gains). This investigation will show how these growth effects come about via an increase in the pace of investment, and especially – in countries with insufficient savings capacity – through direct investment attraction. The hypothesis that goods flows can substitute capital flows should, in light of this, be discarded. This supposition, which favours complementarity between flows of goods and flows of factors, sustains that growth is not necessarily accompanied by a reduction in labour flows.

This paper examines the impact of North-South regional integration policies on growth, direct investment and migration flows, in the light of recent theoretical and empirical studies. It shows that many grey areas still exist in this field, owing mainly to uncertainties surrounding the processes of economic convergence and development. The uncertainties in question are strikingly illustrated by recent events affecting emerging countries (the Asian crisis and its repercussions).

The paper is designed as follows. The first part sets down the main arguments for migratory behaviour, as they have been catalogued by microeconomic theory, and discusses the impact of regional integration policies on these arguments. It concludes that North-South regional integration offers a serious alternative to migration only if it has a chance to markedly change the living

---

1.   4, rue d'Enghien, 75010 Paris. dial@compuserve.com

2.   4, rue d'Enghien – 75010 Paris. dial@compuserve.com

3.   Avenue Jean-Baptiste Clément, 93430 Villetaneuse. mouhoud@seg.univ-paris13.fr

conditions and expectations of South country populations within a fairly short period of time – in less than a generation. The second part focuses on the consequences of open trade on South countries' long-term growth. It concludes that the beneficial effects of regional integration on growth come about through technology transfers and investment. The third part is devoted to the effects of regional integration on direct investment. It shows that inherent in present regional integration processes is the risk of disqualifying countries that are short on human and social capital and have small-sized domestic markets.

1.   Migratory behaviour and openness

Knowledge of international migratory behaviour seems to be fairly thin. Microeconomic models propose several key variables. However, since empirical data and econometric studies are scarce, the soundness of these models and the relative impact of the variables are hard to gauge. The first part of the paper, using a few "canonical" models, discusses the potential impact of regional integration policies on migration flows. Its conclusion is that a substantial and fairly distributed stimulation of earnings and employment in developing countries can offer at least some hope of reducing migration flows.

a)   *Wages, unemployment and inequality*

The Harris and Todaro model

The base model is the Harris and Todaro static model (1970). The potential migrant compares pay for his work in his home region (w_1) with the hoped-for pay in the destination region (w_2^e). Migration occurs if:

$$w_2^e > w_1$$

In Harris and Todaro, expected wages equal wages multiplied by the immediate probability of finding a job:

$$w_2^e = (1 - u_2)w_2$$

Given the relative size of the economies in question, North-South regional integration has a very limited impact on North labour markets. The *induced* variation in the putative wages in the North is thus relatively smaller than variation in pay in the South. It is therefore worth turning the picture around and looking instead at pay expectancy in the emigration region (w_1^e). The manner of formulating pay expectancy is somewhat special, since it ignores both the time spent in unemployment and the length of time spent in each job. It is as though people had permanently renewable labour contracts – "as though individuals went to the hiring hall every day".

Duration of unemployment and effect of growth

As Stiglitz (1974) points out, the Harris and Todaro model is special in that, when there is *turnover*, the frequency of job-hunting plays no part. A more complete model would be expressed as:

$$w_1^e = \frac{w_1.(1/q_1)}{t_1 + (1/q_1)} = \frac{w_1}{1 + t_1 q_1}$$

t_1 being the expected duration of unemployment and $1/q_1$ being the average duration of a job (*turnover*). Everything depends in this case on the way duration of unemployment is represented. If the re-employment process does not depend on the length of unemployment (Poisson process), the following is obtained:

$$w_1^e = \frac{w_1(1-u_1)}{1 - \dfrac{g_1 u_1}{q_1 + g_1}}$$

g_1 being the rate of employment growth. Where employment growth is zero ($g_1=0$), the Harris and Todaro model is used.

If the duration of the unemployment model is a "queue" model, something slightly more complicated is obtained:

$$t_1 = (1/g_1)\ln\left[1 + \left(\frac{u_1}{1+u_1}\right)\left(\frac{g_1}{q_1 + g_1}\right)\right]$$

Once again, the Harris and Todaro model is used where $g_1=0$.

Whatever the assumption, the relation obtained between hoped-for pay and expected growth in employment is, for a given rate of unemployment, positive. Growth in employment increases the immediate probability of finding a job. An increase in job creation improves hoped-for pay faster than in the Harris and Todaro model and so quickly alters the propensity to emigrate.

The role of inequality

Even if the international income differential remains constant, a rise in inequality in the sending country increases the probability of migration among the poorest workers and decreases it among those who are better off. That this probability should depend less than proportionately on individual differences in hoped-for pay, owing to the fall-off in the marginal utility of income, is enough to provoke increased migration flows. Of the other theories on migratory behaviour that refer to wage inequalities, it is worth mentioning the relative deprivation theory whereby migration is made to depend on the income gap between the migrant and a reference group. In this view also, all else being equal, a rise in domestic inequality increases the probability of migration.

b)   Migration costs, timing decisions and uncertainty

Migration costs

Recent theories endeavour to formalise migration costs. They begin by introducing monetary costs. Migration occurs if wage expectancy is greater than the sum of the local wage and the fixed costs of migration:

$$w_2^e - w_1^e > c$$

The model broadens to comparisons of utility and non-monetary costs:

$$U^e(w_2, x_2) - U^e(w_1, x_1) > c$$

The variables x_1 and x_2 refer to non-monetary ingredients in utility, corresponding to each location: psychological comfort and enjoyment of public assets. It is interesting to observe that access to public assets, present in the utility function of the agents (variables x_1 and x_2), can be a strong argument for migration, particularly if these public assets are an important component of welfare. Migration behaviour, in an inter-temporal context, can then be expressed as follows:

$$\int_t^T \left[U^e(w_{2,h}) - U^e(w_{1,h})\right] e^{-\rho(t-h)} dh > \int_t^T c_h^e e^{-\rho(t-h)} dh$$

This holds for permanent migration decided upon at date t, to take place at time T.[4]

Migration costs are a control variable in migration policies. Fixed departure cost is influenced by border controls. Subsequent costs, incurred during the migrant's stay, are influenced by residency permit policies, the prevention of illegal immigration and the "overall climate" in the immigration country. Literature on migration also places quite strong emphasis on the effects of networks. Migration costs then tend to vary negatively with the number of migrants, up to a certain point, at which the contrary effects of congestion appear and costs rise with the number of migrants (Saint-Paul, 1997).

Agent heterogeneity can be introduced at either the preference (utility function) or migration cost level (Faini, 1996), which amounts to much the same thing. Take the example of the Harris and Todaro model applied to migration costs, and express it in terms of multiplication. Individual probability in favour of migrating is expressed as:

$$\frac{N_1}{N_1 + N_2} = P\left[\ln\left(\frac{w_2^e}{w_1}\right) > c\right] = \Phi\left[\ln\left(\frac{w_2^e}{w_1}\right)\right]$$

ϕ being the migration costs distribution function, N_2 the number of migrants and N_1 the number of non-migrants in the economically active population. For example, the choice of a hoped-for logistic distribution of migration costs c and standard deviation σ leads to a highly classical exponential migration function with migration elasticity proportionate to σ:

$$\frac{N_1}{N_2} = \Lambda \left(w_2^e / w_1\right)^{\sigma \sqrt{3}/\pi}$$

These simple calculations show how not only mean migration cost but also *cost disparities* (σ) influence migration flows.

---

4.   Variables x_1 and x_2 are overlooked, deferring their effect by staggering the costs of migration over a period of time.

The role of exchange rates

Where international migration is concerned, it is worth noting that the two sets of pay are not expressed in the same currency. Here a difference between permanent and temporary migrants may be introduced. A permanent migrant (*ex ante*) who does not send back remittances will compare the purchasing power of the respective wage rates in each region. This gives, using Harris and Todaro:

$$U^e\left(w_2/p_2, x_2\right) - U^e\left(w_1/p_1, x_1\right) > c$$

Where the migrant intends to use part of his income in his home country, either by transfers to his reference group or as savings, the model introduces the currency exchange rate. On the assumption that the migrant expects to earmark a part *s* of his permanent income for spending in his home country, the following may be written:

$$U^e\left[(1-s)w_2/p_2 + s\,e_{12}\,w_2/p_1, x_2\right] - U^e\left(w_1/p_1, x_1\right) > c$$

The greater *s* is, the more the exchange rate will influence migration. One may note that the two foregoing equations differ only to the extent that the exchange rate deviates from purchasing power parity ($e_{12} \neq p_1/p_2$).

Is it reasonable to assume that the rate of remittances is fixed? Length of stay has an effect on the decrease in remittances. Migrants also seem to modulate their remittances in step with exchange rate variations. If the remittance is evaluated in the home country currency, the preceding model is expressed as:

$$U^e\left[(w_2 - \overline{R}/e_{12})/p_2, x_2\right] - U^e\left(w_1/p_1, x_1\right) > c$$

The role of uncertainty

The inter-temporal nature of the choice to migrate gives an absolutely central role to assumptions concerning expectations, whether they relate to differences in expected utility or to migration costs. If agent expectations are false, they can be corrected as time passes.

In the case where uncertainty concerns the utility differential, the migrant may do better by waiting and migrating only if a positive differential is confirmed for the second period and paying the cost of migrating only when this is the case. Procrastination has an "option value", in the investment theory sense (Burda, 1995). The interest of this theory is that it links migratory behaviour to uncertainty over future income differentials. Beyond a certain threshold of uncertainty, the migrant does not leave at the first opportunity, even though the current income differential may be great. He postpones his migration. At a time of great uncertainty over the results of policies or over domestic income trends, it is thus possible to observe migration flows which bear only a faint relation to the current income differential. It is therefore more likely that migration will be postponed if migrants assume that international openness will enhance positive expectations of welfare in the home country. On the other hand, if this weak differential turns out to be an illusion (failure of open trade policies; improved living conditions for migrants in the destination country), migration will occur at a later date. According to this view, a difficult macroeconomic transition period (see below) could take place without a heavy increase in migration.

Another theory founded on uncertainty stresses risk diversification strategies within the source family group when loan or insurance markets are incomplete (Stark, 1991). It makes a special point of introducing pecuniary remittances. The utility of the source household in the case of an individual's non-migration may, in the case of a primo-migrant, and simplifying Lambert's presentation (1994), be expressed as:

$$U_1 = U\left[w_1\left(1 + \varepsilon_1\right)\right]$$

In the case of migration: $U_2 = U\left[w_1\left(1 - 1/n_1 + \varepsilon_1\right) + s\,w_2^e\left(1 + \varepsilon_2\right)\right]$

n being the number of members in the household, ε_1 the uncertainty relating to domestic income, and ε_2 the uncertainty relating to the migrant's income. The decision to migrate stems from a comparison between the expectations of the two utilities. Choosing a risk-aversion functional form then makes it possible to express utility expectations as a function of w_1, or of w_2^e, and variations in ε_1 and ε_2. Increased uncertainty over domestic income increases the probability of migration. Here, it is the uncertainty that occasions migration, whereas in the option value theory it is liable to delay it. Uncertainty over the income from emigration inhibits migration.

c)   *Effects of openness on migration variables*

Wages and employment

Standard general equilibrium models, when applied to real cases, generally provide rather disappointing projections of the long-term microeconomic efficiency gains generated by liberalisation of trade – in the region of 2-3% of GDP on average (Brown *et al.*, 1994; Goldin *et al.*, 1993; Rütherford *et al.*, 1994). For the Maghreb or sub-Saharan Africa, some estimates are even lower than that or frankly negative (see Goldin *et al.*, 1993, for example, on the impact of the Uruguay Round on the two regions). It should be remembered that on the whole these models are concerned only with the microeconomic efficiency gain generated by international specialisation that is more closely attuned to comparative advantages (greater closeness in level to the frontier of production) and have nothing to say in terms of growth. Sections 2 and 3 are devoted to the effects of growth, which form the heart of the matter.

The relative labour-intensiveness of sectors that benefit from open trade and that are hurt by it needs to be carefully examined. In the case where import substitution or non-tradable asset sectors are highly labour-intensive, it is indeed possible that the lowering of tariff barriers may lead to an overall drop in wages and hence to a durable increase in migration (Schiff, 1995). The particularity of certain kinds of work may also engender complementarity between trade liberalisation and migration (Venables, 1997). Skilled labour, for instance, may have greater opportunities for redeployment internationally than domestically. If the sectors punished by the reform are specific-labour factor intensive, an increase in the international mobility of this factor may occur.

The substitutability of migrants and natives on the immigration region's labour market is another basic variable (Ethier, 1985). Variations in job or wage discrimination, resulting from a new migration policy, can have an impact.[5] A policy that curbs "dumping" induced by the hiring of

---

5.   In France and the United States, however, available empirical data do not reveal serious wage discrimination (see Trejo, 1997, on Mexicans in the United States). In France, on the other hand, significant job-access inequalities exist.

undeclared labour produces mixed results, since it directly affects the anticipated wage level. On the one hand, it raises the cost to employers of migrant labour and, on the other, it generates an increase in wages. The substitutability of immigrant for native labour then comes into play, since more limited opportunities for dumping may persuade North employers to substitute native for migrant labour.[6]

Migration costs

Schiff (1995) examines several reasons why migration costs may be influenced by growth and, incidentally, by international openness. In the models, a fall in migration costs temporarily spurs migration flows until they reach their equilibrium level. This shows as a "migration hump". Geographical aggregation has an interesting effect. If trade openness tends to favour sectors located in regions where migration costs are highest (rural sectors) and disadvantage sectors with low costs (urban sectors), manpower will more frequently tend to depart, as the average cost of migration decreases. One may likewise suppose that, for certain agents, *domestic* migration movements occasioned by open trade (sectoral reallocations) will mean that part of the cost of international migration (especially the psychological cost, and possibly the cost of transport and information) has already been paid.

Income redistribution and reallocation costs

Traditional economic theory has it that trade liberalisation engenders specialisation in natural resource-intensive and/or unskilled labour-intensive sectors in less developed countries. Earnings for these factors tend to rise compared with that for skilled capital and labour. One might therefore think that the distributive consequences of trade liberalisation are largely favourable. This, however, means forgetting that the countryside is a special case. If farm exports of the North (or of other developing countries) enter into competition with local produce, the lowering of protection will lead to a drop in landowners' earnings. The effect on small peasant food-crop farmers, suppliers of unskilled labour but owners of their own land, is uncertain, and so could well be negative. Within the standard framework, the income curve of poor small peasant-farmers who are distant from the market therefore seems crucial to the distributive problem. Empirical studies conducted since the late 1970s on the functional distribution of income have reached mixed conclusions. Very often, especially in Latin America, income distribution appears to develop in the opposite direction to that predicted by traditional theory (see the essays referred to by Davis, 1996). Davis offers an explanation with what he calls "cones of diversification". Since countries produce only a limited cone of products, factor price equalisation works only among countries that produce in the same cone (Asia and Latin America, for example).

However this may be, it is now considered that, in the long run, international openness on the part of developing countries combines a broad redistribution of incomes with a fairly paltry overall gain in efficiency. Rodrik (1996) uses the term *political cost-benefit ratio* to describe this association.[7]

---

6. Whatever the case, the effects of such a policy, in a standard equilibrium model, depend on the assumption chosen with regard to wage formation. Such a framework, where the North labour market is greatly simplified, seems unsuited to dealing with these matters. Other approaches, such as that of Epstein *et al.* (1998), seem preferable. It formalises the immigrant labour market (legal and clandestine) into a partial equilibrium, by examining, for example, the role of residency permit duration. The trade-off between protection and migration is studied by Ethier (1985), who uses imperfect substitutability, and Müller (1997) in the case of a dualist labour market. Müller emphasises the link between temporary migration and job discrimination inside the Swiss guest-worker system.

7. He shows, in a highly simplified example, that without fiscal offsets, abolition of customs duties can result in a redistribution of $5 for an efficiency gain of $1.

This broad redistribution of incomes is also associated with a strong sectoral reallocation of factors (move towards specialisation), as the very disaggregated model of Rütherford *et al.* shows in the case of Morocco. It must be remembered in this regard that the findings of the theoretical and applied models deal only with *net* flows of factors. The corresponding gross flows are probably much bigger, as labour market studies on employment movements among firms and sectors in the United States and in Europe have shown. This reallocation is produced, on the one hand, by the opening and closing of firms and establishments and, on the other, by the physical displacement of factors and the "reskilling" of factors (job training, for example). Standard models usually overlook these reallocation costs, which can be very high when factor markets are segmented and mobility between one sector and another is difficult. Such "frictional" costs translate into unemployment or added charges and can offset the expected benefit from reform, particularly among categories with the least mobility potential. They also add to uncertainties concerning incomes that, as shown above, can have a more or less marked effect on migration flows. These uncertainties are further accentuated by the threat of financial destabilisation, which accompanies transition periods.

The transition period

In smaller and less developed countries, customs duties continue to account for a large share of fiscal revenues (a quarter in Morocco in 1991). The transition to free trade, therefore, demands a real displacement of taxes – a heavy increase in domestic taxation. All things equal, the offsetting variation required from indirect taxation will obviously be lower if the tax-rate base is broad in proportion to imports. This means that a poorly structured economy will lay the burden of a tax and customs transition on a small number of products and businesses. A transition of this kind runs a high risk of failure.

If the cut in customs tariffs is drastic enough, and local products are only imperfectly substitutable for imports, the transition to free trade will be accompanied, at the consumer level, by a fall in import prices in relation to the price of domestic formal and informal products. *Ex ante*, the tax and customs transition will thus have an effect equivalent to that of a revaluation of the real exchange rate. This is why transition is often accompanied by an offsetting currency devaluation aimed at restoring the long-term foreign balance.[8] As shown earlier, devaluation can temporarily accentuate the urge to emigrate. A key objective of the tax and customs transition is to attract private foreign capital (direct investment). A successful transition should therefore eventually enable the real exchange rate to stabilise. The reform may also be accompanied by an inflow of public foreign capital (aid or loans) which serves temporarily to rebalance the external accounts.[9]

At any rate, it is important not to downplay the potentially destabilising influence of reforms in external taxation, when a country's macroeconomic management capacities are defective and when there is a lack of major productivity gains in the tradables sectors (a precondition for increasing the country's competitiveness and attracting direct investment). Rodrik (1996) recalls how gradual the trade liberalisation of the East and South-East Asian countries was, and how it was preceded by a consolidation of state macroeconomic management capacities and a rapidly paced accumulation of factors (physical and human capital). By comparison, certain Latin American and African countries have had to enact, within five years, reforms which the Asian countries took over twenty years to implement.

---

8. Penetration by imports is greater than the extra growth in exports, mainly because trade liberalisation is more often than not asymmetrical, customs tariffs being much higher in South than in North countries. Moreover, the agreement concluded between the European Union and its Maghreb partners barely touched on agricultural products.

9. These financial flows will nevertheless be offset in the long run by flows in the opposite direction, repatriation of profits (private capital of multinational corporations) or debt repayments.

Conclusion

While microeconomic migration theory has progressed far beyond the Harris and Todaro model (1970), it still proposes a multitude of disconnected models, few of which have been empirically tested. These models call into play, not only wage rates and job opportunities, but also exchange rates (in the case of temporary migration), income disparities, the availability of public non-tradable assets and uncertainty over present and future income. The latter variable, although probably important, produces contradictory effects depending on which theory is adopted. The role of inequalities and the availability of public assets have not yet been evaluated. In the final analysis, the wage and employment outlook continues to be the central and unambiguous argument behind migration behaviour. Static efficiency gains associated with trade liberalisation are relatively small and can be cancelled out by the politico-economic costs of the transition period. These prospects are better examined within the dynamic framework of growth and foreign direct investment theories.

2.   The challenge of openness and its effects on growth

a)   *International openness in neo-classical growth theory*

The properties of the neo-classical growth model in a closed economy are familiar. In the absence of technical progress, the decline in the marginal productivity of the factors of production ensures convergence towards a stationary regular state of per capita production. Furthermore, during the transition phase, the originally less well-endowed economies grow more quickly, generating a catch-up effect.

In an open economy, these features are not questioned and the egalitarian predictions of the neo-classical model are even reinforced. The small country hypothesis indeed allows for the supposition that the interest rate is constant and, in that case, that convergence towards stationary equilibrium is instantaneous.[10] What is more, the equilibrium capital stock is higher than in an economically self-sufficient regime and, if the agents are not too impatient, the same is true of the level of per capita consumption.[11]

Introducing international migration makes it possible to enrich the analysis. Barro and Sala-I-Martin (1995) integrate into the model of Solow and Swan (1956), then into the formalisation of Cass and Koopmans (1965), the possibility of receiving new arrivals endowed with physical or human capital. If the migration flow is sustained over a long period,[12] the equilibrium growth rate will be positively (/negatively) affected by immigration (/emigration). However, this effect will be entirely attributable to the increase in manpower, and the equilibrium levels attained will be smaller as migration is heavier. On the other hand, if the capital endowment of the new arrivals is relatively small, the process of convergence towards the stationary condition will be hastened. Braun (1993) goes further in investigating the inclusion of migratory phenomena in the neo-classical growth model by admitting international capital mobility and supposing that decisions to migrate stem from an attitude of inter-temporal optimisation. He furthermore considers that there is a fixed factor in the

---

10.   Here is repeated, within a dynamic framework, the conclusions of the standard international trade model, which predicts instantaneous convergence of rates of pay upon trade liberalisation.

11.   For a formal demonstration and some additional findings, see, for example, Barro and Sala-I-Martin (1995).

12.   On the supposition, for example, that it is exogenous (for example, independent of economic conditions) or that the per capita equilibrium stock of capital is such that incentives to migrate continue.

economy, which undergoes a congestion effect as the population increases. In this view, incentives to migrate dwindle during the transition phase and the migration flow dries up little by little. As in the open model without manpower mobility, the economy ends up converging towards a stationary state.

Faini (1996), escaping from the neo-classical framework, shows how assumptions concerning labour factor mobility can condition convergence. The author uses a two-country model, each country producing tradable and non-tradable goods. Production of the non-tradable good takes place with increasing returns using capital only. Production of the tradable good needs, for its part, non-tradable goods, labour and capital. In this sector, returns are such that accumulable capital is utilised with non-increasing returns. Sustained long-term growth is therefore impossible and, without migration, the dynamics of transition exhibit a phenomenon of convergence. Once migration becomes possible, the country initially possessing the greatest stock of capital grows the fastest since it benefits from the increasing returns in the non-tradable sector. Pressure on wages will then favour immigration. A divergence of growth rates is observable in the short term between the two economies, and this is threatened in the long term only by the availability of manpower liable to migrate.

In the neo-classical growth model, openness, even if it involves factors and goods, has no particular impact on long-term growth potential. What it does affect, however, is welfare and the dynamics of transition. Recent formalisations, deriving from "the new international economics"[13] and "endogenous growth theories", present a very different picture. The introduction of market imperfections, non-diminishing returns or external effects fundamentally changes the preceding findings (Faini, 1996). As regards growth models, four types of mechanisms are called into play:

– Openness, through its effect on specialisation, influences the equilibrium growth rate.

– Growth in trade favours technology transfers and so stimulates the growth process in least developed countries.

– Market integration makes it possible to benefit from economies of scale in the increasing return sector. This is, generally speaking, a research and development sector.

– The development of trade eliminates duplication of effort in research (the fact that resources are devoted to the development of similar products in two different places).

In the special context of North-South regional integration, these mechanisms are not all equally relevant. The two last points, for instance, refer more to cases where production techniques and specialisation are alike in different countries. This work is quite well exemplified by the models of Rivera-Batiz and Romer (1991*a* and 1991*b*), Grossman and Helpman (1991*a*), and Taylor (1994) in the case of distinct technologies or, more recently, Walz (1997) with a three-bloc model. Laffargue (1993) offers a detailed review of these contributions. The mechanisms involved in the first two cases, however, deserve further explanation.

---

13. Baldwin and Seghezza (1996*b*) show, for example, that the presence of market imperfections in the standard dynamic framework modifies some of its characteristics. In the neo-classical model, more particularly, openness leads to a win-lose situation during the transition phase (the least endowed country grows faster and the most endowed country grows more slowly). The introduction of elements of monopolistic competition into the tradable sector, assumed to be relatively capital-intensive, makes it possible to alter this outcome and to generate win-win situations which, according the authors, are more consistent with observations from the post-war period. In these models, openness to trade has the effect of favouring the process of accumulation and accelerating the dynamics of transition towards a stationary regular state characterised by a larger stock of equilibrium capital in all countries.

b)   *Specialisation geared to comparative advantages*

Lucas (1988), in his landmark contribution, proposes a preliminary approach to the dynamic effect of specialisation within a situation of international competition. He begins by considering a self-supporting economy which produces two types of goods, and where the accumulation of human capital occurs through a process of on-the-job learning. The problem of inter-temporal maximisation facing the agents is expressed as:

$$\begin{cases} MaxU(C_1,C_2) = (\alpha_1 . C_1^{-\rho} + \alpha_2 . C_2^{-\rho}) \\ C_i(t) = h_i(t) . u_i(t) . N(t) \\ \dot{h}_i(t) = h_i(t) . \delta_i . u_i(t) \end{cases}$$

Ci being final consumption of good *i*

hi the specific human capital used for producing good *i*

ui the time devoted to forming the human capital of type *i*

δi-1 the depreciation rate of the human capital

$i=1.2 \; \delta_1 > \delta_2$

Under these conditions it may be shown that the dynamic properties depend on the elasticity of substitution σ:

- If $\sigma \leq 1$, the tendency will be towards stable mixed production.

- If $\sigma > 1$, choice of specialisation is entirely determined by initial endowments, meaning that there will be specialisation in production of the good where performance is best. At length, production will consist exclusively of this good.

It is extremely instructive to introduce international trade into this rather primitive model. Assuming that there is a continuum of small countries faced with an identical relative trade price $p=p_2/p_1$, the author shows that the countries will specialise in producing the good for which they possess a static comparative advantage. If $h_1/h_2 < p$ (/ $h_1/h_2 > p$), they will exclusively produce good 2 (/good 1). In terms of dynamics, it is apparent that the countries specialised in the production of good 1 (/ 2) have a constant endowment of h_2 (/ h_1) and a growth rate for factor h_1 equal to δ_1 (/ h_2 equal to δ_2). In this situation, openness to trade enhances the initial comparative advantages. However, if the growth potential of production of good 1 is notably stronger than that of good 2, it is possible that the price p will vary to such an extent that it would be advisable for certain countries to change their specialisation (this possibility implies that $\sigma < 1 - \delta_2/\delta_1$). This notwithstanding, in cases where $\sigma > 1$, it is certain that initial specialisations will not be altered, and it can be shown that the countries best endowed with the factor h_1 will have a higher growth rate.

Comparable results have been obtained by Feenstra (1996), who concludes that countries with a low capacity for growth-generating innovation will be penalised by open trade, and by Matsuyama (1991), who shows how exploitation of comparative advantages in traditional sectors can deprive industry or research of resources and curb growth.

Quah and Rauch (1990) take the model of Lucas and adapt it by assuming the existence of complementary intermediate goods. In a closed economy, growth is then constrained by the development potential of the least dynamic sector. With openness to trade, this constraint is removed and greater specialisation in the more technology-intensive intermediate goods may be observed, with a consequent increase in growth. This conclusion applies only to countries not specialising in the production of the least dynamic goods.

It is finally worth mentioning the work by Stokey (1991) and Young (1991) who depart somewhat from the previous framework while continuing to admit the effects of learning. The accumulation of human capital is subject to an external effect and makes possible the production of better quality goods which consumers prefer. A distinction is then drawn between two economic entities, the North and the South, according to their initial endowment in human capital. In a situation of self-sufficiency, there is a single equilibrium growth rate that depends primarily on preferences for the present (negatively) and (positively) on the efficiency of production of human capital. The transition to an open economy reduces the relative price of human capital-intensive goods. The authors then show that the South will produce a range of low-quality goods whereas the North will specialise in more human capital-intensive goods. In this situation, the economies of both entities will continue to grow at constant rates, but these rates will be less similar than they would have been without trade. Openness fosters a process of divergence.

A contradictory finding obtained by Grossman and Helpman (1991*b*) may be pointed out, using a three-sector (traditional, technological, and R&D) learning model and two types of labour (skilled and unskilled). The traditional sector is alone in using unskilled labour whereas the R&D sector increases the productivity of the technological sector and favours the accumulation of human capital. The authors proceed to show that countries holding an initial comparative advantage in production of the technological good will, with open trade, be tempted to devote more resources to the latter and will thereby suffer a decline in their growth rate. Although this mechanism predicts that the North will perhaps not benefit from open trade, it does not indicate that the South will gain from it.

Pecorino (1992) does reach this finding. He shows that the existence of economic rents hobbles growth potential by reducing the human capital available for productive activities and by inducing agents to invest in human resources that are specific to the quest for rent. According to this view, trade liberalisation, by curtailing trade rents, will stimulate the growth process.

c)   ***Technology dissemination***

Another mechanism by which openness is liable to affect the long-term growth process of South economies has to do with the dissemination of technology. It is expected that foreign direct investment (FDI) should play a special role in this regard. Foreign firms would – by taking part in the privatisation of large existing companies, entering into joint-venture agreements with local firms or carrying out green-field FDI – bring with them their know-how and management structures, thereby easing the transition towards modern forms of organisation. Technological catch-up could then take place by short-circuiting – skipping the investment-intensive stages of R&D and directly latching on to the new technology of existing products and processes. Such FDI should help transform sectoral specialisations and raise their R&D and skilled labour content.

The technological dissemination process described by Phelps (1962) provides an understanding of this mechanism. It has recently been brought to the fore again by the new growth theory. This is especially evident in the work of Grossman and Helpman (1991*b*), revisited by Barro and Sala-I-Martin (1995).[14] As earlier, a distinction is made between two countries. The first (the leader country) develops new intermediate goods through efforts at innovation, while the second (the follower country) lays hands on the technology thanks to a less expensive process of imitation. In each country *i*, production is a function of the availability of the technology (that is, of the diversity of the intermediate goods):

---

14.   See also the work by Wang (1990), who applies the hypothesis of Findlay (1978) – according to which direct investment enables the pace of technical progress to accelerate via an effect of "contagion" spreading through the whole economy – in a standard neo-classical model.

$$Y_i = A_i L_i^{1-\alpha} \sum_{j=1}^{Ni} (Xij)^\alpha$$

Supposing that the activities of research and imitation are monopolistic (the price of the good is fixed) and that there is free access to these sectors (the cost is equal to the discounted value of profits), it can be demonstrated that the growth rate of each of the economies is:

$$\gamma_i = (1/\vartheta)[r_i - \rho] = (1/\vartheta)\left[(L_i/\varphi_i)\left(\frac{1-\alpha}{\alpha}\right)(A_i)^{1/(1-\alpha)} \alpha^{2/(1-\alpha)} - \rho \right]$$

φ_1 (/φ_2) being the cost of innovation (/imitation) for a new good.

The model's dynamic properties therefore depend essentially on the costs φ_1 and φ_2:

–   If it is supposed that the costs of innovation and imitation are fixed, so that $\varphi_2 < \varphi_1$, the growth rate of the follower country will be higher than that of the leader country and there will be a catch-up process. Country 2 will grow faster and will end up imitating all the goods developed by country 1. At equilibrium, the economies will differ only in their functional parameters. In other words, if they have the same production technologies and the same quantity of manpower, they will reach equivalent equilibrium levels.

–   It may also be supposed that the cost of innovation is fixed and that the cost of imitation positively depends on the rarity of the new products. Posit, for example, that $\varphi_2 = f(N_2/N_1)$ with $f'(.)>0$ and $f''(.)<0$. It may then be shown that a ratio N_2/N_1 exists which enables the costs of research and imitation activities to be equalised. In the long run, the two countries will converge towards the same equilibrium growth rate, but the levels attained and the welfare of the two populations will be different.

Regional integration is liable to affect the cost of imitation in two opposite ways: *a)* by imposing quality standards and enforcing property rights, and; *b)* by facilitating access to the technology developed by the leader country. The former effect would tend to raise the costs of reproducing the technology, whereas the second would work the other way around. Depending on the result, regional integration would or would not favour the growth process in the South country. The effect would be exerted, however, only during the transition period and only on equilibrium levels. The effects of openness discussed here do not differ fundamentally therefore from those derived from the standard neo-classical model.

On this point, Pissarides (1997) suggests that the effect of integration differs in at least one respect from the standard analysis. It can, he writes, lead to an increase in wage inequalities. The author uses the preceding model to distinguish between two types of labour: skilled and unskilled. He also supposes that the process of imitation in country 2 employs only skilled labour. Under this assumption, openness – here determined from the expansion of the whole range of goods liable to be imitated[15] – causes a relative increase in skilled wages during the transition phase. This means that the accumulation of human capital will be stimulated and the migration of skilled labour stemmed.[16] In the

---

15.   Which, under certain conditions, amounts to a reduction in the cost of imitation.

16.   This mechanism contradicts the finding of Haque and Kim (1995). The authors make the supposition that individuals have two periods in their lives. When they are young, they spend part of their time on learning, and then they decide on the country where they will exercise their activity. The decision to migrate is taken in the light of a fixed cost, a parameter of assimilation and the wage differential. The inclusion of a fixed cost associated with migration is all-important in that it makes expatriation all the more remunerative in that the level of human capital is high. The authors conclude by demonstrating that migration permanently lowers the per capita growth rate in the sending country through a brain-drain

longer term, however, the benefits accruing to skilled labour will tend to cancel themselves out and the wage ratio will return to its original level.

If it is supposed that innovation activities are protected by property rights, imitation in the South is doomed. The North's R&D sector will alone have the power to transfer technology. The transfer could take place through direct investment, through an adjustment process whose cost is postulated as equal to φ_3.[17] Although these changes may seem minor, they have important consequences for the answers given by the technological dissemination model:

- If it is assumed that the South country, closed to begin with, opens to direct investment, the activity of adaptation becomes highly lucrative and North investors will initially devote all their efforts to it. When balance among rates of return is restored, R&D activities will resume and any new product will immediately be adapted. In comparison with the self-supporting situation, the South country will, under openness, benefit from a long-term increase in growth, which was not the case earlier.

- What is more, the world equilibrium growth rate is stimulated by the joint introduction of property rights and open trade. In this scenario, North innovators can internalise all the profits from their activity and will so be encouraged to devote more resources to it.

Recently, Ben-David and Loewy (1995) took the representation of the trade liberalisation process a step further by building a multi-country model capable of explicitly simulating the impact of lower entrance duties. In this formalisation, the dissemination of technical progress is directly linked with increased trade. It depends on the share of exports in total production and the skill level acquired by the partners. In this model, where each economic entity produces a single good, which it trades with all the others, technical progress stimulates the accumulation of human capital, the sole factor of production. Following a reduction in customs duties, growth during the transition phase increases to equilibrium. The same is true for the equilibrium levels. These conclusions continue to be valid even where the economies and liberalisation are asymmetrical.

d)   What should be remembered about the theoretical effects of openness on growth?

Assessment of the expected effects of openness to trade and regional integration, taking the new theories of growth in an open economy as a yardstick, may seem to be a somewhat questionable exercise. Yet the contribution of this work, when set against the feebleness of the neo-classical theory's predictions, is by no means negligible. In the standard framework, the decline in the marginal productivity of the accumulable factor ensures unconditional and instantaneous convergence of income, regardless of the openness and manpower mobility situation. At equilibrium, the growth rate will depend solely on technical progress and population growth. Welfare will be (positively) affected by open trade. These conclusions come back to those of classic international trade models, whose evaluation is often disappointing. The theories of endogenous growth enable this framework to be transcended and pave the way for new assessments of the effects of openness.[18]

---

effect. The benefit derived by the immigration country from new human resources dwindles and finally cancels itself out.

17.   This cost should be lower than the cost of innovation and also lower than the cost of imitation φ_2. It may be reasonably supposed that the companies which develop new products are in the best position to modify them.

18.   Laffargue (1993, p. 25) concludes his presentation by saying that, "The importance of the literature on endogenous growth cannot be overestimated. The models of calculable general equilibrium used to study the effects of distortions in the developing economies often attribute a fairly limited increase in well-

A first series of endogenous growth models, based on Lucas (1988), stresses the importance of the growth potential linked with static comparative advantages. In these models, growth rate disparities among countries may be permanent and may even widen. Regional integration would contribute to growth only in countries holding an initial comparative advantage in the factor essential to producing the most dynamic good, usually human capital. It would therefore accentuate the properties of hysteresis.

These were the findings which led Barro (1993) to write: "Therefore, as a general conclusion, we can say that countries, which already have a reasonable level of endogenous technical progress and may compete in a relatively fair situation with other developed economies, are urged by the new growth theory to reduce protection, as a way to promote growth. Developing countries, nonetheless, have to protect their sectors which can generate high levels of spillover, if they seek to achieve higher rates of economic growth."

A second body of work focuses on the effect of technological dissemination, the extension of which is a source of sustained long-term growth. The results here are relatively equivocal. They tend to show that open trade is favourable to long-term growth since it allows technology to be disseminated. Protection of property rights and the free movement of capital also appear as favourable elements.

For FDI to produce a positive effect on the receiving country, however, various conditions have to be met. The transfer of knowledge liable to spur improvement in the factors of endogenous growth is certainly beset with limits.

One central question is knowing whether FDI is placed in well-enough developed sectors, that is, in areas close to or complementary with the specialisations of the receiving country's enterprises, or whether it is like "a cathedral in a desert", hardly at all in touch with the local economy (Cantwell, 1992).

As regards the developing world, Wang and Blömstrom (1992) show that technological dissemination in the receiving country depends not only on the size of FDI flows but more importantly on its capacity of absorption; which is largely a question of the availability of a skilled workforce and the state of the country's infrastructure.

It could be concluded that, after a reading of this literature, the gamble on openness by developing countries poorly endowed with human capital depends necessarily on the prospect for greater access to technology and foreign direct investment. Moreover, if the sectors concerned by this investment are skilled labour-intensive, the depreciative effects of openness on the return from human capital may possibly be attenuated. For this reason, the inflow of direct investment, besides favouring growth, would have the added advantage of limiting movements of skilled labour.

The question now is to establish whether or not this theoretical insight is corroborated by empirical studies.

---

being to large-scale trade liberalisation or to moves towards a more neutral tax system. One reason for this finding would seem to be that these models do not pay heed, except perhaps in an *ad hoc* fashion, to the dynamic effects of these measures. It is to be hoped that the technical framework developed by the theory of endogenous growth will enable these gains to be better discussed".

e)   *Empirical assessments of the link between openness and growth confirm the importance of domestic and foreign investment*

In the 1950s and 1960s, the issue of openness was little disputed. The protectionist paradigm dominated the developing world and most industrialisation policies, preached and practised, were grounded on minimal openness to trade and the protection of fledgling industries (Prebish, 1950). In the mid-1970s and later during the 1980s, development economists, faced with the non-viability of self-centred policies, began recommending strategies based on market reform and openness to international trade. A large number of empirical studies were then launched to underpin this new approach (see Edwards, 1993 for a complete digest of this work).

The ground-breaking contribution by Michaely (1977) was among the very first cross-section econometric studies. The author ranked a sample of 41 countries by growth rate, per capita production and rate of growth of the share of exports in GDP from 1950 to 1973. A rank-correlation analysis (Spearman test) brought to light a positive and significant relation between the rankings, suggesting that the most outward-looking countries grow more rapidly.[19] Krueger (1978), for her part, proceeded somewhat differently by constructing a qualitative indicator linked to the different types of trade regime, which she then used to explain export and GDP trends in a 10-country sample from 1954 to 1972. She showed that trade liberalisation had a positive effect on growth but that this effect was primarily indirect – that it was expressed through an increase in exports.

These studies were criticised, however, for their lack of conceptual underpinning and more especially for failing to identify the main factors of growth. Numerous authors then set about calculating growth equations, inferred from neo-classical production functions, that included an indicator of openness. Feder (1983) supposed, for example, that export sector development was a source of technical progress for the non-tradable sector. The rate of GDP growth would then depend on the rate of investment, population growth rate and the volume and growth of exports. The model's calculation, applied to a sample of 31 semi-industrialised countries, confirmed the existence of a significant and positive external effect related to exports. The studies along the same lines by Balassa (1985), Ram (1985, 1987), Rana (1988), Kohli and Singh (1989) or Syrquin and Chenery (1989) broadly corroborated these first findings.[20]

This work was not to be taken as gospel, however, for at least two reasons (Krugman, 1994; Rodrik, 1995). For one thing, the direction of the causality displayed in the growth equations was not clear. As Edwards (1993) put it, "Do countries with rapidly growing exports have a higher rate of growth, or is it that faster growing countries have a more dynamic export sector?" For another, the indicators used to represent the conditions of openness were often conceptually and empirically vulnerable to criticism. According to Rodrik (1995), two sorts of measurement problems deserve to be mentioned: "The trade-regime indicator used is typically measured very badly. ... Openness in the sense of lack of trade restrictions is often confused with macroeconomic aspects of a policy regime, notably the exchange-rate stance."

Yet despite quality problems with the indicators, the consistency of the findings must be admitted. Edwards (1997), for example, performs a series of calculations involving nine different indicators[21] in a regression dealing with 93 countries. Out of the eighteen equations tested, all but one

---

19.   Similar results were obtained by Balassa (1978), for example, using a different sample.

20.   See Edwards (1993) for a detailed treatment of these studies.

21.   Sachs and Warmer Openness Index, World Development Report Outward Orientation Index, Leamer's Openness Index, Average Black Market Premium, Average Import Tariff on Manufacturing, Average Coverage of non Tariff Barriers, The Heritage Foundation Index of Distortions in International Trade, Collected Trade Taxes Ratio, Wolf's Index of Import Distortions.

exhibit a positive effect of the openness variable, and thirteen express a significant coefficient. It is this relative evenness in the findings that leads Rodrik (1995) to temper his criticism: "Measurement and conceptual issues aside, it is perhaps reassuring that so many studies using so many different indicators tend to confirm that countries with fewer price distortions, particularly on the trade side, tend to growth faster. Even if we are not convinced by any single study, should we not be swayed by all of them taken together?"

Various authors using different techniques have tackled the problem of causality. Jung and Marshall (1985), for example, apply a Granger-style causality test to panel data and conclude that, in 22 cases out of 37, it is impossible to be sure of the direction of causality between export growth and per capita production growth. Esfahani (1991) calculates a set of simultaneous equations stipulating GDP, export and import growth. He does not manage to demonstrate an effect of openness on growth.

The truth of the matter, according to the broad synthesis published by Levine and Renelt (1992), seems to be that openness does not produce an independent effect but that this effect is achieved essentially through investment. The authors conclude their essay with this sentence: "These results suggest an important two-link chain between trade and growth through investment".[22] Recent work by Baldwin and Seghezza (1996a) confirms this analysis. They calculate a system of two simultaneous equations acting in cross-section on a sample of countries whose manufacturing firms were exporters in 1989. The system evaluated, deduced from a theoretical formalisation, is expressed as:

$$\left(\frac{\dot{Y}}{Y}\right)_j = b_{11} - b_{12}\left(\frac{Y}{L}\right)_j - b_{13}h_j + b_{14}\left(\frac{\dot{K}}{Y}\right)_j + b_{15}(xH)_j + b_{16}h_j + e_1j$$

$$\left(\frac{I}{Y}\right)_j = b_{21} - b_{22}\ln\left(\frac{Y}{L}\right)_j - b_{23}\ln(xH)_j + b_{24}\ln h_j - b_{25}o_jt^* - b_{26}o_jt + e_2j$$

$$\beta_{kl} > 0, \forall k \, \forall l$$

Y being GDP, L population, η the population growth rate, ξ_H the per capita human capital ratio, h and k per capita human and physical capital investment, respectively, o_j the imports/GDP ratio which country j would have in a free trade environment, τ the domestic trade barrier factor,[23] and τ^* the foreign trade barrier confronting domestic exports.

The calculation shows i) that the impact of trade barriers (domestic and foreign) is negative – they deter investment – and ii) that the mechanism by which trade affects growth is not direct – trade affects growth through its impact on investment.

Last, it is interesting to note that empirical studies confirm the determining role of investment in the influence exerted by openness on growth. It would seem worthwhile therefore to investigate the relation between foreign direct investment (FDI) and per capita productivity growth.

22. We may also quote the recent study by Weinhold and Rauch (1997) who postulate a chain of causality among openness, specialisation and productivity growth. They construct three indicators of specialisation for 39 countries and 28 sectors of industry. The findings clearly confirm the effects of specialisation on productivity growth, chiefly in developing countries.

23. If $\tau = 1$, trade is completely free.

Unfortunately, data availability problems have meant that empirical studies assessing this relation are few and far between. Mention may be made of a study by Alonso-Gamo *et al.* (1997) dealing with the Arab countries. The authors offer an assessment covering seven countries (Algeria, Egypt, Jordan, Mauritania, Morocco, Syria and Tunisia), each of which supplied four sets of observations covering five-year periods from 1970 to 1990. While the econometric findings confirm a positive and significant effect of openness on investment, FDI apparently did not affect growth. An explanation may perhaps lie in the conditions surrounding this investment, especially as regards infrastructure and the supply of skilled manpower.

Another study that may be mentioned is that by Borensztein *et al.* (1994) which offers an in-depth appraisal of the relation between FDI and growth carried out on a 69-country sample from 1970 to 1989. Three types of finding are worth noting here:

- Foreign direct investment increases total investment but without producing a crowding-out effect. On the contrary, there would seem to be relative complementarity between domestic and foreign direct investment.

- FDI is positively correlated with per capita productivity growth, meaning that, for each additional percentage point in the FDI/GDP ratio, growth rate is higher by 0.8 point.

- When a term crossing FDI with a school enrolment variable (here the average years of secondary schooling for boys) is introduced, the latter is found to have a positive effect on growth. Furthermore, the independent effect of FDI disappears, even when endogeneity problems are taken into account.

These findings lead the authors to conclude: "The most robust finding of this paper is that the effect of FDI on economic growth is dependent on the level of human capital in the host economy. (…) The contribution of FDI to economic growth comprises two effects. First, FDI increases the overall level of investment, attracting higher levels of domestic investment. (...) And second, FDI is more productive than domestic investment, a result that does depend on the interaction with human capital" (Borensztein *et al.*, 1994).

It would seem then that, despite disagreements, empirical studies are reasonably united in affirming that trade liberalisation has a positive and appreciable impact on productivity gains and production growth. It would seem also that the link is largely mediated by investment. A closer look at the foreign component of investment reveals a noteworthy impact of FDI on growth. Growth appears to depend on the total availability of investment and a locomotive effect on domestic investment. It seems also that the availability of skilled manpower is an essential condition for FDI efficiency.

It now remains to be seen what the determinants of this technology-intensive investment are and, more especially, whether trade openness is enough to attract it.

3.   Relation between direct investment and trade liberalisation

It is important to know, within the context of this subject and from a theoretical and empirical standpoint, to what extent trade liberalisation between a regional union (the EU countries) and less developed countries (those around the Mediterranean seaboard, for example) generates FDI flows in the latter's direction. Most studies take an exogenous view when dealing with the massive increase of FDI in countries aspiring to sign a free trade agreement or lining up as candidates for the enlargement of a regional union (EU, NAFTA), after they open up to trade.[24] This implicitly amounts to adopting the hypothesis that a complementary relation exists between trade and FDI. But in the case of a substitution relation justified by the prior existence of tariff-avoidance ("barrier-jumping") direct investment, should not opening to trade then result in a decline in FDI?

It is first important to distinguish very clearly between transfers of activity by multinational enterprises from their base countries in the course of operations to conquer local and regional markets, and transfers of activity related to simple differences in factor endowment, which entail re-importation of end products. This latter category does not necessarily involve transfers of capital (FDI); it is often more a matter of international out-sourcing contracts. Once these two motivations of multinational enterprises have been detached from one another, one can begin considering the relation between FDI and international trade in each case, and concentrate on the study of FDI determinants.

Where firms are based in countries other than members of the trading bloc, the problem can be posed in terms of a trade-off between direct investment and exports to the bloc. Indeed, as the theory of customs unions shows (Viner, 1950), diversion of trade can occur to the detriment of non-member countries, which formerly exported to bloc countries. The latter then react by substituting FDI for trade flows (tariff-jumping investment). This investigation is most concerned with direct investment among member countries of a trading bloc, as may be studied from the effects of the European single market. There are two further types of response: either firms from most developed countries in the regional zone transfer their standard or waning production activities to the newly joined countries in order to profit from a comparative cost-advantage or to meet demand for less sophisticated goods; or the transfers of activity by firms towards the countries in question are subject to a trade-off between proximity and regional concentration of the firms' activity. The new economic geography provides answers by incorporating externalities of "agglomeration" into the models.

After reviewing the main stylised facts concerning macro- and microeconomic trends in international direct investment and their determinants (Section 3a), the investigation will give an account of the theoretical and empirical studies that emphasise the substitution relation between FDI and trade (Section 3b). It will then describe the studies – more numerous, especially on the empirical side – which opt for a relation of complementarity. Next, it will turn to the problems of trade-offs by multinational enterprises between proximity and concentration, insisting on the marginal character of vertical FDI founded on differences in factor proportions. It will also deal with the site distribution of firms in a regional zone, using economic geography approaches (Section 3c).

a)   ***Main stylised facts concerning FDI***

Even though industrialised countries already accounted for the lion's share of direct investment inputs, this share grew appreciably during the 1980s.[25] Direct investment flows also took on an increasingly hybrid character, reflecting the dual movement of convergence of the overall technological level of industrialised countries and of their accentuated technological specialisation. Several essays demonstrated a relation between countries' technological advantages and direct investment inputs (Dunning, 1988; Kogut and Chang, 1991), whereas Pearce, Islam and Sauvant (UNCTAD, 1992) did not find any significant correlation between direct investment flows among industrialised countries and relative sectoral wage costs.

---

24.   More recently, Cogneau *et al.* (1998) have endeavoured to endogenise this direct investment in a general equilibrium model that is calculable as a lowering of the FDI risk premium, after the work of Rodrik (1991).

25.   Developing countries' share of direct investment inflows shot up abruptly in 1993. The upsurge seems to have been governed mainly by cyclical determinants (UNCTAD, 1995).

All the same, the sudden jump in the proportion of investment flows directed towards developing countries in the early 1990s did not necessarily signify a continuation or upsurge in movements to locate abroad for comparative cost reasons. It is worth noting, however, that over 90% of these direct investment flows were concentrated in ten or so rapid-growth developing countries that offered both attractive local outlet potential and a highly efficient communication infrastructure endowment. This thereby reconciled de-location for cost minimisation reasons with flexibility and versatility in responding to demand fluctuations.

The share of FDI in primary sectors is receding in favour of FDI in manufacturing industry and above all in service activities. Within the manufacturing industry, FDI is increasingly concentrated in technology-intensive sectors, in marketing and advertising expenditure-intensive sectors and, third, in sectors where oligopolistic interdependence is strong, the three descriptions being superimposable. Most FDI is likewise now horizontal in character (Markusen, 1995), whereas until the late 1970s its nature or logic was rather vertical (logic of vertical international segmentation of production processes). So it is that, while almost 30% of world trade (and 40% of OECD-country trade in manufacturing) consists of intra-firm commerce, most of the output of multi-national enterprise subsidiaries is sold in the host country. These changes in the scale, nature and geographical and sectoral orientation of FDI are matched by changes in its *main determinants* – there being a very definite erosion of the traditional FDI determinant of factor endowment or wage cost differences (EEC, 1993; Markusen, 1995).

As for the *modalities* or *shape* of FDI, there has been an increase in intermediate forms (joint venture agreements, strategic alliances, take-over mergers, and so forth) to the detriment of the creation of majority-owned subsidiaries. Many studies attest to the boom in the number of co-operative (joint venture) agreements concluded since the 1980s.[26] These agreements, mostly international, are heavily concentrated in knowledge-intensive sectors (technology, R&D, skilled manpower) and especially in information technology, new materials and biotechnology. The studies underscore the very important role played by considerations of technological complementarity among countries with a similar endowment.[27] The authors of these studies go on to interpret the alliances among firms belonging to different technological sectors as a method for "conglomerating and combining stores of knowledge".[28] In short, FDI has quickly and strongly developed under new forms and among countries with similar factor endowment and per capita income, and with limited trade barriers.

b)   *The theoretical FDI/trade relation: substitution or complementarity*

Models positing substitution between exports and FDI rest for the most part on microeconomic firm theories (except in Mundell). The investigation will now demonstrate how substitution operates theoretically, first among countries with different factor endowments

---

26.   See, amongst others, Chesnais (1988), Hagedoorn and Schakenraad (1993), and for a rapid overview, see Nunnemkamp *et al.* (1994).

27.   31% of the 587 agreements involving European groups recorded from 1980 to 1988 by the CEREM concerned the production of technological knowledge.

28.   Chesnais (1988) points out that 53% of the 1,883 agreements recorded from 1982 to 1985 involved technology transfers and the integration of R&D activities. Hagedoorn and Schakenraad (1993) show that 60% of the alliances observed had R&D cost sharing or know-how acquisition as their primary motivation. Market access or modification of market structures were reported as the primary motive in only 30% of cases. The ranking list of motives varies by sector. Market access predominates in industry. Technology-related motives rank high in biotechnology, new materials, industrial automation, computer software and, to a lesser degree, in the aircraft industry.

(Mundellian approach within a HOS framework), then in a time frame ("optimal timing" theory). It will then show how the new theory of multinational enterprises in imperfect competition treats the impact of formation of a trading bloc on direct investment and export flows of non-member countries towards bloc countries.

Models tending to favour complementarity fall into various categories: macroeconomic, industrial-economic, and spatial-economic.

Substitution in a Heckscher-Ohlin-Samuelson (HOS) framework

If substitution exists between direct investment and international trade (Mundell, 1957), it is by reason of the hypothesis of identical production functions in perfect competition. Take, for example, two countries A and B. Country A is relatively rich in capital K, while B is relatively rich in labour L: $K_A/L_A > K_B/L_B$ Two goods, X (capital-intensive) and Y (labour-intensive), are manufactured in the two countries in a context of complete free trade in goods and capital. Specialisation (incomplete) develops according to the principle of comparative advantages: A in the manufacture of good X, and B in the manufacture of good Y. The application of an international relative price for the two goods creates an equilibrium in which the exports of the one balance the imports of the other. The Stolper-Samuelson theorem leads to equalisation of factor prices. Mundell supposes the introduction by country B of a customs duty on imports of good X from country A. This brings about an increase in the relative price in country B, since protection is applied to the capital-intensive good. The difference in return on capital (relatively scarce in B) results in a transfer of capital from A to B. The outcome is a transformation of the two countries' factor endowments (good X is produced more in B and its production declines in A, and *vice versa* for good Y) which leads logically to an elimination of comparative advantages. Capital flows from A to B continue for as long as the marginal productivity of the capital remains different between A and B. Protectionism is what triggers the movement of capital from A to B. Country B, importer of capital, must produce an additional quantity of goods for export in order to pay for the capital imported from A.

Income and production remain unchanged in the two countries; it is only the trade in goods that diminishes. There is indeed substitution between trade and capital flows. As shown by Markusen (1983), Mundell was the first to present this notion in formalised fashion. International mobility of capital would end up eliminating differences in factor endowment among economies, thereby leading to a world without FDI and without trade.

The difficulty with this type of analysis stems from reasoning in terms of production factor mobility versus mobility of goods and therefore overlooks the existence of the multinational enterprise and its strategy choices. The theory of company multinationalisation (Hymer, 1976) was initially developed for the purpose of contesting international trade theory. It explicitly introduces the multilateral enterprise as possessor of a specific advantage ("ownership advantage" in imperfect competition) which internalised transaction costs (Coase-Williamson) instead of relying on the market ("internalisation"), although it would later be recognised that location advantages strongly resembled the notion of comparative advantages when it came to choosing a host country ("localisation"). The new so-called "eclectic" theory (Ownership-Localisation-Internalisation) of company multinationalisation put forward by Dunning (1988) thus conjugated several direct investment cause variables corresponding to different levels of analysis. Variables dealing with specificity (ownership), referring to advantages deriving from the imperfect competition peculiar to the firm's sector, raise the question of the multinational's very existence despite delocation costs. Variables concerning internalisation raise the question of choice between the market (exporting) and organisation (FDI) depending on the specificity of assets, the frequency of transactions and market failures.

Variables concerning location give an insight into how the choice of host country is made in the light of what is known about the first two types of variables. It is then likely that *an ambiguous relation between FDI and exports* will be obtained *if the level of analysis is macroeconomic* only or restricted to production factor mobility. On the other hand, exploitation of all three levels would very likely make it possible, at a given stage of technological development, to distinguish between HOS sectors where a substitution relation comes into play and Schumpeterian sectors where a relation of complementarity predominates. Other approaches make the two types of flows alternate in the course of time.

The theory of optimal timing and the product cycle: sequential alternation

The theory of optimal timing of FDI (sequential theory) under which exports form a springboard for FDI again reflects the notion of substitution between FDI and exports. Opening up to trade would first facilitate exports to LDCs and then attract FDI flows (Agarwal *et al.*, 1991). This theory is based on the notion that, on the assumption of increasing returns, location abroad represents a fixed cost offset by diminishing variable costs (Buckley and Casson, 1985). Exports, licensing and FDI are successive alternative modes for conquering a foreign market (in ascending order of fixed costs and descending order of variable costs) (Agarwal *et al.*, 1991).

This approach predicts a gradual shift from exports to licensing and then to FDI, in pace with the expansion of the foreign markets. In the case of sectors where licensing entails excessive costs or risks, there would be a direct transition from exports to FDI.

This sequential theory implies that a substitution relation exists between FDI and exports. The theory of "optimal timing of FDI" is also incompatible with the theory of trade barrier-jumping FDI.[29] Trade relations enable firms to build up knowledge on both the supply and specific demand situation for a particular product in a country. Vernon's product cycle theory (1966) may be classified as such a thesis. The author himself threw doubt on his theory in 1979,[30] on account of the shortening of cycles combined with the increased pace of technological innovation, and the fact that this sort of diachronic sequence did not occur in certain sectors. International direct investment could start as soon as a new product was launched.

Substitution of FDI for trade flows may, however, appear at the microeconomic level when multinational enterprises see countries, to which they previously exported, form a regional union which excludes the enterprise's country of origin.

Impact of the formation of regional blocs

The regional integration process induces firms from countries that are not members of the bloc to replace their export strategy by an FDI strategy. The FDI in question is tariff barrier-jumping

---

29. A theory that is moreover refuted by the econometric test of Agarwal *et al.* (1991).

30. The theory supposes a diachronic sequence: the innovating firm serves its domestic market in the product-launch phase (monopolistic rent), then exports it because it is imitated by its domestic competitors in the product growth phase. It carries out FDI in the initial export market to fight against the erosion of its innovation rent, and finishes by delocating the manufacturing of the good to the least technologically advanced country, once the product has become commonplace. FDI in developing countries therefore necessarily occurs at the end of the product cycle. In oligopolistic sectors, multinational enterprises can launch a new product on the world market straight away and manufacture it in the host countries without going through the export stage.

investment linked to the trade flow diversion effect (of the Viner type) created by the non-integration into the trading zone of the country substituting FDI for exports. For example, enlargement of the European Union to the East will not necessarily entail an increase in intra-zone FDI (unless an interest is shown for economic geography). What is likely to increase is extra-zone FDI (American or Japanese, for instance).

Motta and Norman (1993) developed a three-country model to study this situation. The three countries are designated as H, P and A. Countries H and P decide to form a regional union. They are imagined as being identical in size and consumer taste structure. In each of the two countries, a domestic firm (designated h in country H and p in country P) produces. These firms both supply their domestic market and export to the other country in the bloc. Let c^H be the marginal cost in country H, supposed as being lower than that, c^P, of the firms in country P. The cost of exporting between H and P equals t per unit (transport costs and tariff and non-tariff barriers – the latter raise production costs). The strategies of firms h and p for supplying country A may be ignored in this hypothesis of constant marginal production costs.

Demand in the trading bloc (H and P) is expressed as $Q = S(v-p)$, p being the price of the good, Q overall demand, v consumer affordability and S the size of the market. Outside the trading bloc, country A has two firms (designated as 1 and 2) which produce at marginal costs c^1 and c^2 considered as identical ($c = c^1 = c^2$). Firms 1 and 2 export to or invest in the regional zone formed by H and P.

Under these conditions, the problem of choosing between FDI and exports (or of substitution between trade and FDI) is posed not only in terms of the different options' costs to the firms but also in terms of oligopolistic reactions.

–   If the firms decide to export, they bear a unit cost $\tau > t$ such that $c^P < c^H < c + \tau$.

–   If the firms decide to invest in H and/or in P, they bear a fixed installation cost G per unit of production created. But once the FDI has been made, the firms benefit from a specific advantage owing to the fact that they produce at a cost ρc^H or ρc^P with $\rho < 1$. The lower ρ is, the more profitable is the FDI. Likewise, the faster G (installation cost) is recouped (that is, the greater S/G is), the more advantageous is the FDI.

It is further supposed that exporting from a trading bloc country is more advantageous than exporting from outside the bloc, that:

$$c + \tau > \rho c^H + t > \rho c^P + t$$

then the two firms thus have four options as regards selling in countries H and P:

1. Exporting to both countries.

2. Investing in one of the two countries (H, for example) and re-exporting from this host country to the other country (P).

3. Investing in P and re-exporting from P to H.

4. Investing directly in both countries.

The strategies adopted result from a two-stage process in which firms 1 and 2 first choose their system for penetrating the markets of P and H. In the second stage, firms 1 and 2, h and p determine their supply in accordance with the decisions taken by firms 1 and 2 in the first stage. The size of the regional zone and the amount of the common customs duty (common external tariff) are determining factors in the choice of system of penetration. The degree of integration (measured by t)

influences the choice of the country of location in the event that the firm chooses FDI. An increase in the common external tariff τ obviously favours direct investment to the detriment of exports.

The possibility of a difference in production costs between P and H induces firms *1* and *2* to delocate production to P in order to benefit from its lower production cost. An increase in customs duties would then favour concentration of FDI in the regional zone.[31]

When the specific advantage of multinational firms is great (low ρ), however, direct investment is always given preference over exporting. But, seeing that the variation in production costs among delocated units $\rho(c^H - c^P)$ is smaller when ρ is low, the firms will split their FDI among the countries in the zone in order to ease competitive pressure (intensified by concentration of FDI). A familiar conclusion is reached, namely that the more a trading bloc grows in size, the more direct investment becomes a substitute for exports.

In this type of model, FDI from countries which are not members of the trading bloc increases and takes the place of trade flows. The countries in the regional zone that offer a comparative cost advantage can benefit from a concentration of locations of non-member country firms' units of production, since they belong to the same regional market as the one the firms are hoping to serve.

The Motta and Norman model (1993) produces a further result:

– Where the integration process becomes strong (*t* decreases), direct investment concentrates in countries offering the lowest production cost (thanks to a productivity or comparative cost advantage).

– Where there is no appreciable difference in production cost, direct investment is spread in order to reduce competitive pressure.

In sum, this model stresses the effects of substitution at the corporate level, although it does not exclude relations of complementarity between FDI and trade flows at the macro-sectoral level.

Complementarity in the context of factor/goods mobility

Against the Mundellian approach of substitution among factor flows, Kojima (1978) sets an approach in terms of complementarity. In so doing, he reconciles FDI theory and the theory of international trade based on differences in technology (the neo-technological approach). Kojima's analysis, which is situated at the macro-sectoral level, introduces country comparative advantages when explaining the relations between international (North-South) direct investment and trade flows. International direct investment involves a transfer of capital and technology. If direct investment is made, as it is in Mundell's system in the sector holding a comparative advantage in the source country, a relation of substitution between trade and FDI must be admitted. If, as in Kojima (1978), FDI is made from the source country's sector of comparative disadvantage to the same sector holding a comparative advantage in the host country, a relation of complementarity can develop. The FDI's source country will import the goods originating from the delocations in the country holding the comparative advantage. The latter, on its side, will import capital goods from the investing North country.

Kojima's conclusion may also be found in the model of Helpman (1984). This is a model with two technologically different countries (country *1* being more advanced than country *2*), two factors (labour and R&D) and two goods (one differentiated, the other homogeneous). The differentiated good is characterised by a market subjected to monopolistic competition, while the

---

31. An intuitive adaptation of this model to the Euro-Mediterranean free trade agreement would then reflect the possibility of increased FDI in the regional zone's low-wage or lowest unit cost countries.

second good is subject to perfect competition. The differentiated good is more R&D-intensive, relatively, than the homogeneous good. In the absence of multinational enterprises, at equilibrium, factor prices do not equalise. The relatively rarer factor is better remunerated in each country. Suppose that a firm from country *1* creates a subsidiary in country *2*. It transfers R&D to country *2* until the prices of the two factors equalise and it re-imports the end products from country *2*. This intra-firm trade is the sign of complementarity between FDI and international trade.

Markusen (1983) shows that, in work such as Mundell's (1957), the substitution relation between factor mobility and international trade rests on the assumption that differences in factor endowment are the sole driving force of international trade. It is possible to show that, even in a two-country, two-factor, two-goods (2x2x2) model, the relation between factor mobility and international trade can be complementary in a framework based on technology differences among countries. The relation between factor mobility and international trade is also complementary in the system of Schmitz and Helmberger (1970), in which the commodity exports of developing countries require prior FDI from industrialised countries.

Including the multinational enterprise and the micro-macro interconnection

The model of Motta and Norman (1993), although it demonstrates a substitution relation between FDI and exports at the microeconomic level, does not do so at the macroeconomic or macro-sectoral level, at which a relation of complementarity should normally be confirmed. There is a second lesson to be drawn from this model. When a regional zone member country hosts a multinational enterprise, trade (exports) with its trading partners grows thanks to export flows (from *H* to *P*, for example) generated by the subsidiary. This parallels a finding by Rowthorn (1992) who shows that the creation of a customs union increases FDI received by its member countries from outside countries and that this boosts intra-bloc trade flows. In other words, the relation of substitution between external FDI and exports appears to be soundly based theoretically at the microeconomic level.

The eclectic approaches by Dunning (OLI) objectively favour the substitution relation. The advantage of internalisation, as a variable determining the choice of founding a multinational firm by FDI, or, what amounts to much the same thing, locating subsidiaries abroad, necessarily replaces trade flow (internalisation of the multinational's set-up through FDI is preferred to going through the market-exporting).

The existence of a complementarity (or substitution) relation depends largely, in sum, on the determinants of direct investment and its sectoral logic. More analytically, the firm performs a trade-off between, on the one hand, concentrating its production and serving markets by export flows and, on the other, moving closer to point-of-sale (proximity). The trade-off is therefore more a choice between FDI and sales by subsidiaries (intra-firm trade).

The concentration/proximity trade-off (CPT)

Brainard (1993a) developed a general equilibrium model to explain the expansion of multinationals through exports or direct investment as the outcome of a trade-off between the advantages of concentration and of proximity.[32] He posits a two-country (*A* and *B*) economy with two sectors, one agricultural and homogeneous (good *Y*), the other manufacturing and differentiated (goods *Q*). The differentiated sector is characterised by production in several stages, and has specific

---

32.   This is again the Dunning-style (1988) OLI (Ownership-Location-Internalisation) framework mentioned earlier.

R&D and manufacturing expenses.[33] It is therefore eligible for a trade-off between exports and location abroad or, in other words, proximity and concentration (or again, trade and investment). According to the value of the parameters, therefore, firms in the differentiated sector penetrate the foreign market by exports and direct investment. The existence of this sector gives rise *ipso facto* to a number of different equilibria.

Thus arises a sort of general case, in a world comprising not only end products but also intermediate goods, and a continuum of intermediate solutions between the two extremes: at one end, total domination by factor endowment considerations and purely inter-branch trade both in end products and intermediate consumptions; and, at the other end, total domination by considerations of proximity with direct investment completely replacing intra-branch trade in end products but existing side by side with intra-branch trade in intermediate consumptions. Brainard (1993a), extending his supposition to a large number of countries, surmised that international trade patterns may be ordered by the size of differences in factor endowment. Inter-branch trade predominates among countries that are different in this respect, whereas intra-branch trade predominates among countries that are similar.

The findings of the theoretical models do not add up to a general law of complementarity or substitution between the two types of flows. The answers depend on the assumptions made: perfect or imperfect competition; level of analysis (micro- or macro-sectoral); and, determinants (market, or differences in costs). The empirical work on assessing the impact of trade liberalisation on FDI flows concludes on the whole, however, that relations of complementarity predominate. This is particularly evident when looking at the effects of European integration on FDI.

c)   *Empirical studies: preponderance of complementarity*

Nature of the FDI/trade relation in the European integration context

Dunning (1997a), in a recent article, provides an exhaustive inventory of the empirical studies dealing with trade flow inter-relations since the advent of the Common Market and then the European single market.

On the Common Market's effects on the FDI placed in European Community countries, whether from outside or by Member states, studies carried out in the 1960s and 1970s reveal two sorts of seemingly contradictory effects:[34]

–   Reduction in tariff-jumping FDI *and hence a decrease* in defensive import-substitution DI.[35] The source countries for this kind of FDI could supply Member state markets simply by exporting. This was a substitution effect.

–   An indirect or secondary effect, under which trade integration induced a general improvement in income and business competitiveness within the zone in question and, subsequently, a multiplication of profitable investment opportunities along with an

---

33.   At both levels, there are increasing returns of scale, but this advantage, which should act in the direction of export-led penetration of the foreign market, is countered by transport costs supposedly reflecting the drawbacks of distance (transport proper, customs barriers, cultural and linguistic differences and so forth).

34.   From a methodological viewpoint, Dunning criticises these studies for taking a longitudinal – the study of chronological series – rather than a cross-section approach to data (Dunning, 1997a).

35.   Refers to imports from the viewpoint of the target market, here the FDI receiving country.

enhancement of local firms' ability to carry out direct investment (Dunning, 1997a). Dunning dubs this indirect effect a wealth effect.

According to Dunning, studies dealing with the period before preparations for the single market show that, except for some defensive import-substitution DI, most DI (intra-EC and from non-EC members) was either beneficial for foreign trade or neutral (Dunning, 1997a).

Dunning makes two basic assumptions, which he then examines:

–   The single market should *a priori* have an ambiguous effect on intra-zone DI and a positive effect on DI from non-member countries (Dunning, 1997a).

–   The single market should *a priori* bring about a diversion effect of FDI in line with production costs and, more generally, according to supply variables in the different possible locations, whereas demand variables (notably market size and growth) should conversely reduce its relative volume (Dunning, 1997a).

Several indicators for checking substitution/complementarity between FDI and trade may be used. Strong similarities between the geographical distribution of trade flows and FDI flows point to complementarity between the two kinds of flows or indices of FDI and trade intensity may again be used (Petri, 1997). For example, where intensity $FDI_{ij}/FDI_j > 1$ and $X_{ij}/X_j > 1$, FDI and exports from country i to country j – the target country – are relatively greater than those from other countries to country j.

The target "country" here is the European Community. Studies show that non-member countries have placed large amounts of defensive FDI capable of substituting for trade (Dunning, 1997a).

If, on the other hand, country-by-country econometric studies are used, the complementarity relation is often apparent. Henry (1994) econometrically demonstrates a degree of complementarity between France's exports and its FDI stock, at least for much of its dealings with OECD countries. There is a positive correlation between the tendential changes in French FDI stocks and France's propensity to export.

This apparent complementarity has two possible explanations:

–   It stems from a combined response to variations in world demand for French products, whether they are produced in France itself or in affiliates abroad. Complementarity is apparent in the sense that, in the absence (or slackening) of growth in demand for French products, intra-branch substitution may occur. Since the goods are the same, any increase in delocated production cuts into exports.

–   It signifies intra- or inter-branch support by FDI for exports. FDI can in fact either be used for the production of finished goods using intermediate goods made in France or to set up networks for distributing products made in France. (See box 1 on Henry's study of French FDI abroad).

An econometric study by Petri (1997) of the four most important FDI source countries in 1990 shows that the FDI/trade relation is by and large complementary. Without committing itself to a causal relation between DI and foreign trade (unlike Henry's study), it shows that regional concentration of FDI and of trade is determined by the same factors.

Before the advent of the single market, most DI in the EC countries had its source in non-member countries (Dunning, 1997a). Correlatively, intra-EC trade was more inter-firm than intra-firm. American corporations had meanwhile developed and integrated their subsidiaries within the EEC, thereby stimulating a flourishing Europe-wide intra-firm trade. The implementation of the single market then witnessed an accompanying rise in intra-EU FDI and intra-EU intra-firm trade.

Sectoral data show that DI from non-member countries is clearly concentrated in services infrastructure sectors, above all financing, banking, insurance and distributive trade activities (Dunning, 1997a). This attests to the fact that DI placed in the EU countries is very largely motivated by market access.

Generally speaking, according to Dunning, both the literature and the facts lead to the conclusion that MNEs especially develop in sectors having certain features: high R&D intensiveness; large proportions of skilled staff in the workforce; production (relying on economies of scale) of technologically-advanced and complex intermediate goods; production of highly differentiated end products for which demand is income-elastic; and, low co-ordination costs for intra-firm relations among units spread across several different countries (EEC, 1993 ; Dunning, 1997*a*).

Now that the relations of complementarity or substitution within the framework of trade liberalisation have been verified, it is time to present the empirical studies aimed at assessing the effects of European regional integration (single market) on FDI.

Effects of regional integration (single market) on FDI

Despite all the obstacles[36] to isolating the European single market's specific effects on the volume and modalities of intra- and extra-European FDI in the European Community, two kinds of approaches used in recent econometric studies may be categorised (Dunning, 1997*b*):

- The first involves building a model in which the variable "single market" is added to the classic FDI causal variables and trying to evaluate its significance in residual fashion.

- The other more deductive and predictive approach consists in testing a certain number of particular assumptions concerning the effects of regional integration of FDI as drawn from the multinational firm and international trade theories.

The methods seem fairly close to one another: the same analytical and measurement problem, and the construction of a "proxy" for integrating non-quantifiable variables.

Work by Clegg (1995), or Pain and Lansbury (1996), has clarified the significance of those variables unrelated to the single market which influence FDI in the EU. It is a case where the values of the residual (non-dependent) variables may be considered as a proxy for the single market or for its importance, leaving aside its effects on the value of other causal variables.

A different method is to calculate the impact of regional integration (single market) variables on the variables (independent of the single market) which themselves determine FDI. This is the method used by UNCTAD (UNCTAD, 1993) to deal with FDI in the European Community and the other industrialised countries.

It may thereby be deduced – as shown in the essays by Clegg (1995) or by Pain and Lansbury (1996) (see Figure 1) – that 20 to 27% of the increase in FDI over the period examined (1987-92) was attributable to the single market. This was done by estimating GNP variation due to the completion of the single market at 6%, as simulated in the report by Cecchini *et al.* (1988), and by using the calculations of Julius (1990) and UNCTAD (1993) on FDI elasticities (from 3.5 to 4.5%) in relation to GNP variations.

The authors find that (overlooking the negligible exchange rate variable) the other four variables explain 90% of FDI fluctuations in both the EU and the other industrialised countries.[37] The most significant of them is the market size (GNP) variable – the value of the coefficients is greater for Europe than for other industrialised countries. The share of domestic investment in GNP is also

---

36. Much depends on the type of FDI (defensive or aggressive) examined, the factors specific to the host country, the method of measuring the single market, and the assumptions made on what would happen without a single market (construction of an "anti-world").

37. The value of the explanatory variables' coefficients is always correct.

significant and is positively correlated to FDI[38] with regard both to FDI in the EU and FDI going to other industrialised countries. The study measures FDI elasticity in response to changes in the value of the independent variables. It finds that an increase in both GNP and the rate of domestic investment (GFCF/GNP) is accompanied by a 4% growth in FDI flows.

Figure 1. **Indirect effects of the single market on FDI**

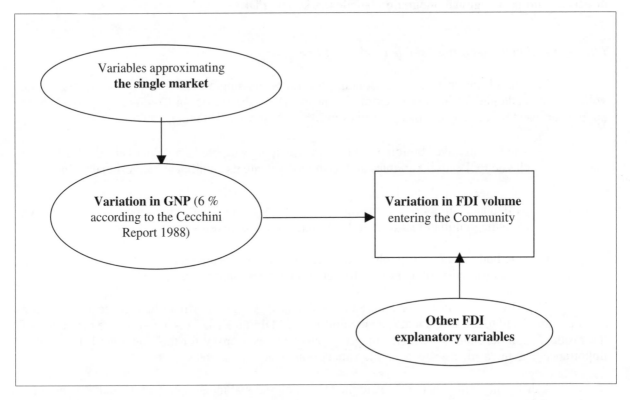

The study's concluding observation is that the growth rate of FDI going to EU countries is higher than that of FDI going to other industrialised countries, and that growth rates of GNP and of the investment/GNP ratio are also higher.

The essay by Srinivasan and Mody (1998) limits itself to an examination of Japanese and American FDI in 35 receiving countries (including ten EC members) over the period 1977-92. Four types of FDI determining factors are considered:

– The classic factors (approximated by the size of the receiving country's market, the cost of labour and the cost of capital).

– Factors of agglomeration (approximated by per capita electricity and telecommunications infrastructure).

– Factors of trade restriction (approximated in reverse by the degree of openness of the receiving country's economy and a "dummy" variable representing the European single market).

– Country-risk factors (as customarily assigned to LDCs).

---

38. Which suggests possible complementarity between domestic investment and FDI entering the EU over the reference period.

For the classic factors, the market size variable is significant and positively correlated to FDI, while the labour cost variable is significant but negatively correlated to FDI. The variables linked with the agglomeration factors are significant and positively correlated in EU countries but not in other industrialised receiving countries. The trade openness variables are significantly and positively related to FDI, but the country-risk variables are not. Introduction of the single market "dummy" variation improves the equation's explanatory capacity. When the country-risk variable is omitted, the other three variables explain 70% of FDI variation in EU countries. The single market's favourable effect on the entry of American and Japanese FDI is corroborated by other econometric studies on FDI originating in a larger sample of investing industrialised countries (Clegg, 1995; Buigues and Jacquemin, 1994; Pain and Lansbury, 1996). The latter essay even detects an effect of FDI being diverted to the EU on account of the single market.

Taken together, the studies confirm the European single market's positive effect on the increase of FDI inflows. Most of FDI, however, is direct investment for the purpose of penetrating the European market. There is no reason to think that the less advanced countries (say the South of the Mediterranean) will experience an influx of FDI once they join a regional zone (the European Union, for example) or sign free-trade agreements.

In conclusion: complementarity or substitution?

The theoretical analysis of the FDI/trade relation has made great progress. Early work produced contradictory results. The relation of substitution between FDI and trade first appeared in models where the motivation for FDI was market conquest (Hymer, 1976), and then in oligopolistic competition models (Rowthorn, 1992). They introduced the idea whereby firms in a country *A* previously exporting to two countries *B* and *C*, which decide to form a trade zone excluding country *A*, can substitute FDI for export flows.

Complementarity appears in the case of delocations inspired by differences in production costs, generally among countries having dissimilar factor endowments. Complementarity of this kind involves several kinds of flow. From a dynamic and sequential viewpoint, the country receiving assembly segment-tasks delocated by the North firm becomes the exporter of the good to the North country (Kojima, 1978). Or the North firm delocates part of the production process to the South country which, after exporting components, re-imports the end product. There is complementarity and simultaneity between FDI flows and trade flows.

More recent models reach less clear-cut conclusions. FDI and exports are substitutable or complementary according to the assumptions made and the choice of level of analysis (micro- or macro-sectoral). For the latter, it is enough to widen the angle of study of market penetration behaviour.

Oddly, empirical studies tend to come down on the side of the complementarity relation, even in cases where FDI is motivated by market access. This seems consistent with the stylised facts concerning FDI, whereby its primary determinants are more and more often market access and access to specific scientific and technical skills. Differences in factor endowment explain only a marginal part of FDI. How do the new theories of multinationalisation of firms explain these paradoxes? One answer lies in not limiting attention to the relation between FDI and trade but broadening it to the relation between exports (concentration) and the activities of MNE subsidiaries (proximity).

The single market has a positive effect on the increase in FDI in the European Community. There is no reason to conclude however, that the inclusion of LDCs in the European Union, and, *a fortiori*, the signing of a simple free-trade agreement between the EU and these countries, will result in an increase of FDI in their direction capable of bringing into play the dynamic mechanisms described in Section II.

d)   *Regional integration and location of productive activities: contribution of the new economic geography*

Why does direct investment not necessarily flow to low-wage countries in the integrated zone or to countries entering into a free-trade agreement with the zone, following the logic of differences in factor endowment? To put it differently, postulating a cost difference-related inflow of FDI simply because trade or even the terms of direct investment have been liberalised (example of NAFTA) is to forget that multinationals only very rarely and only in a few sectoral niches invest abroad and re-import the product (reverse import flow). Factual analysis increasingly rejects the difference-in-factor-endowment determinant and even cost differences in the delocation strategies of multinational enterprises (Mouhoud, 1992 and 1996; Henry, 1994; Markusen, 1995). Julius (1990) calculated that, in Brazil as in the European Union, sales by American subsidiaries on the local market were five times greater than exports of the local production back to the United States. These considerations all cast doubt on the use of factor endowment differentials to explain multinational corporate expansion.

Brainard, for instance, taking a theoretical model (1993*a*), which he had tested empirically (1993*b*, 1993*c*), attempted to explain why an ever-growing proportion of FDI involves the industrialised countries as investors but also and above all as recipients, and why the trade-off between concentration and proximity seems to determine firms' choice of investment destination. The literature dealing with the new economic geography and with regional integration mentions other factors governing location of multinational firms (Krugman, 1991; Baldwin and Venables, 1995; Markusen and Venables, 1996). It must nevertheless be emphasised that very little empirical work is available for testing the theoretical findings of these models.

Taking the redistribution effects (agglomeration/decentralisation) of the location of firms (activities) into account in the context of an integrated regional zone made up of regions (points in space, not countries) supposes the existence of non-linear inequality or catch-up processes. For lack of data, especially for Europe, the insights of the new economic geography have, unfortunately, only rarely been empirically tested.

One of the issues raised by this literature (Baldwin and Venables, 1995) is the extent to which regional integration is accompanied by agglomeration/concentration effects in certain areas of the regional zone and knowing whether inequalities can be an element in attracting firms.

It is undeniable that regional integration alters the distribution of activity within the integrated zone, so affecting regional inequalities. With perfect competition, regional integration reduces differences in factor prices and leads to their convergence within the integrated zone. The presence of imperfect competition and increasing returns of scale can change, and even reverse, this effect. Economies of scale induce firms to make a strategy choice, based on a trade-off between proximity and concentration inside the integrated zone, of where to locate their production. The trade-off depends on trade barriers and wage differentials. Regional inequalities can thus result from integration.

Imagine three countries whose markets are of different sizes. Two of the countries form a regional bloc, with the result that transaction costs between them fall. What inferences can be drawn as to the location of industry and, hence, labour demand and relative wages in each of the integrated countries?

106

The authors (Baldwin and Venables, 1995) treat the subject in three stages: the effects of integration on the profitability of firms in the different countries; the effects of integration on the displacement of production resulting from a change in the number of firms following changes in profit levels; and the determinants of the extent of the effects, and their impact on welfare.

Each country has two sectors. Sector X, where competition is imperfect, manufactures differentiated goods with increasing returns of scale. Sector Z, where competition is perfect and returns of scale are constant, manufactures a homogeneous good which is tradable at lower cost and acts as money. Only one factor of production – labour – is considered. The typical consumer of country j has a function of indirect utility $v_j(P_j,1,E_j)$, 1 being the output price of sector Z, E_j consumer expenditure and P_j the price index for the varieties of good X for sale on market j. The price index takes the following CES form:

$$P_j = \left(\sum_{k=1}^{3} \left[n_k (p_{kj} \tau_{kj})^{1-\sigma} \right] \right)^{\frac{1}{1-\sigma}}, \sigma > 1$$

n_k being the number of varieties offered by country k, p_{kj} the price charged by the producer, τ_{kj} the transaction cost factor (type "Samuelson iceberg") of producing in k and selling in j,[39] and $p_k \tau_{kj}$ the price of sale of these varieties in country j. On the demand side, $E_j^X(P_j,E_j)$ is the total expenditure of country j in sector X; consumer expenditure on a variety of product X is:

$$c_{kj} = (p_{kj}^i \tau_{kj})^{-\sigma} P_j^{\sigma-1} E_j^X (P_j, E_j)$$

On the supply side, each firm produces a single variety of good X and the authors suppose that each firm is ignorant of the effect of its action on the industry as a whole. Profit for any one firm in sector X in country j is therefore:

$$\pi_j = \sum_{k=1}^{3} p_{jk} x_{jk} - x_j b_j - f_j, \quad x_j \equiv \sum_{k=1}^{3} x_{jk}$$

technology having a fixed cost f_j and a constant marginal cost b_j. The firms are considered as playing a "segmented market" game, that is, they compete against one another on each market separately. A first-order condition for profit maximisation is obtained by:

$$p_{jk} = \frac{\sigma}{\sigma-1} b_j$$

The number of firms operating in each country n_k, is determined, at long-term equilibrium, by the zero profit condition:

$$\sum_{k=1}^{3} \frac{x_{jk}}{\sigma-1} = \frac{f_j}{b_j}$$

The equilibrium scale at firm level is thus expressed as:

$$\bar{x} = (\sigma-1) f_j / b_j$$

---

39. $0<\tau<1$. This being so, a proportion of the goods $(\tau_{kj}-1)/\tau_{kj}$ disappears in transit. Production is therefore greater than effective consumption.

Demand functions may be expressed in the form:

$$p_k x_{kj} = E_j^x \frac{\theta_{kj}}{\sum_{i=1}^{3} n_i \theta_{ij}}, \quad \theta_{ij} \equiv \frac{p_i x_{ij}}{p_j x_{jj}} = \left(\frac{b_i \tau_{ij}}{b_j}\right)^{1-\sigma}$$

θ_{ij} measuring the ratio of country i firm sales to country j to country j firm sales to country j. θ_{ij} sums up relative costs.[40]

With these elements in hand, it is possible to determine the number of firms and production volume in each country. The authors, for the sake of simplicity, suppose that the two integrated countries are symmetrical, that $\theta_{12} = \theta_{21} = \theta$, and $\theta_{i3} = \theta_{3i} = 0$, in erecting prohibitive trade barriers against non-union countries, and that $p_1 = p_2$, $i = 1.2$. They deduce the equations for total sales by a representative country 1 firm (equal by symmetry to those of a representative country 2 firm), and by a country 3 firm:

$$x_1 = \frac{1}{p}\left[\frac{E_1^X}{n_1 + \theta_{21}n_2} + \frac{E_2^X \theta}{\theta_{12}n_1 + n_2}\right] \text{ and } x_3 = \frac{1}{p_3}\left[\frac{E_3^X}{n_3}\right]$$

Equilibrium in an industry is such that $x_i = \bar{x}$. If $x_i > (<)\bar{x}$, profits are positive (negative).

Four results are obtained:

- The profitability of firms is zero in the extreme cases of self-sufficiency and free trade. In between the two, profit is positive or negative according to whether consumer spending is higher in country 1 than in country 2. It follows that, for a constant number of firms, sales per firm in the small economy will follow a U-curve function for transaction costs, which fall then rise during the integration process.

- The lowering of trade barriers induces a movement of firms from the small to the large country, until trade is totally liberalised, at which time location becomes indeterminate.

- Where transaction costs are high, wages are similar in the two countries. Conversely, when costs fall, the large market becomes more attractive. In order for the same number of firms to stay on the territory, wages must be raised in the small country and lowered in the large country. If costs drop too far, wages in the two countries will realign.

- The small economy gains in welfare from full integration, in that it has access to more varieties without having to bear transaction costs.[41]

If one reasons within an agglomeration framework, that is, one in which an increase in the number of firms present on a location improves the return of the firms already there, the same conclusions are not necessarily achieved, since multiple equilibria may appear. In order for the agglomeration effect to be possible, externalities must be introduced (although it is not a sufficient condition): for example, technological ones limited in space, or financial ones connected with the imperfect competition environment. It is important, however, to distinguish between externalities related to costs and those related to demand. Cost-related externalities can signify that integration induces agglomeration and thereby intensifies the delocation of activities into already developed territories of the regional zone.

---

40. Obviously, $\theta_{ij} = 1$. θ_{ij} equals 0 in a self-sufficient economy and 1 in free trade.

41. A similar result is obtained in Krugman and Venables (1995).

Within this non-monotonous perspective, several configurations are possible. It is not at all clear that the newly integrated country, or that country with which trade is liberalised, will attract productive activities or even retain those it has. In the long run, however, it could again benefit from a dispersion of the regional zone's activities.

Conclusion

This paper has tried to settle the question of the substitution of trade flows for international migration flows through the indirect effects of regional integration on growth. Openness only indirectly stimulates growth via the inflow of FDI, or of a certain type of FDI. This sequential process has therefore been broken down into three parts:

- How does trade openness act on migration and what is it at the microeconomic level that determines the choices of a given individual in modifying his decision to emigrate?

- What, in the new growth models, are the dynamic effects of regional integration and, more precisely, what role does the dissemination of knowledge (implicitly correlated with FDI flows) play in these models?

- Given that FDI inflows should foster growth, it is still necessary for a relation of complementarity to exist between trade openness and FDI. In other words, what conditions are needed for FDI to flow to the less-advanced emigration countries which join a regional bloc made up of immigration countries?

The investigation has tried to answer these questions by interrogating recent theoretical models, discussing their often contradictory findings and setting them against empirical studies where these exist. If the conclusions from these three categories of questions are placed end to end, the intuitively positive impact that trade openness should have on growth, on welfare and ultimately on international migration is far from evident on either the theoretical or the empirical plane.

With regard to the first question, microeconomic migration theory proposes a plethora of models that are neither unified nor, in the majority of cases, empirically tested. As these models put it, the wages and job outlook continues to be the unambiguous central argument for migration behaviour. The static efficiency gains associated with trade liberalisation are relatively small, and can be imperilled by the politico-economic costs of the transition period.

For this reason, these realities are better examined in the dynamic framework of growth and foreign direct investment theories. While direct investment, in the theoretical models of endogenous growth, is sometimes a force for convergence and catch-up, the impact of direct investment on growth strongly depends on the kinds of knowledge transferred by the multinationals and hence on the type of sector in which FDI is carried out. The more technological knowledge-intensive the sector is, the more FDI can have a positive traction effect on specialisation and growth, providing that the host country has a sufficient stock of human capital with which to begin.

The empirical studies, despite their many methodological failings, confirm the positive and significant impact of trade liberalisation on productivity gains and production growth. This impact comes about mostly via domestic investment, itself spurred by FDI. The issue of whether or not a relation of complementarity exists between openness to trade and international direct investment thenceforth becomes crucial.

Like the connection between liberalisation of trade and FDI, an equivocal relation is often obtained if the level of approach used is that of production factor mobility or is exclusively macroeconomic. FDI and exports are substitutable or complementary according to the hypothesis and the analytical level (micro- or macro-sectoral) chosen.

Empirical studies on the effects of European integration on intra-European FDI and FDI from non-member countries confirm a relation of complementarity, and even a positive effect of the single market on FDI. There are no grounds for thinking, however, that where the emigration countries are concerned, the fact of joining a regional union with the industrialised countries or, *a fortiori*, signing a simple free-trade agreement will result in an increase of FDI capable of propelling growth mechanisms.

The new economic geography models indeed show that a reduction in transaction costs can, if the initial situation is detrimental to the peripheral countries (locations already relatively concentrated, internal economies of scale, and so forth), bring about a cumulative process of divergence among the countries in the regional zone. Recent work also stresses, however, the existence of strong non-linearities and the reversibility of the process of polarisation/concentration of activities.

In the end, a positive long-term relation can under certain conditions exist between regional integration, direct investment and growth, favouring employment and growth in the emigration countries best endowed with human and social capital. Yet the temptation to migrate to the North will remain strong for so long as the process of globalisation/polarisation continues to marginalise most developing countries. Whatever assumption is made, simple openness to trade will not suffice to engender a process of convergence and economic development, which still largely depends on domestic factors.

BIBLIOGRAPHY

Section 1: Migratory behaviour and openness

BORJAS, G.J. (1987)
"The economics of immigration", *Journal of Economic Literature*, Vol. 32, No. 4, pp. 1667-1717.

BOURGUIGNON, F. and MORRISSON, C. (1991)
External Trade and Income Distribution, OECD, Paris.

BROWN, D.K. *et al.* (1994)
"An Assessment of Extending NAFTA to Other Major Trading Countries in South America", mimeo, Research Consortium on North American Trade and Investment (3rd annual meeting), Toronto.

BURDA, M. (1995)
"Migration and the option value of waiting", CEPR Discussion Paper No. 1229.

DAVERI, F. and FAINI, R. (1996)
"Where do migrants go? Risk-aversion, mobility costs and the locational choice of migrants", CEPR Discussion Paper No. 1540.

DAVIS, D. (1996)
"Trade liberalization and income distribution", NBER Working Paper No. 5693.

DRAPIER, C., JAYET, H. and RAPOPORT, H. (1997)
"Les motifs des migrations et des transferts associés. Une revue de la littérature centrée sur les conséquences attendues pour les pays en développement", *Revue Région et Développement*, No. 6.

EPSTEIN, G.S., HILLMAN, A.L. and WEISS, A. (1998)
"Creating illegal immigrants", CEPR Discussion Paper No. 1796.

ETHIER, W.J. (1985)
"International trade and labor migration", *American Economic Review*, Vol. 75, No. 4, pp. 691-707.

FAINI, R. (1996)
"Increasing returns, migration and convergence", *Journal of Development Economics*, Vol. 49, pp. 121-136.

FAINI, R., GRETHER, J.M. and de MELO, J. (1997)
"Globalization and migratory pressures from developing countries: a simulation analysis", CEPR Discussion Paper No. 1660.

GOLDIN, I. *et al.* (1993)
> *Trade Liberalization: Global Economic Implications*, OECD–World Bank, Paris, Washington, D.C.

HARRIS, J.R. and TODARO, M. (1970)
> "Migration, unemployment and development: a two-sector analysis", *American Economic Review*, Vol. 60, No. 3, pp. 126-142.

LAMBERT, S. (1994)
> "La migration comme instrument de diversification des risques dans la famille ivoirienne", *Revue d'économie du développement*, No. 2, pp. 3-38.

MÜLLER, T. (1997)
> *Migration, Dual Labor Markets and Social Welfare in a Small Open Economy*, Cahier 97-13 of the CREFA, Laval University.

O'ROURKE, K. (1996)
> "Trade, migration and convergence: a historical perspective", CEPR Discussion Paper No. 1319.

RODRIK, D. (1996)
> "Understanding economic policy reform", *Journal of Economic Literature*, Vol. 24, pp. 9-41.

RUTHERFORD, T.F., RUTSTRÖM, E.E. and TARR, D. (1994)
> "L'accord de libre-échange entre le Maroc et la CEE : une évaluation quantitative", *Revue d'économie du développement*, No. 2, pp. 97-133.

SAINT-PAUL, G. (1997)
> "Economic integration, factor mobility and wage convergence", CEPR Discussion Paper No. 1597.

SAPIR, A. (1983)
> "Foreign competition, immigration and structural adjustment", *Journal of International Economics*, No. 14, pp. 381-394.

SCHIFF, M. (1995)
> "Politique commerciale et migration internationale à court et moyen terme", *Revue d'économie du développement*, No. 1, pp. 3-25.

STARK, O. (1991)
> *The Migration of Labor*, Blackwell, Oxford.

STIGLITZ, J.E. (1974)
> "Aternative theories of wage determination and unemployment in LDSs: the labor turnover model?", *Quarterly Journal of Economics*, Vol. 88, No. 2, May, pp. 194-227.

TAPINOS, G. (1974)
> *L'économie des migrations internationales*, Colin, FNSP, Paris.

TREJO, S.J. (1997)
> "Why do Mexican–Americans earn low wages?", *Journal of Political Economy*, Vol. 105, No. 6, pp. 1235-1268.

VENABLES, A. (1997)

"Trade liberalization and factor mobility: an overview", mimeo, London School of Economics, Centre for Economic Performance Discussion Paper 352, London.

ZÉNOU, Y. (1995)

"Chômage urbain et migration dans les pays en développement : une approche théorique", *Revue d'économie politique*, Vol. 105, No. 2, pp. 293-314.

Section 2: The challenge of openness and its effects on growth

ALONSO-GAMO, P., FEDELINO, A. and HORVITZ, S.P. (1997)

"Globalization and growth in Arab countries", IMF Working Paper No. 97/125.

BALASSA, B. (1978)

"Exports and economic growth: further evidence", *Journal of Development Economics*, Vol. 5, No. 2, pp. 181-189.

BALASSA, B. (1985)

"Exports, policy choices and economic growth in developing countries after 1973 oil shock", *Journal of Development Economics*, Vol. 18, No. 2, pp. 23-35.

BALDWIN, R.E. and SEGHEZZA, E. (1996a)

"Trade-induced investment-led growth", CEPR Discussion Paper No. 1420, London.

BALDWIN, R.E. and SEGHEZZA, E. (1996b)

"Testing for trade-induced investment-led growth", NBER Working Paper Series No. 5416, Cambridge, MA.

BARRO, R. (1993)

"Some implications of new growth theory for economic development", *Journal of International Development*, Vol. 5, No. 5, pp. 531-558.

BARRO, R. and SALA-I-MARTIN, X. (1995)

Economic Growth, McGraw-Hill, New York, N.Y.

BEN-DAVID, D. and LOEWY, M. (1995)

"Free trade and long-run growth", CEPR Discussion Paper No. 1183.

BORENSZTEIN, E., DE GREGORIO, J. and LEE, J.W. (1994)

"How does foreign direct investment affect economic growth?", IMF Working Paper No. 94/100.

BRAUN, J. (1993)

Essays on Economic Growth and Migration, Ph.D, Harvard University.

CANTWELL, J. (1992)

"Innovation and technological competitiveness", in P. J Buckley and M. Casson (eds.), *Multinational Enterprises in the World Economy*, Edward Elgar, Aldershot, pp. 20-40.

CASS, D. (1965)
"Optimum growth in an aggregative model of capital accumulation", *Review of Economic Studies*, No. 32, pp. 233-240.

EEC (1993)
"New location factors mobile investment in Europe", Final Report, *Regional Development Studies*, No. 6.

EDWARDS, S. (1992)
"Trade orientation, distortions and growth in developing countries", *Journal of Development Economics*, Vol. 39, No. 1, pp. 31-57.

EDWARDS, S. (1993)
"Openness, trade liberalization and growth in developing countries", *Journal of Economic Literature*, Vol. 31, pp. 1358-1393.

EDWARDS, S. (1997)
"Openness, productivity and growth: what do we really know?", NBER Working Paper Series No. 5978.

ESFAHANI, H. (1991)
"Exports, imports and economic growth in semi-industrialized countries", *Journal of Development Economics*, Vol. 35, No. 1, pp. 93-116.

FAINI, R. (1996)
"Increasing returns, migrations and convergence", *Journal of Development Economics*, Vol. 49, pp. 121-136.

FEDER, G. (1983)
"On exports and economic growth", *Journal of Development Economics*, Vol. 12, Nos. 1-2, pp. 59-73.

FEENSTRA, R. (1996)
"Trade and uneven growth", *Journal of Development Economics*, No. 49, pp. 229-256.

FINDLAY, R. (1978)
"Relative backwardness, direct foreign investment, and the transfer of technology: a simple dynamic model", *Quarterly Journal of Economics*, Vol. 92(1), pp. 1-16.

GROSSMAN, G.M. and HELPMAN, E. (1990)
"Comparative advantage and long run growth", *American Economic Review*, No. 80, pp. 796-815.

GROSSMAN, G.M. and HELPMAN, E. (1991*a*)
Innovation and Growth in the Global Economy, MIT Press, Cambridge MA and London.

GROSSMAN, G.M. and HELPMAN, E. (1991*b*)
"Trade, knowledge spillovers, and growth", *European Economic Review*, No. 35, pp. 517–526.

HAQUE, N. and KIM, S. (1995)
Human Capital Flight: Impact of Migration on Income and Growth, IMF Staff Paper Vol. 42, No. 3, pp. 577–607.

JUNG, W. and MARSHALL, P. (1985)
"Exports growth and causality in developing countries", *Journal of Development Economics*, Vol. 18, pp. 1–12.

KOHLI, I. and SINGH, N. (1989)
"Exports and growth: critical minimum effort and diminishing return", *Journal of Development Economics*, Vol. 30, No. 2, pp. 391–400.

KOOPMANS, T.C. (1965)
On the Concept of Optimal Economic Growth. The Econometric Approach to Development Planning, Amsterdam.

KRUEGER, A. (1978)
Foreign Trade Regimes and Economic Development: Liberalization Attempts and Consequences, Cambridge, MA, Ballinger Publication for NBER.

KRUGMAN, P. (1994)
"The myth of Asia's miracle", *Foreign Affairs*, Vol. 73(6), pp. 62–78.

LAFFARGUE, J.P. (1993)
"Croissance endogène, ouverture sur l'extérieur et développement. Point de vue récent", *Revue d'économie du développement*, No. 3, pp. 4–27.

LEVINE, R. and RENELT, D. (1992)
"A sensitivity analysis of cross-country growth regressions", *American Economic Review*, Vol. 82, No. 4, pp. 942–963.

LUCAS, R. (1988),
"On the mechanics of economic development", *Journal of Monetary Economics*, No. 22, pp. 3-42.

MATSUYAMA, K. (1991)
"Increasing returns, industrialization, and the indeterminacy of equilibrium", *Quarterly Journal of Economics*, Vol. 106, No. 2, pp. 617-650.

MICHAELY, M. (1977)
"Exports and growth: an empirical investigation", *Journal of Development Economics*, Vol. 4, No. 1, pp. 49–53.

PECORINO, P. (1992)
"Rent seeking and growth: the case of growth through human capital accumulation", *Canadian Journal of Economics*, Vol. 25, No.°4, pp. 944-956.

PHELPS, E.S. (1962)
"The new view of investment: a neoclassical analysis", *Quarterly Journal of Economics*, Vol. 76(4), pp. 548-567.

PISSARIDES, C. (1997)
"Learning by trading and the returns to human capital in developing countries", *The World Bank Economic Review*, Vol. 11, No. 1.

PREBISH, P. (1950)

The Economic Development of Latin America and Its Principal Problem, United Nations, New York.

QUAH, D. and RAUCH, J. (1990)

"Openness and the rate of economic growth", mimeo, University of California, San Diego.

RAM, R. (1985)

"Exports and economic growth: some additional evidence", Economic Development and Cultural Change, Vol. 33, No. 2, pp. 261–64.

RAM, R. (1987)

"Exports and economic growth in developing countries: evidence from times series and cross-section data", Economic Development and Cultural Change, Vol. 36, No. 1, pp. 51–72.

RANA, P. (1988)

"Exports, policy change and economic growth in developing countries after the oil shock: comments", Journal of Development Economics, Vol. 28, No. 2, pp. 261–64.

RIVERA-BATIZ, L.A. and ROMER, P.M. (1991a)

"International trade with endogenous technological change", European Economic Review, No. 35, pp. 971–1004.

RIVERA-BATIZ, L.A and ROMER, P.M (1991b)

"Economic integration and endogenous growth", Quarterly Journal of Economics, Vol. 106, No. 2, May, pp. 531-555.

RODRIK, D. (1995)

"Trade policy and industrial policy reform", in J. Behrman and T. Srinivasan (eds.), Handbook of Development Economics, Vol. 3B, pp. 2925–2982, North Holland.

SOLOW R. (1956)

"A contribution to the theory of economic growth", The Quarterly Journal of Economics, Vol. 70, pp. 65-94.

STOKEY, N.L. (1991)

"Human capital, product quality and growth", The Quarterly Journal of Economics, No. 106(2), pp. 587-616.

SWAN T.W. (1956)

"Economic growth and capital accumulation", Economic Record, No. 32, pp. 334-361.

SYRQUIN, M. and CHENERY, H. (1989)

"Three decades of industrialization", The World Bank Economic Review, No. 3, pp. 145–181.

TAYLOR, S. (1994)

"'Once off' and continuing gains from trade", Review of Economic Studies, No. 61, pp. 589-601.

WALZ, U. (1997)

"Growth and deeper regional integration in a three-country model", Review of International Economics, Vol. 5, No. 4, pp. 492–507.

WANG, J.-Y. (1990)
"Growth, technology transfer, and the long-run theory of international capital movements", *Journal of International Economics*, Vol. 29 (3-4), pp. 255-271.

WANG, J.-Y. and BLOMSTROM, M. (1992)
"Foreign investment and technology transfer: a simple model", *European Economic Review*, Vol. 36(1), January, pp. 137-155.

WEINHOLD, D. and RAUCH, J. (1997)
"Openness, specialization and productivity growth in less developed countries", NBER Working Paper Series No. 6131.

YOUNG, A. (1991)
"Learning by doing and the dynamic effects of international trade", *Quarterly Journal of Economics*, No. 106, pp. 369–405.

Section 3: Relation between direct investment and trade liberalisation

AGARWAL, J., GUBITZ, A. and NUNNENKAMP, P. (1991)
Foreign Direct Investment in Developing Countries – The Case of Germany, Kieler Studien, No. 238, J.C.B., Mohr (Paul Siebeck), Tübingen.

BALASSA, B. (1961)
The Theory of Economic Integration, George Allen & Unwin, Paris.

BALDWIN, R.E. and SEGHEZZA, E. (1996)
"Testing for trade-induced investment-led growth", NBER Working Paper No. 5416, January, p. 21.

BALDWIN, R.E. and VENABLES, A.J. (1995)
"Regional economic integration", *Handbook of International Economics*, Vol. 3, pp. 1597-1644.

BARRELL, R. and PAIN, N. (1997)
"The growth of foreign direct investment in Europe", *National Institute Economic Review*, Vol. 160, No. 2/97, April, pp. 63–75.

BLOMSTROM, M. and ZEJAN, M. (1991)
"Why do multinational corporations seek out joint ventures", *Journal of International Development*, Vol. 3, No. 1, pp. 53–63.

BORENSZTEIN, E., DE GREGORIO, J. and LEE, J.W. (1995)
"How does foreign direct investment affect economic growth?", NBER Working Paper No. 5057, March.

BRAINARD, S.L. and RIKER, D.A. (1997)
"Are U.S. multinationals exporting U.S. jobs?", NBER Working Paper No. 5958, March.

BRAINARD, S.L. (1993a)
"A simple theory of multinational corporations and trade with a trade-off between proximity and concentration", NBER, Working Paper No. 4269, February.

BRAINARD, S.L. (1993*b*)

"An empirical assessment of the proximity-concentration trade-off between multinational sales and trade", NBER Working Paper No. 4580, December.

BRAINARD, S.L. (1993*c*)

"An empirical assessment of the factor proportions explanation of multinational sales", NBER Working Paper No. 4583, December.

BRAINARD, S.L. (1997)

"An empirical assessment of the proximity-concentration trade-off between multinational sales and trade", *American Economic Review*, Vol. 87, No. 4, pp. 520–544, September.

BUCKLEY, P.J. (1993)

"Contemporary theories of international investment", *Revue économique*, Vol. 44, No. 4, July.

BUCKLEY, P.J. and CASSON, M. (1985)

"The optimal timing of foreign direct investment", *The Economic Theory of the Multinational Enterprise: Selected Papers*, pp. 98–122, London.

BUIGUES, P. and JACQUEMIN, A. (1994)

"Foreign direct investment and exports to the european community", in M. Mason, and D. Encarnation (eds.), *Does Ownership Matter? Japanese Multinationals in Europe,* Oxford University Press, Clarendon Press, Oxford, New York, Toronto and Melbourne, pp. 163-199.

CANTWELL, J.A. and DUNNING, J.H. (1991)

"MNEs, technology and the competitiveness of European industries", *Aussenwirtschaft*, No. 46(1), April, pp. 45–65.

CANTWELL, J. (1992)

"Innovation and technological competitiveness", in Peter J. Buckley and Mark Casson, (eds.) *Multinational Enterprises in the World Economy*, Elgar, Aldershot, U.K, pp. 20-40.

CECCHINI, P. (1988)

The European Challenge: 1992. The Benefits of a Single Market, Wilwood House, Aldershot.

CHESNAIS, F. (1988)

"Les accords de coopération techniques entre firmes indépendantes", *STI Review* N°4, OECD, Paris, December.

CLEGG, J. (1995)

"The determinants of United States Foreign Direct Investment in the European Community: a critical appraisal", University of Bath, mimeo.

COGNEAU, D., DUMONT, J.-C. and IZZO, P. (1998)

"Intégration régionale, investissements directs et migrations dans l'espace euro-méditerranéen : enseignement d'un modèle d'Equilibre général calculable", *Migrations, libre-échange et intégration régionale dans le Bassin méditerranéen*, OECD, Paris.

DUNNING, J.H. (1988)

Explaining International Production, Unwin Hyman, London, pp. xvii, 378.

DUNNING, J.H. (1993)

The Globalization of Business – The Challenge of the 1990s, Routledge, London.

DUNNING, J.H. (1997*a*)

"The European internal market programme and inbound foreign direct investment", *Journal of Common Market Studies*, Vol. 35, No. 1, March, pp. 1–30.

DUNNING, J.H. (1997*b*)

"The European internal market programme and inbound foreign direct investment", *Journal of Common Market Studies*, Vol. 35, No. 2, June, pp. 191–223.

EEC (1993)

"New location factors: mobile investment in Europe", Final Report, *Regional Development Studies*, No. 6.

ETHIER, W.J. and MARKUSEN, J.R. (1996)

"Multinational firms, technology diffusion and trade", *Journal of International Economics*, Vol. 41, No. 1-2, August, pp. 1-28.

FLAM, H. and HELPMAN, E. (1987)

"Vertical product differentiation and North-South trade", *The American Economic Review*, Vol. 77, No. 5, December, pp. 810–822.

FREEMAN, C. and HAGEDOORN, J. (1995)

"Convergence and divergence in the internationalization of technology", in J. Hagedoorn (ed.), *Technical Change and the World Economy: Convergence and Divergence in Technology Strategies*, Elgar, Aldershot, U.K, pp. 34-57.

GREENAWAY, D. (1993)

"L'investissement direct dans la Communauté", *Economie européenne*, No. 52, pp. 113–141.

GROSSMAN, G.M. and HELPMAN, E. (1991)

"Quality ladders and product cycles", *Quarterly Journal of Economics*, No. 106, pp. 557-586.

HAGEDOORN, J. and SCHAKENRAAD, J. (1993)

"Strategic technology partenering and international corporate strategies", in K.S. Hughes (ed.), *European Competitiveness*, Cambridge University Press, Cambridge, New York and Melbourne, pp. 60-86.

HATZICHRONOGLOU, T. (1994)

The Performance of Foreign Affiliates in OECD Countries, OECD, Paris.

HELPMAN, E. (1984)

"A simple theory of international trade with multinational corporations", *Journal of Political Economy*, Vol. 92, No. 3, June, pp. 451–471.

HENRY, J. (1994)

Investissement direct et exportations : existe-t-il un lien ?, Bulletin de la Banque de France, No. 9, September.

HUFBAUER, G. and STEPHENSON, S. (1995)
"Competitive advantages in the world economy", in H. Siebert (ed.), *Locational Competition in the World Economy*, Mohr (Siebeck), Tubingen, pp. 45-63.

HUMMELS, D. L. and STERN, R.M. (1994)
"Evolving patterns of North American merchandise trade and foreign direct investment, 1960-1990", *World Economy,* Vol. 17, No. 1, January, pp. 5-29.

HYMER, S.H. (1976)
The International Operations of National Firms: A Study of Direct Foreign Investment, MIT Press, London.

JULIUS, D. (1990)
Global Companies and Public Policy: the Growing Challenge of Foreign Direct Investment, Council on Foreign Relations Press for the Royal Institute of International Affairs, Chatham House Papers, New York, pp. xiii, 126.

JUNGNICKEL, R. (1993)
"Globalization and international division of labor: the role of technology and wage costs", paper presented for the IILS 3rd Forum Meeting, 16-17 September, Geneva.

KINDLEBERGER, C.P. (1987)
International Capital Movements: Based on the Marshall Lectures given at the University of Cambridge 1985, Cambridge University Press, Cambridge; New York and Melbourne, pp. vi, 9.

KOGUT, B. (1995)
"Platform technologies and national industrial networks", in J. Hagedoorn (ed.), *Technical Change and the World Economy: Convergence and Divergence in Technology Strategies*, Elgar, Aldershot, U.K, distributed in the U.S. by Ashgate, Brookfield, Vt., pp. 58-82.

KOGUT, B. and CHANG, S.J. (1991)
"Technological Capabilities and Japanses Foreign Direct Investment in the United States", *Review of Economics and Statistics*, Vol. 73, No. 3, August, pp. 401-413.

KOJIMA, K. (1978)
Direct Foreign Investment: A Japanese Model of Multinational Business Operations, Croom Helm, London.

KRUGMAN, P. (1979)
"A model of innovation, technology transfer, and the world distribution of income", *Journal of Political Economy*, Vol. 87, No. 2, pp. 253–266.

KRUGMAN, P. (1990)
Rethinking International Trade, MIT Press, Cambridge, MA, and London.

KRUGMAN, P. (1991)
Geography and Trade, Gaston Eyskens Lecture Series, MIT Press, Cambridge, Mass. and London, Louvain University Press, Louvain, Belgium, p. xi, 142.

KRUGMAN, P. and VENABLES, A.J. (1995)
"The seamless world: a spatial model of international specialization", NBER Working Paper 5220, August, p. 31.

LIN, A. (1995)
"Trade effects of foreign direct investment: evidence for Taiwan with four ASEAN countries", *Weltwirtschaftliches Archiv*, Vol. 131, No. 4, pp. 737–747.

LONGHI, C. and QUÉRÉ, M. (1993)
"Local systems of innovation and territorial dynamics", *Revue économique*, Vol. 44, No. 4, July, pp. 713–724.

MARKUSEN, J.R. (1983)
"Factor movements and commodity trade as complements", *Journal of International Economics*, Vol. 14, No. 3/4, May, pp. 341–356.

MARKUSEN, J.R. (1995)
"The boundaries of multinational enterprises and the theory of international trade", *Journal of Economic Perspectives*, Vol. 9, No. 2, Spring, pp. 169–189.

MARKUSEN, J.R. and VENABLES, A.J. (1996)
"The increased importance of multinationals in North American economic relationships: a convergence hypothesis", in M.B. Canzoneri, W.J. Ethier, V. Grilli (eds.), *The New Transatlantic Economy*, Cambridge University Press, Cambridge, New York and Melbourne, pp. 169-89.

MAZIER, J. (1995)
"Intégration européenne et investissements directs à l'étranger", *Revue du Marché commun et de l'Union européenne*, No. 385, February, pp. 112–126.

MOATI, P. and MOUHOUD, E.M. (1994)
"Information et organisation de la production : vers une division cognitive du travail", *Economie appliquée*, Vol. 47, No. 1, pp. 47–73.

MOTTA, M. (1994)
"International trade and investments in a vertically differentiated industry", *International Journal of Industrial Organization*, Vol. 12, No. 2, pp. 179–196, June.

MOTTA, M. and NORMAN, G. (1993)
"Does economic integration cause foreign direct investment?", Working Paper University Pompeu Fabra, Barcelona.

MOUHOUD, E.M. (1992)
Changement technique et division internationale du travail, Economica, Paris.

MOUHOUD, E.M. (1993)
"Technical change, comparative advantages and industrial plants relocation", *Revue d'économie politique*, Vol. 103, No. 5, Sept.-Oct, pp. 733–761.

MOUHOUD, E.M. (1996)
"Délocalisation dans les pays à bas salaires et contraintes d'efficacité productive", *Monde en développement*, Vol. 95, No. 1.

MOUHOUD, E.M. (1997)
"The links between migration, free trade and regional integration: specific characteristics of the CEECs", *Migration, Free Trade and Regional Integration in Central and Eastern Europe*, OECD/WIFO, Vienna.

MOUHOUD, E.M. (1998)
"Investissements directs étrangers, migrations et intégration régionale", *Migrations, libre-échange et intégration régionale dans le Bassin méditerranéen*, OECD, Paris.

MUCCHIELLI, J.L. (1985)
Firmes multinationales, mutations et nouvelles perspectives, Economica, Paris.

MUNDELL, R.A. (1957)
"International trade and factor mobility", *American Economic Review*, Vol. 47, pp. 321–335.

NEVEN, D. and SIOTIS, G. (1996)
"Technology sourcing and FDI in the EU: an empirical evaluation", *International Journal of Industrial Organization*, Vol. 14, No. 5, pp. 543–560, July.

NUNNENKAMP, P., GUNDLACH, E. and AGARWAL, J. (1994)
Globalisation of Production and Markets, Institut fur Weltwirtschaft an der Universitat Kiel Kieler Studien, Vol. 262, Mohr (Siebeck), Tubingen, pp. xii, 187.

OECD (1997)
Activities of Foreign Affiliates in OECD Countries – Statistical Data 1985-1994, Paris.

PAIN, N. and LANSBURY, M. (1996)
"The impact of the internal market on the evolution of European Direct Investment", NIESR, London, mimeo.

PETRI, P.A. (1997)
"The regional clustering of foreign direct investment and trade", *Transnational Corporations*, Vol. 3, No. 3, pp. 1-24

RIVERA-BATIZ, L.A. and ROMER, P.M. (1991)
"International trade with endogenous technical change", *European Economic Review*, Vol. 35, No. 4, May, pp. 971-1001.

RODRIK, D. (1991)
"Policy uncertainty and private investment in developing countries", *Journal of Development Economics*, Vol. 36, No. 2, October, pp. 229–242.

ROWTHORN, R.E. (1992)
"Intra-industry trade and investment under oligopoly: the role of market size", *Economic Journal*, Vol. 102, No. 411, March, pp. 402-414.

SCHMITZ, A. and HELMBERGER, P. (1970)
"Factor mobility and international trade: the case of complementarity", *American Economic Review*, Vol. 60, No. 4, September, pp. 761-767.

SRINIVASAN, K. and MODY, A. (1998)
"Japanese and U.S. firms as foreign investors: do they march to the same tune?", *Canadian Journal of Economics,* Vol. 31, No. 4, October, pp. 778-799.

SWEDENBORG, B. (1990)
"The EC and the locational choice of Swedish multinational companies", Industrial Institute of Economic and Social Research, Working Paper 284, Stockholm.

UNCTAD (United Nations Conference on Trade and Development), (1991, 1992, 1993, 1994, 1995)
World Investment Report, United Nations Publications, New York.

UNCTAD (1995)

"Foreign direct investment in Africa / UNCTAD", Division on Transnational Corporations and Investment, UNCTAD, Geneva.

UNCTAD (1997)

World Investment Report, 1997: Transnational Corporations, Market Structure and Competition Policy, United Nations Publications, New York and Geneva, pp. xxxv, 381.

VERNON, R. (1966)

"International investment and international trade in product cycle", *Quarterly Journal of Economics*, No. 80, pp. 190–207.

VERNON, R. (1979)

"The product cycle hypothesis in a new international environment", *Oxford Bulletin of Economics and Statistics*, Vol. 41, No. 4, November, pp. 255-267.

VINER, J. (1950)

The customs union issue, Stevens, London.

WORTMANN, M. (1990)

"Multinationals and the internalisation of R&D: new developments in German companies", *Research Policy*, Vol. 19, No. 2.

Comments on the paper by
Denis Cogneau, Jean-Christophe Dumont **and** *El-Mouhoub Mouhoud*

by
John P. Martin
OECD

This is a very rich and ambitious paper. The authors survey a very wide body of theoretical and empirical studies covering at least three separate topics:

–   The determinants of international migration.

–   The role of openness in the "new growth theories".

–   The links between foreign direct investment (FDI), trade liberalisation and growth.

The authors have done us all a great service by surveying a vast number of studies under these three headings, and trying to distil the main conclusions. At the same time, it is not always easy to follow the central thread of the argument underlying the paper, which seeks to link the three sections together.

However, it seems to me that the central issue which the paper seeks to address is the following: how does trade liberalisation and/or regional economic integration involving the countries of the North and South affect the incentives for migration from the South to the North? Once we keep this question to the fore in our minds, I think one can see the links between the three parts of the paper.

The first part of the paper works within a standard static neo-classical framework to show that the welfare effects of trade liberalisation/regional economic integration are likely to be "small" (maybe of the order of 1 to 2% of GDP). Hence, this theoretical framework suggests that moves to foster trade liberalisation and/or regional economic integration are likely to have little impact on the incentives for labour to move from the South to the North. As a result, the authors conclude that if we want to understand how trade liberalisation/regional economic integration could potentially have a significant impact on North-South migration, we must turn to a different class of theoretical models, the so-called "new growth" or "endogenous growth" theories.

These theories, with their emphasis on externalities, particularly in production, and on the role of product differentiation and market structure, can lead to outcomes whereby trade liberalisation/regional economic integration leads to a permanent, or at least a prolonged, rise in the growth rate. As the authors highlight, many of the "new growth" models emphasise favourable spillovers coming from human capital accumulation and diffusion of knowledge, technological spillovers, often associated with FDI. But, as the authors note, while it is possible to derive favourable growth effects from such channels, especially for the South, this outcome is not guaranteed in theory. However, drawing on a few studies, the authors argue that a crucial ingredient in the story relates to "the capacity of the South to absorb technology" which, in turn, is positively related to the human capital stock in the South and the state of its infrastructure.

The authors then turn to a review of the empirical literature on the links between trade liberalisation and growth. They conclude from this review that "openness" (their shorthand term for trade liberalisation/regional economic integration) does not have a direct impact on growth and convergence; instead, its effect is indirect via openness serving to raise domestic investment. The authors then go on to argue that the empirical evidence suggests that FDI has a significant effect on growth though this latter conclusion is disputed by the econometric results reported by *Florence Toutain* in a separate paper presented in this publication.

The final part of the paper seeks to assess the links between regional economic integration, FDI and growth. In particular, it seeks to assess whether there is likely to be substitution or complementarity between FDI and trade flows. Once again, their review of the theoretical literature on this question does not yield an unambiguous prediction. However, they argue that the empirical literature, especially that focusing on European integration, suggests that complementarity is the most likely outcome.

So where does this review of the recent literature leave us in terms of the incentives to migrate from the South to the North? It seems to imply that only if trade liberalisation/regional economic integration between the North and the South gives rise to large-scale FDI to the South would there likely be a significant reduction in the incentives to migrate. However, the authors conclude that such a large increase in FDI to the South is unlikely, hence trade liberalisation/regional economic integration is unlikely to choke-off migration pressures from the South in the near future.

This conclusion is disappointing for those who hope that the process of globalisation will prove to be a main spur behind North-South convergence. But perhaps it is a bit premature to write off the possibility?

Convergence within the EU: the case of the periphery countries

The effects of European integration over the past three decades on the periphery countries, Greece, Ireland, Portugal and Spain, should provide us with some food for thought on this topic. Ireland joined the European Community in 1973 with the United Kingdom, and Greece, Portugal and Spain joined in 1986.

If we use GDP per capita, measured in purchasing power parities (PPPs) as an indicator of convergence in living standards over the period 1970-97, Table A permits us to draw two conclusions:

– All four periphery countries have experienced some convergence over the period to the EU average.

– Ireland has outstripped the other three countries in the convergence process, especially since 1990. Ireland, which had an income per capita only 60% of the EU average in 1970, had equalled the EU15 average by 1997. This is the Celtic tiger roaring away! At the same time, Ireland has experienced net immigration over the past decade, something which has only happened once before in the past 150 years.

So what forces set the Celtic tiger loose and are there any lessons from this experience for the subject of this conference? The first point to make is that there is a lively on-going debate among Irish economists on the origins of the Celtic tiger, and whether it is likely to continue to roar ahead or turn out to be a paper tiger. The list of potential causes for the Celtic tiger is long: a rapid rate of human capital accumulation, generous EU structural and cohesion funds, and better macro-economic policies and control over the public finances are often cited. In addition, there is no denying that FDI has played a large role in recent Irish success, with much of this investment coming from the United States.

Now, some commentators have attributed the rapid growth in FDI to a favourable tax regime in Ireland for foreign capital, while others have stressed the attraction of a young and relatively well-educated work force which is English-speaking. In addition, there has been a significant improvement in the basic infrastructure in Ireland (roads, telecommunications, etc.) over the past decade thanks, at least in part, to EU funds.

In sum, it is possible to envisage significant complementarity between trade, foreign direct investment, growth and employment; such a virtuous circle can have major impacts on the incentives to migrate. But a virtuous circle, as the authors stress, is by no means a foregone conclusion. It seems, in line with some of the conclusions drawn from the literature survey by the authors, that investments in human capital accumulation and the basic infrastructure are likely to yield large dividends in the process. It may be that favourable tax treatment for foreign capital can also be a key element in such a strategy — though this gives rise to obvious difficulties within a common market or economic union. Finally, a sound macroeconomic environment is also a must in any successful strategy.

Table A. **Convergence in the European periphery, 1970-1997**

	GDP per capita in PPPs (EU15 = 100)		
	1970	**1990**	**1997**
Greece	58	59	68
Ireland	60	74	100
Portugal	52	60	71
Spain	73	76	78

Source: OECD (1998).

TRADE LIBERALISATION, FOREIGN DIRECT INVESTMENT AND GROWTH IN SEMI-INDUSTRIALISED COUNTRIES: OVERVIEW AND EMPIRICAL ANALYSIS

by
Florence Toutain
École nationale de la Statistique et de l'Administration économique (ENSAE), Paris

Introduction

The liberalisation of trade in goods and services in southern countries is a source of optimism in terms of regulating migration flows. The intermediate objective of this medium- to long-term process is to achieve growth generated by trade liberalisation and to increase foreign direct investment (FDI). Assuming that growth and employment can slow down emigration, what potential effects can liberalisation have on economic growth and to what extent can FDI stimulate growth and job creation. It is, however, difficult to measure the effect of FDI on employment, since it is usually a dynamic and indirect process. The number of jobs directly created by subsidiaries of multinationals in southern countries often appears negligible. This study will therefore focus primarily on the growth objective.

The aim of this paper is not to study the direct link between liberalisation and growth, which has long been controversial. Many critics have emphasised the shortcomings of empirical work on the subject, necessitating the use of precise and varied instruments to assess trade policies, the degree of integration and the nature of trade. A key study by Edwards (1997) nevertheless confirms the positive effect of liberalisation on growth, as measured by nine different indices.

A fairly narrow definition of liberalisation will be used here, since it will be measured simply in terms of foreign trade in gross domestic product (GDP) unit. The main focus will be on the role FDI plays in the growth process.

After giving an overview of FDI flows to southern countries and job creation by multinationals (Section 1), the investigation will then discuss the factors determining FDI and, in particular, the effect of trade liberalisation on FDI inflow. The aim is to identify the main criteria used by investors when choosing a location and, particularly, to measure the consequences of liberalisation on foreign investment inflow in terms of complementarity or substitution (Section 2). Finally, Section 3 will evaluate the impact of FDI on growth, including the interaction of FDI with human capital and domestic investment.

1. An overview of FDI

a) *FDI polarisation and orientation: a brief analysis*

The 1980s saw a significant increase of FDI towards southern countries. In 1990, however, southern countries received only 10% of total FDI, as against 33% in the mid-1970s. In addition, FDI was unevenly distributed among regions. Latin America still received a large portion of FDI in southern countries (22% in 1985 and 30% in 1990), and Asian countries became increasingly attractive in the mid-1980s (45% of the total), with Singapore, China, Malaysia and Thailand heading the list. This phenomenon forms part of the vertical integration process, inspired in large part by factors linked to production costs in the world economy. The relocation of manufacturing has become widespread. At the same time, FDI has expanded in the services sector, particularly for wholesale, transport and insurance.

After declining in 1991 and 1992, worldwide FDI has been rising sharply in the 1990s. Although still mainly directed to OECD countries, it is also increasingly going to southern countries. The growing appeal of the newly industrialised countries in general and of Asia in particular largely accounts for this renewed interest.

Asian countries have experienced a massive inflow of industrial capital since 1991. They already accounted for 50% of FDI in southern countries for the period 1985-90 and, in 1996, this percentage rose to 63%, representing USD 85 billion. China, for example, received less than two billion dollars before 1990 and USD 40.2 billion in 1996 (see Table 1 at the end of the article). After China come Singapore (USD 9.4 billion), Indonesia (USD 7.9 billion, see UNCTAD, 1997) and Malaysia (USD 4.1 billion). It is important to note that, since trade was liberalised in 1988, Vietnam has received a significant part of FDI for the region (USD 2.1 billion in 1996, see UNCTAD, 1997).

In terms of FDI, Latin America comes in second place after Southeast Asia. The region received USD 39 billion in 1996, or 11% of the world total and 30% of all capital aimed at southern countries. In 1997, the region received almost 45% of all FDI to southern countries. While in the early 1990s FDI was directed towards Argentina, Peru and Venezuela, as a result of the wave of privatisations, it subsequently shifted towards the extractive (Chile and Brazil), automobile (Mexico and Brazil) and transport/communication industries (Peru).

A closer look at Mexico, the largest receiver of FDI in the region, shows that FDI inflow rose during the 1993-95 period, essentially due to investment from NAFTA and the EU, particularly France. Between 1985-92 and 1993-95, FDI in Mexico doubled. In terms of sectors, investment in manufacturing has dropped since 1992 (46% of the 1995 total) while investment in the services sector is on the rise. The automobile sector experienced a boom in 1993-94, but dropped back in 1995 (11% of FDI in manufacturing). The chemicals sector continues to receive a large part of FDI aimed at manufacturing (25% in 1995). At the same time, office machinery, computers and communications equipment reached similar levels to that of food and metal products in 1995, or around USD 650 million. The percentage of FDI in services, which represented 27% in 1986-90, soared to 52% in 1995 notably due to holding companies (USD 1.2 billion) and investment in trade and repair. Telecommunications has become increasingly important since 1990, with USD 350 million on average for 1993-95.

Increases in FDI in Peru, Argentina and Venezuela in 1993-94 were largely due to the privatisation of telecommunications, air transport and oil companies. The fact that a large percentage of foreign investment in the region is aimed at privatisations means that investment flows vary significantly from country to country and year to year. There is, however, an overall trend within the manufacturing sector toward high technology products and a swing from the manufacturing to the services sector.

Eastern Europe has received massive international capital inflows since 1991, mainly from Europe (Germany) and the United States. These capital flows are nevertheless focused on Hungary, Poland and the Czech Republic (70%) and generally correspond to privatisation policies. In the Czech Republic, investment is mainly aimed at transport, telecommunications and motor vehicle construction. Poland, on the other hand, presents a different scenario: foreign investment, on the rise since 1990, is mainly aimed at the agri-food industry, trade and repair.

Africa remains the least attractive region and receives an ever-smaller percentage of total FDI in southern countries (11% for 1981-85, 6% for 1991-93, and 3.8% in 1996). The distribution of FDI has changed since the 1980s: Southern Africa's share has decreased (it represented only a quarter of FDI world stocks in 1995), while North Africa's has increased, mainly due to the influence of European investors. FDI is nevertheless highly concentrated in certain areas. In sub-Saharan Africa, Nigeria received 61% of FDI in 1993-95. In the North, Egypt accounted for 48% of flows to the region for the same period.

Turkey, the second largest recipient in the Mediterranean, saw regular increases in its FDI up to 1991, when it reached USD 1.9 billion, before stabilising at around USD 830 million. This investment, about 60% of it from Europe, mainly involved metal and mechanical products, even though services are receiving growing attention (trade and repair accounted for 24% of the total during 1992-97, against 48% for metal and mechanical products). The other main recipients of FDI are Israel, Morocco and Tunisia. Algeria, Syria and Libya have proven to be less attractive, with the little FDI they do receive concentrated in few activities.

b)   ***FDI and employment: a brief introduction***

The employment situation has continued to deteriorate in countries facing international competition in the past ten years. The effects of making export and foreign investment the main priorities are difficult to evaluate in terms of job creation. This problem requires an analysis of multinationals operating in countries receiving FDI, but overlooks the inter-company and inter-sector crowding-out or spill-over effects it may have on the host country's economy. Second, such an analysis only brings to light the effects of FDI at a given time, while FDI, in fact, typically has medium- to long-term effects through technological externalities.

A study by El Mekki Karoui (1998) on the impact of FDI on employment in Tunisia over the past few decades sheds some light on the subject. It shows that job creation resulting from FDI differs from one sector to the next. Manufacturing, agriculture, and tourism were the main sectors studied. The largest number of projects are usually found in the manufacturing sector. These manufacturing projects also create the most jobs and are most efficient in terms of volume and cost (capital invested per job created). The textile and clothing industry accounts for 77% of jobs created between 1973 and 1995 and 73% of all manufacturing investment. The author warns, however, that these results are subject to two caveats. First, most manufacturing companies, 89% to be exact, make use of "on-the-job" training, which places limits on the type of training given and has very little spill-over effect.[1] Second, most of these jobs are concentrated in the offshore textile industry, which is wholly foreign-owned, and have the limited impact of low-paid employment. Their effects, in terms of training, organisational capacity and initiative, will therefore remain limited.

A comparative study of manufacturing multinationals in Mexico and Turkey offers other employment models. Table 2 gives 1993 figures for employment, the number of companies and the value added (in millions of dollars) for the main sectors, as measured by number of jobs and projects. Only those companies that are majority foreign-owned are included.

---

1.   On-the-job training is practical rather than theoretical in nature, and trainees are seen as a cheap form of labour. Employers usually refuse to allow trainees to attend theoretical training courses.

Comparing the profiles of these two countries allows for several remarks. First, a considerable difference exists in the level of employment and number of projects, since there are 10 times more multinationals in Mexico, and they employ 23 times the amount of people, than in Turkey. Nevertheless, differences in terms of value added are much smaller – 1 to 4. This difference in terms of value added in relation to the number of employees may lead one to think that, although there is relatively little investment in Turkey, and few jobs created, the investments made make a larger contribution to domestic production than in Mexico. Such an interpretation, however, needs to be put in context, since the oil refinery and coal by-products sector accounts for one-fourth of manufacturing value added by multinationals in Turkey (but employs only 1 126 people). Apart from these differences, the same sectors are in the lead in both these countries, in terms of the number of projects, employees, and value added. The motor vehicle industry, which is highly concentrated by its very nature, is the largest employer in Turkey. It is followed by the chemical industry, which accounts for 20% of manufacturing jobs and 20% of value added.

In Mexico, these two sectors are of secondary importance in terms of employment, but chemicals, rubber and plastic products account for more than one-fourth of value added by manufacturing multinationals. Multinationals (80% of them from the United States) which manufacture electrical machines are the largest employers (one-third of all manufacturing jobs), but only make up 13% of manufacturing value added. The contribution of the textile industry, which is the most labour-intensive, has stagnated since the early 1980s. Since the early 1990s, the number of jobs in this industry has even dropped in Turkey. The food sector, with a large number of companies from Europe, the United States and South America, is also stagnating.

It is therefore clear that FDI has an immediate impact, which differs from country to country, both in terms of the level and distribution of the impact. Job creation differs from sector to sector in Mexico, Tunisia and Turkey and, even in the same sector, employment levels vary from country to country. It is important to know that the number of jobs created in the services sector is usually small compared to manufacturing jobs. For example, services accounted for only 10% of all jobs created by multinationals in Mexico in 1993, in spite of high growth in the sector.[2]

Overall, while still favouring the manufacturing sector, FDI is rapidly moving towards medium- and high-technology fields, while certain traditional labour-intensive sectors are stagnating or even dropping off. As a result, one has to be careful when evaluating the true impact of FDI on factors of production, even though manufacturing FDI seems to result in some job creation. It is essential to consider the crowding-out and spill-over effect of FDI on domestic investment, technological externalities and the real vocational training effect.

Even if one assumes that FDI has a positive effect on the economic performance and/or productivity of the host country, the capacity of the various host countries to attract FDI nevertheless differs sharply. FDI is mostly directed towards large countries with a high growth potential, or those with advantages in terms of production cost and the availability of labour. Nevertheless, analysing FDI in terms of factor proportions seems less relevant today. In addition, according to Brainard (1993), the choice made by multinationals between FDI and exports should also be seen as a choice between proximity and concentration. The fact is that multinationals are primarily interested in market considerations, and those factors influencing their choice of location should be the focus of this investigation.

---

2.   In Mexico, the number of jobs in the commerce, repair, hotel and restaurant sectors rose three-fold between 1985 and 1993, but dropped in the finance, insurance and business services sectors.

2. Factors determining FDI and the impact of trade liberalisation: an empirical approach

a) *Determinants*

Foreign investment essentially serves two purposes: penetrating domestic markets and exploiting comparative advantages, with production mainly intended for export. Two types of factors need be taken into account: market factors and cost factors, or, more generally speaking, supply factors in the host country.

In terms of market factors, the size of the host market undeniably receives the most empirical support. Reuber *et al.* (1973) has shown a positive correlation between per capita FDI and GDP. Edwards (1991) further showed that, between 1971 and 1981, direct investment from OECD countries aimed at southern countries was channelled to large markets. This factor, which can also be explained in terms of population size or density, is even more important when investment is linked to the production of goods destined for the domestic market. FDI achieves market penetration using the advantage of proximity (Brainard, 1993) even in the absence of trade barriers. As a matter of fact, advantages include the absence of customs duties and lower transport costs, but also benefits due to an improved distribution network and greater cultural and linguistic compatibility.

Market growth often appears as the second most important factor influencing investors' decisions.[3] It has, however, received little empirical support in terms of the southern countries.

The quest for low production costs has often been described as one of the most important aspects considered in choosing a location for a production site. According to the product life-cycle theory (Vernon, 1966), production can be relocated to southern countries during the standardisation phase of a product. This only applies if price elasticity of demand for the product is strong, and if the manufacturing process is labour-intensive. Comparative advantages (Kojima, 1978) and particularly competitive wages, were shown to explain investment in southern countries. Riedel (1975) noted that relatively low wage costs were one of the main determinants of export-oriented FDI to Taiwan. A number of studies conducted in the 1970s and 1980s, such as those by Schneider and Frey (1985), Swansborough (1972) and Root (1978) have shown a negative relationship between FDI and wage costs. Lucas (1990), seeking to explain why industrialised countries do not invest more in southern countries, demonstrated that, while labour costs are lower in southern countries, marginal productivity is also lower, due to the quality of human capital.

Investment stimulated by the existence of mineral and agricultural resources remains predominant in certain regions and countries (sub-Saharan African and the Middle East). In the case of Africa, those countries exporting oil[4] consistently received more than 60% of FDI flows during the 1970s. On a global scale, however, this type of investment is becoming rare.

Other important factors need to be addressed, such as the degree of industrialisation, the level of existing infrastructure (Wheeler and Mody, 1992) and the quality of the human capital. Chan and Mason's cross-sector study of FDI (1992) in 48 southern countries in 1987 shows that the countries attracting the most investment are those that are most industrialised, largest in size, have political and military relations with the United States, and a strong central government. Empirical studies demonstrate the importance of government credibility (Seven, 1992), since this will determine

---

3. According to a study of 311 executives of multinational firms and experts conducted in France by the Ministry of Economy and Finance (International Investment Delegation) in 1996.

4. Algeria, Angola, Cameroon, Egypt, Gabon, Libya, Nigeria and Tunisia.

the success of policy incentives. These policies, however, only come into play once the host country meets basic performance criteria (Lim, 1982; McMillan, 1995). By the same token, political instability appears to discourage direct investment only when the country's economy already shows signs of weakness, but is not, in itself, a factor determining investment (Edwards, 1991).

A brief analysis of existing studies brings to light certain factors that may influence FDI flows: economic performance, level of industrialisation, liberalisation, the existence of exploitable natural resources, country size (which may signify the existence of a large domestic market), geographical location (which may provide access to a regional market), low costs, the level of existing infrastructure, as well as factors such as tax incentives, administrative structures and stability. In view of the fact that the present focus is the effect of trade liberalisation, the investigation will only consider a few of these factors.

An attempt has been made to estimate the effect of several variables on FDI rates (net flow of direct investment/GDP, **FDI** in the regressions)[5] by means of a cross-sectional analysis of panel data for 29 semi-industrialised or recently industrialised countries.[6] Data span the years from 1975 to 1995, which have been divided into four periods: 1975-80, 1981-85, 1986-90 and 1991-95. The limited nature of the sample is due to the dearth of available information, particularly pertaining to recent years. Dividing data into 5-year time segments serves to compensate for missing data, but is especially meant to eliminate some short-term variations. Data from various sources were used, notably the *International Financial Statistics* of the IMF (1998), the *World Development Indicators* of the World Bank (1997), and Summers and Heston's *Pen World Table* (1993), updated in 1994.[7]

Estimated equations were not derived from a single, well-defined theoretical model, but involved measuring the effect of certain key variables. Some aspects were disregarded, due to lack of available data. Per capita gross domestic product (**GDPC**) and the rate of economic growth (**GGDPC**) were used as indicators of the country's economic performance. Per capita GDP, measured in constant dollars (base year 1985), has an *a priori* ambiguous effect on FDI rates. In view of the fact that most FDI comes from industrialised, high-income countries and goes first and foremost to countries with a similar degree of development, one would expect a positive correlation between GDPC and FDI. On the other hand, high per capita income also reflects high labour costs – an *a priori* negative factor for FDI. One would, however, expect that, overall, per capita income and the rate of economic growth would have a positive effect. Economic growth is measured using data in constant international prices (base year 1985). At the same time, an inverse measure of competitiveness is used here based on price levels (**PLVL**), produced by the ratio of the GDP deflator (parity of purchasing power) to the official exchange rate (Summers and Heston, 1994). Concerning the market size assumption, either population size or GDP expressed in constant international prices is used. These two variables are expressed in logarithmic form in order to reduce differences between countries (**LgPOP** and **LgGDP**). Once again, the effect is ambiguous. A positive effect would imply that the domestic market penetration factor is dominant, but it must be borne in mind that size may also have a negative effect on the amount of

---

5. FDI data are based on IMF balance of payment calculations. They are based on the international definition initially developed in 1993 by the IMF. However, the data are subject to problems created by national definitions of FDI. The data notably do not include transactions where title to property does not change, such as inter-company transactions.

6. The countries included in this sample are: Algeria, Bolivia, Brazil, Chile, China, Colombia, Egypt, Greece, Hungary, India, Indonesia, Ireland, Korea, Malaysia, Mexico, Morocco, Paraguay, Peru, the Philippines, Poland, Portugal, Singapore, South Africa, Spain, Thailand, Tunisia, Turkey, Uruguay and Venezuela.

7. Data taken from the Summers and Heston database only go up to 1992. Therefore, only two years will be considered for the last period.

direct investment. The volume of investment is higher in a large country than in a small country, but expressed as a percentage of economic activity, its impact may be negative due to a levelling-off effect.

The economic structure of countries was assessed using the value added by manufacturing and services as a percentage of GDP (**VAIND, VASERV**). The first is a measure of a country's degree of industrialisation, whereas the value added by services provides an indication of a more advanced stage of economic development. Also considered is the domestic investment rate[8] (**GDFI**), derived from the *World Development Indicators* (World Bank, 1997), to determine if there was a need for investment and to provide an indirect evaluation of infrastructure levels. The percentage of GDP accounted for by government consumption in real terms (**GOUV**), taken from the Summers and Heston table, was also considered to determine government involvement. Variables reflecting educational level (rate of primary and secondary schooling or average number of years of schooling for the population over 25 years of age) have been used as an estimate of the skill levels of the labour force. But since the rate of primary and secondary schooling was not significant, only the average number of years of schooling for persons over 25 years of age was used, taken from the UNDP (ONU, 1994) tables (**ETUD**). Other variables used include export growth rates (**GEX**) and indicators of the relative importance of major export categories (countries exporting primary commodities, services, manufactured goods or with diversified exports, respectively designated as **PRIM, SERV, MANUF** and **DIV**). Only the first three categories were used in the regressions. Finally, regional variables were introduced, namely **ASIE** and **AMSUD**.

To avoid any ambiguity regarding the direction of causality and problems relating to endogeneity, lagged data was used for certain variables, such as trade liberalisation, GDP and economic growth rate. As a result, only three periods were analysed. Lagged variables carry the prefix L.

The first series of regressions (1.1 to 1.4) uses the ordinary least square method with pooled data. The results are shown in Table 3. The figures in parentheses show the t-test values. First, a positive relation is found to exist between direct investment and per capita GDP, and a negative relation between FDI and market size, whether calculated using the logarithm of GDP or population size. In other words, when market size increases, FDI rates tend to decline. In addition, the positive relation between FDI and per capita GDP can be interpreted as investor preference for high-income countries. It should be noted that this effect persists even when this variable is expressed in constant international prices. This suggests that low labour costs are perhaps not an essential determinant of investment, and that investors tend to give more consideration to market characteristics. Price levels, however, have a negative effect on FDI, demonstrating that investors are nevertheless influenced by competitiveness factors. It is also clear that the FDI rate is higher in countries that export manufactured goods, where manufacturing accounts for much of the value added. Asian countries are the leaders in this regard. The number of years of schooling has also a negative influence on FDI. This may indicate that investors do not require qualified labour, and confirms El Mekki Karoui's theory regarding Tunisia. This may, however, also have resulted from a sampling bias.[9] It can further be noted that the dynamic nature of economies, whether in terms of growth in exports or income, does not seem to be a significant factor. Government spending and the domestic investment rate are also insignificant. A Fisher test confirmed that these coefficients have a combined zero effect.

---

8.   Fixed gross domestic investment, in other words, domestic investment less stock flows. Public investment linked to military spending is excluded, and is reported as government consumption.

9.   The effect of educational level remains negative, even when substituting a dichotomous variable reflecting educational level for the ETUD variable.

Introducing fixed effects for the various periods has little impact on the results obtained. The same variables are significant and have the same sign effect. Overall, the quality of the regression improves, since the determination coefficient increases, the variation coefficient decreases slightly and the variables gain in significance, except in the case of competitiveness. The effects observed are also sharper. In terms of the period effect, a strong negative effect can be observed for the second period (1986-90), while estimated constants for the first and third periods remain close to zero. At the same time, the significance of domestic investment rises. Observing a regression of only the significant variables (regression 1.6) shows that the investment rate is positive at the 0.15 level of significance.

b)   The impact of liberalisation

The effect of trade liberalisation on FDI flow is the focus here. There is, *a priori*, a substitution effect caused by trade liberalisation and, in particular, the drop in customs duties on imports. This, however, only impacts FDI from countries affected by trade agreements, designed to bypass trade barriers. The expected result of FDI in export industries would be positive in light of the fact that a low level of import protection can be more attractive than a rebate system. In addition, as the market expands, so does FDI from countries outside the agreement, in order to break into markets of countries with the best comparative advantages. Finally, comparative advantages, in the form of economic integration and a freer flow of factors of production, may result in the reallocation of FDI within the region.

Another effect may be viewed from a dynamic perspective. Regional trade agreements bring about a more efficient diffusion of technology within a region and result in economies of scale in a greatly expanded market. Such economies of scale make the market more competitive internationally. Increased exposure to international competition further stimulates productivity. These incentives, which increase with the degree of regional integration, stimulate growth (see above) and augment the area's economic potential, creating an increasingly favourable climate for investment. For these effects to be positive, however, a certain threshold stage of development needs to have been attained to enable the absorption of investment.

It is therefore necessary to measure the extent of trade liberalisation as one of the factors determining the location of direct investment. A comparison between FDI flows to the relatively free markets of some Asian countries and the fairly protected Latin American markets (at least until very recently) shows that the Asian markets attract FDI aimed at exports, while the Latin American markets generally attract FDI aimed at the domestic market (UNCTAD, 1996). These findings are supported by another study showing that, in 1992, exports accounted for 45% of the total sales of Japanese subsidiaries in the Asian manufacturing sector, while for Japanese subsidiaries in Latin America, exports only accounted for 23% of sales.

Few empirical, *post facto* studies have been conducted regarding the effects of regional agreements, since only a few of them (EEC, the US-Canadian free-trade agreement and EFTA) have been in effect for some time, and these mainly involve northern countries. What is clear, however, is that the effects vary greatly depending on the investors concerned and on whether or not they are affected by trade agreements. A comparison between the 1980s (1982-85 and 1986-90) and the early 1990s shows a strong regional division of FDI flows, with investment from the European Union focused on EU countries, investment by Asia going to Asian countries, and the role of local investors increasing within NAFTA. Regarding North-South agreements[10] (NAFTA and the expansion of the

---

10.   Jovanovic (1995), in a study based on FDI flows in southern countries participating in a South-South regional integration programme between 1960 and 1993, demonstrated that no significant link existed.

EEC to include Greece, Spain and Portugal), it is difficult to measure the impact of regional agreements on inflows of FDI, since this is largely linked with international economic fluctuations.

A comprehensive study of the impact of trade agreements on FDI flows calls for a bilateral analysis, identifying trading partners from countries that are not parties to trade agreements. This type of data, however, is not available for the semi-industrialised countries, and the fact that these agreements are recent also limits the analysis. More generally, measuring the degree of an economy's liberalisation creates a number of problems. (see Edwards, 1997). There is, in fact, no comprehensive criterion and one must rely at best on partial indicators of trade policies and distortion (customs duties and black market premium) or variables such as the percentage of GDP accounted for by foreign trade. This variable can, however, according to Leamer (1992), be determined by many factors other than the level of protectionism applied by the government, such as a country's size and its comparative advantages.

The influence of import duties on FDI flows was examined in a sub-sample for which the data were available. Customs duties seemed to have no significant impact. Foreign trade was therefore used as a percentage of GDP (*OPEN*) to measure the degree of trade liberalisation. This variable, which one would expect to have a positive effect, raises the same problems as those discussed above. Many factors are taken into consideration in this study, however, including market size, the economic structure and exports. The ratio of trade to GDP was also used for the previous period, to avoid problems in determining the direction of causality. This left one major problem, namely that this variable does not reflect the existence of trade policies or agreements. It merely shows the complementary relationship that exists between trade and foreign investment.

The results obtained (Table 3, regressions 1.8 and 1.9) are striking: whether using pooled regressions or fixed effects, the highly significant influence of liberalisation overpowers almost all other variables. In the pooled regressions, which are not presented here, only the inverse variable of competitiveness is significant, and negative, as in earlier regressions. Once period effects are included, competitiveness is no longer significant and the logarithm of GDP has a slight positive significance, whereas it had been negative in previous regressions. Trade levels appear as an essential determinant of FDI. The coefficient is estimated at 4.9, which means that a rise of 1 point in trade corresponds to a 5% increase in the FDI rate, which is considerable. The period effect is also significant, with each of the three periods having a distinct effect. The FDI rate is lowest during the second period (1986-90) and highest during the third period (1991-95). A Fisher test to determine whether the combined effect of the global and period constants is zero (that is, periods 1 and 2, since the third is 0) confirmed the null hypothesis.[11]

There is, in fact, a high degree of correlation between trade liberalisation and most of the explanatory variables (see Table 4). In addition, the study of multicollinearity of the model, conducted using variance inflation factors (VIF) and the Belsley, Kuh and Welsch indicators, shows that there is a collinearity problem between the rate of liberalisation and market size, and to a lesser extent, between competitiveness and per capita income (see Table 5). When a standardised model is used, this diagnostic is not as alarming. This multicollinearity may then only be due to a size effect on condition indices.

The step-wise method has been used to draw up a new model incorporating only significant variables. Results obtained are similar to those in regression 1.9. The degree of liberalisation is more significant than in regression 1.8, but the coefficient is lower. The period effect remains highly

---

11.   Performing a total regression brings competitiveness to the fore, and sharply decreases the significance of market size. The justification for this approach, however, appears questionable in light of the above.

significant, analogous to that observed in regression 1.8. The only other variable that is significant at the 0.05 level is market size, which has a positive effect. The effect of market size observed in the first series of regressions (1.1 to 1.7) has thus been invalidated. In fact, at constant levels of trade liberalisation, this may be interpreted as an argument in favour of market penetration. The other variables in this regression are only significant at the 0.15 level. Competitiveness has a lesser positive effect than when foreign trade was disregarded and, all other things being equal, Latin America is particularly attractive to investors. More surprisingly, the domestic investment rate appears to have a negative effect on the rate of FDI. This may be contrary to what one would expect, but can be explained by the strong positive correlation with the degree of liberalisation (see Table 3).

The present study, while not claiming to be exhaustive, has emphasised the impact of certain characteristics of the host countries on the choice of FDI location. First, a very strong correlation exists between the degree of trade liberalisation and FDI inflows. Also, FDI is strongly biased in favour of countries that export manufactured goods. Second, FDI favours countries with high income but low price levels, which offers proof of the existence of both market penetration and competitiveness arguments. The level of industrialisation is also an important factor, but domestic investment does not appear to have a large effect on FDI. Neither economic growth nor government spending appears to be significant. Finally, the level of qualifications of human capital, measured by the average number of years of schooling of the working population, does not impact on the choice of FDI destination, suggesting that FDI principally creates jobs for low-skilled labour. Furthermore, it is important to note that FDI depends in large part on the period under consideration, seeing that it is strongly influenced by factors related to the international economic situation, regardless of the characteristics of host countries. The study now turns to the impact of FDI on growth.

3. The impact of FDI on growth

Although the relation between the degree of trade liberalisation and economic growth is still controversial, most empirical studies agree that liberalisation has a positive impact on growth. Edwards (1997), who used nine different indicators related to trade liberalisation, showed that all but one of the 18 equations tested demonstrated the positive impact of liberalisation. For this study, the direct effects of liberalisation on growth were examined, but no significant correlation was found. It thus seems logical to investigate indirect relationships. Levine and Renelt (1992) pointed out that liberalisation affects growth through its impact on investment. This was supported by a Baldwin and Seghezza study (1995), which found that a protected domestic market discourages investment and therefore slows growth. The investigation will now focus on the interaction between investment and growth and, in particular, on the role played by FDI.

As already demonstrated, liberalisation brings about an increase in FDI. But a high degree of liberalisation is also associated with high domestic investment levels. One of the key effects of FDI is its impact on domestic investment: does FDI stimulate domestic investment or does it have a crowding-out effect?

One of the most important aspects of FDI is that it serves as a vehicle for technology. In fact, technology transfers can take many forms (imports of high-technology products, improved human capital through training abroad, and so forth). FDI, however, is often presented in the literature as the best vehicle for transferring technology, though without any reliable empirical evidence offered. Findlay (1978) hypothesises that direct foreign investment boosts technological progress in the host country through a "contagion effect" produced by the management and production techniques used by foreign firms. Wang (1990) included this notion in his neo-classical growth model, assuming that growth, as measured by increased production, is linked to FDI. As regards endogenous growth, new information can be assimilated in two ways. First, in the case of labour it may lead to improved productivity; second, at the level of capital or consumer goods, it may improve the quality or range of goods produced. Borenzstein *et al.* (1994) developed a model of domestic growth based on this approach, where the level of technological progress is linked to the introduction of new types of capital goods and is the main determinant of long-term growth rates. Foreign firms, which are more advanced, have higher productivity and can introduce new types of goods at a lesser expense, which, in turn, lowers the cost of adapting these technologies to the market.

The relative impact of FDI and domestic investment on growth needs to be evaluated. Is FDI more effective? Does technology transfer take place? In order to answer these questions, several matters must be addressed. The first, which will not be dealt with in this study due to the lack of available data, concerns evaluating the impact of FDI in terms of technology and the degree of integration into the host economy. According to Cantwell (1992), FDI has a positive influence on the host country's economy if there is a strong presence of domestic companies in the sector concerned. FDI increases competition in the host country, thus bringing about a positive hold-over effect thanks to imitation and learning. It is self-evident that FDI, resulting in co-operative efforts and training, has a greater impact than vertical FDI, involving the assembly of imported components, such as in the clothing and textile and electronics industries (see data on the Tunisian textile industry in Table 2). The second important aspect is that, for new technologies to be absorbed, the human capital needs to have reached a certain stage of development. Borensztein *et al.* (1994) studied the impact of FDI on growth by means of a cross-sectional analysis of 69 countries for the period 1970-1989. The authors evaluated the impact of FDI on domestic investment, and concluded that they complemented one another. They further stressed that the positive impact of FDI on growth is mainly due to its impact on human capital. This argument, however, does not appear to be very solid.

The study is based on the following estimation of the growth model:

$$g = c_0 + c_1 FDI + c_2 FDI.H + c_3 H + c_4 Y_0 + c_5 X$$

where g is the per capita GDP growth rate, *FDI* is the FDI rate as a percentage of GDP, H is the level of human capital (as measured by the average number of years of secondary schooling of the male working population), Y_0 is the logarithm for the initial per capita GDP, and X is a range of variables that usually affects growth. The authors observed that coefficient c_1 is negative, but not (or only slightly) significant, while coefficient c_2 is positive. From this they deduced an H–threshold beyond which FDI would have a positive impact on growth. Apart from the fact that the significance of c_1 creates problems in calculating this threshold, there is also the risk of endogeneity, which is unfortunately not stressed by the authors. While the instrumental variables method is used in their study, the authors do not seem to consider the mitigated and somewhat dubious nature of their results. Based on their criteria, it seems that at an average level of education, the two-step effect of FDI becomes negative, or even insignificant.

What is more, the authors conclude that domestic and foreign investments are both effective, while no proof is presented in their study. Finally, a much more serious problem, purely statistical in nature, concerns the probable multicollinearity between the variables affecting FDI. This results in serious errors when estimating the respective effects of variables *H*, *FDI* and *FDI.H*. Tests carried out on the present sample confirm this idea. There is, however, no easy solution to this problem, which will be left aside for future studies. It is nevertheless important to caution the reader to carefully consider the interactions between these three variables. This investigation has largely been inspired by the method used by Borenzstein *et al.* (1994), while focusing on the problem of endogeneity. Additional variables have also been introduced into the model. It should also be pointed out that the education variable used is based on the average number of years of schooling of the population.

a)   ***Preliminary analysis, without taking the endogeneity of FDI into account***

Overall, in order to draw up a growth model, the same variables as those in Section II were used, along with the logarithm of per capita GDP in international dollars, which is lagged in order to initialise income level (the convergence hypothesis). Other variables include the number of years of schooling, as a measure of human capital, which is supposed to have a positive effect on growth; the inverse variable of competitiveness; population growth, which is expected to have a negative effect on growth in per capita income; and government consumption as a percentage of GDP. One would expect the latter to have a negative effect, as a result of a drop in the multiplying effect or a drop in investment. Another variable used is the total domestic investment rate. The variables indicating the main export categories (manufacturing, services or primary products) provide a measure of the effect of specialisation. Finally, the model also includes regional variables (Asia, excluding China, Latin America, and Other, which includes countries in Africa, Central Europe, the Mediterranean and India).

The results obtained (Table 6) using the least squares method illustrate, first, that those countries exporting mainly manufactured goods show the highest growth in per capita income. Apart from the fact that population growth slows growth in per capita income, the outcome indicates that competitiveness influences growth, although only slightly. Finally, a positive correlation is found to exist between total domestic investment rate and GDP growth. This correlation ceases to be significant when introducing the Asia variable, which is significant at the 0.15 level. This phenomenon, once again, advocates the introduction of individual effects, which unfortunately is impossible due to the size of the sample. Another correlation, which only appears in conjunction with the Asia variable, is the negative correlation between the level of education and economic growth rate. This somewhat surprising finding may be explained in several ways.

On the one hand, Asian countries, which have shown the highest growth rates in recent years, have – with the exception of Korea – low educational levels. On the other hand, a country such as the Philippines, with high educational levels, has experienced little, even negative, growth. In fact, many countries with negative growth, for example, those in Latin America and Eastern Europe, have high levels of education. What is more, the variable used only provides a broad approximation of the level of qualification of the labour force, since it is too general in nature. It should instead only consider the number of years of secondary schooling. It is interesting to note that, if this education variable is replaced with a dichotomous variable, the negative relation disappears. In light of the above, it is not possible to conclude that those countries with the least developed human capital have the highest growth rates. Finally, introducing the period variable had no impact on this finding.

This investigation has tried to measure the impact of liberalisation on growth, but this variable is not found to be significant, and has virtually no effect on the other coefficients. When introducing the FDI rate, however, even if it does not differ significantly from zero, a positive impact on the domestic investment coefficient is observed. This may lead one to conclude that FDI improves the effectiveness of total investment. But, when measuring its direct effect, in other words, without taking total investment into account, the results show that it is not significant. On the other hand, when introducing the crossed variable ***ETUD.FDI***, as done by Borenzstein *et al.* (1994), both variables become significant, but with opposite sign effects: positive for FDI and negative for the crossed variable. It is thus clear that applying the least squares method to the sample brings about results that are opposite to those of Borenzstein *et al.*[12]

In addition to the problem of collinearity, created by introducing the crossed variable, the following needs to be noted. First, it is exaggerated to consider the FDI rate as an exogenous variable,

---

12.   Borenzstein *et al.* (1994) observed that the positive relation between FDI and growth was due to the compounded effect of FDI and human capital.

as demonstrated by the results. The instrumental variables method is therefore appropriate. Finally, a detailed analysis of the interaction between the FDI rate and total investment rate is necessary.

The investigation will now turn to the effect of FDI on growth, as measured by several instruments, without considering the domestic investment rate, in order to avoid any overflow effect, and, finally, will consider the relation between FDI and domestic investment.

b)   *The impact of FDI on growth using the two-stage least squares method*

In order to measure the "direct" impact of FDI on growth, the domestic investment rate is excluded from the initial analysis. The two-stage least squares method is used. The independent exogenous variables are the logarithm of per capita GDP (lagged), the number of years of schooling, government consumption, competitiveness, population growth rate and indicators of main exports. The instruments used are the lagged direct investment rate and the value added by manufacturing as a percentage of GDP (also lagged). The fixed period effect and Asia variable differ from the other variables in that they can be used either as additional instruments or as independent variables. These instruments will always be introduced last, and are systematically validated by correlation tests with residuals. The projection of FDI on the independent variables is given in Table 7. In addition, exogeneity tests were systematically done, and resulted in the rejection of the exogeneity null hypothesis (see Table 8).

The impact of FDI without considering the crossed effect with educational level

Regardless of the specification used, FDI does not have a significant impact on growth (regressions 3.2 and 3.3). The main factors explaining growth are manufacturing exports and population growth rate. Competitiveness is also featured, but only in the absence of period effects. Educational level again appears negatively related to growth, and its significance increases when period and regional variables are introduced as additional explanatory variables. The Asia variable is positively related to growth, while the period effect is barely significant. Only the first period appears to be somewhat negative. Thus, according to the initial regressions, FDI does not appear to be directly related to growth in the countries in the sample.

If the domestic investment rate is included as an additional exogenous variable (see 3.01 for projected **FDI** on this new variable), the FDI rate is still not significant, and there is, once again, a positive relation between FDI and domestic investment. This correlation disappears when the Asia variable is introduced, and is amplified when fixed-time effects are present. The period effect increases the degree of variance accounted for, but is not significant. The introduction of domestic investment as an independent variable also decreases the significance of educational level.

It is therefore clear that FDI does not appear to influence growth rates when controlling for problems of endogeneity. Domestic investment, however, has a small positive effect on growth. The spill-over effect of FDI on domestic investment observed earlier in the preliminary regressions was not confirmed with the instrumental variable approach to FDI. This aspect will be considered in more detail in Section 3c.

Introducing a crossed effect

When **ETUD.FDI** is substituted for **FDI**, the results remain largely the same. In spite of the limited scope of this exercise, a crossed effect is introduced in addition to the simple FDI effect. The multicollinearity problem will be dealt with later. This procedure requires modifications to the estimation method. Because the endogeneity of the crossed variable can only be due to FDI, projected FDI values are used on all the instruments to make this composite variable more exogenous, instead of merely projecting FDI.ETUD. Tests conducted demonstrate the endogeneity of FDI and FDI.ETUD, as well as the validity of the instruments used, which are the same as those used in Section 2.

As indicated earlier, when using the ordinary least squares method, introducing a crossed variable makes both variables featuring FDI significant (4.1 and 4.2), although with opposite sign effects (see Table 9). The crossed variable has a positive effect, while the FDI and educational level variable has a negative effect. The significance of these effects increases when the Asia and period variables are introduced, but only the Asia variable has a significant impact. At the same time, the negative impact of government consumption and the positive effect of competitiveness are both stronger when the crossed variable is not considered.

When the domestic investment rate (4.3 and 4.4) is introduced, it is no longer significant and also decreases the significance of the FDI variables, and their impact. The same is true for the educational level variable. The Asia variable remains significantly positive, but the impact of government consumption disappears.

Regarding the problem of multicollinearity, diagnostics are given in the annex for regressions 4.2 and 4.4 (VIF and the Belsley, Kuh and Welsch indicators for the standardised and non-standardised models). First, the condition indices are high for the constant and the logarithm of per capita GDP, but this is a common phenomenon: as soon as one considers broad macro-economic aggregates, a size effect comes into play, without it necessarily being due to multicollinearity.[13] A greater cause for concern is the high condition index values for *ETUD*, *FDI* and *ETUD.FDI*, even when using a standardised model. The impact of these three variables can therefore not be assessed with precision without the use of more sophisticated instruments (the Principal Components Estimator or Ridge Estimator), or redesigning the model. It is important to note that simply excluding one of the variables making up the crossed variable would not be a solution, since that would exclude the possibility of making any comparisons.

The results obtained in this series of regressions, and those obtained by Borenzstein *et al.* regarding the link between human capital and FDI impact, should thus be interpreted with the greatest caution, since it could be due to an econometric artefact. As a result, determining the "direct" result of FDI remains problematic and unresolved by the present study. It is therefore appropriate to consider the indirect effects of FDI, in other words, its effect on growth through its effect on domestic investment.

c)   *The impact of FDI and liberalisation on total domestic investment*

As indicated (regression series 1 and 2), the lagged total investment rate has only a marginal impact on FDI flows. What is more, the domestic investment rate has a positive effect on growth, whether at constant FDI levels or not. The impact of domestic investment may, in turn, result from its interaction with human capital. When introducing a crossed variable, however, any slightly positive effects observed in the previous regressions disappear. The interaction effect thus seems to be unique to FDI. It is nevertheless necessary to consider the impact of FDI on domestic investment in order to check for any crowding-out or spill-over effects.

---

13.   For an evaluation of methods to detect multicollinearity, see Erkel-Rousse (1994).

FDI and domestic investment

The results obtained (Table 10) concerning the relation between FDI and domestic investment are mixed. In regressions 5.1 and 5.2, FDI has a positive impact on the domestic investment rate, but the coefficient is only slightly greater than one. What is more, it drops sharply to below 1 when fixed period effects are introduced. It is therefore particularly difficult to clearly define the impact of FDI on domestic investment. Introducing the ***ETUD.FDI*** crossed variable gives largely the same results, suggesting that there is no interaction between the impact of FDI on domestic investment and human capital. It may therefore be due to the impact of FDI on growth. The (presumed) impact of FDI on growth does thus not necessarily involve domestic investment.

Another important point is that the degree of liberalisation has a significant effect on the domestic investment rate.

With regard to the other independent variables, domestic investment is high in countries with high value added by the manufacturing and service industries (which is hardly surprising), and high exports in the services and manufacturing sectors. Government consumption, however, has a negative impact, as does per capita GDP.

4.   Conclusion

The results of this study show that the impact of FDI on growth is uncertain, in light of the highly endogenous nature of such investment (see Chart 1 next page). FDI does not generally appear to be a factor determining growth, unless one considers its interaction with human capital. But while FDI has a positive impact overall, this is probably due to an econometric artefact. Results should therefore be viewed with the greatest caution.

Total domestic investment, on the other hand, has a positive impact on growth. FDI appears to influence domestic investment only in terms of its direct contribution to it, without having any crowding-out or spill-over effect. It has not, unfortunately, been possible to demonstrate any difference between the effectiveness of domestic and foreign investment, since these two variables were not significant at the same time.

Trade liberalisation plays a role in attracting FDI, but is not a decisive factor in determining growth. The investigation has also shown that liberalisation does not have a direct impact on growth, although it does through domestic investment. Governments should therefore provide incentives for investment, while at the same time remaining reserved about FDI-led growth. It would seem necessary to follow through on this study with a sector-by-sector examination of the impact of FDI on production. That impact is likely to depend largely on the technological content of investment, its real vocational training effects and, above all, on how well it can be integrated into the economy.

Chart 1. **Recapitulative diagram of results**

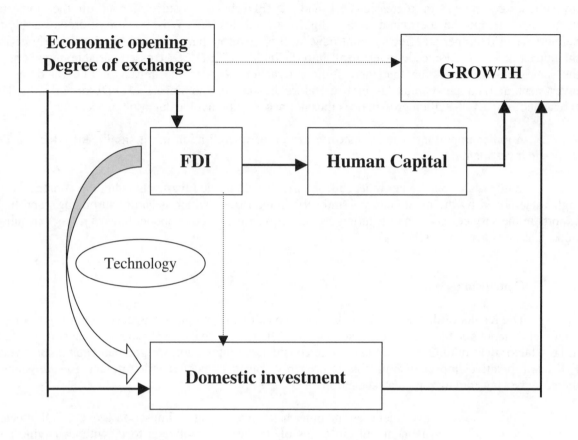

→ Positive effect
⋯▶ Undetermined effect

BIBLIOGRAPHY

BALDWIN, R.E. and SEGHEZZA, E. (1995)
"Testing for trade-induced investment-led growth", NBER Working Paper No. 5416.

BORENSZTEIN, E., DE GREGORIO, J. and LEE, J.W. (1994)
"How does foreign investment affect economic growth?", IMF Working Paper, September.

BRAINARD, S.L. (1993)
"A simple theory of multinational corporations with a trade-off between proximity and concentration", NBER Working Paper No. 4269, February.

CANTWELL, J. (1992)
"Innovation and technological competitiveness", in P.J. Buckley and M. Casson (eds.), *Multinational Enterprises in the World Economy*, pp. 20-40, Edward Elgar, Aldershot.

CHAN, S. and MASON, M. (1992)
"Foreign direct investment and host country conditions: looking from the other side now", *International Interactions*, Vol. 23, No. 4.

DUNNING, J.H. (1973)
"The determinants of international production", *Oxford Economic Papers*, N.S. 25, pp. 289-236.

EDWARDS, S. (1991)
"Capital flows, foreign direct investment and debt equity swaps in developing countries", in H. Siebert (ed.), *Capital Flows in the World Economy: Symposium 1990,* Institut für Weltwirtschaft an der Universität Kiel, Tubingen.

EDWARDS, S. (1997)
"Openness, productivity and growth: what do we really know?", NBER Working Paper No. 5978, March.

EL MEKKI KAROUI, Y. (1998)
"Les effets sur l'emploi", in B. Bellon and R. Gouia (eds.), *Investissements directs étrangers et développement industriel méditerranéen*, Economica, Paris.

ERKEL-ROUSSE, H. (1994)
"Détection de la multicolinéarité dans un modèle linéaire ordinaire", INSEE Working Paper, Paris.

FINDLAY, R. (1978)
"Relative backwardness, direct foreign investment, and the transfer of technology: a simple dynamic model", *Quarterly Journal of Economics*, Vol. 92, pp. 1-16, February.

INTERNATIONAL MONETARY FUND – IMF (1998)
International Financial Statistics (4), Washington, D.C.

JOVANOVIC, M.N. (1995)
"Economic integration among developing countries and foreign direct investment", *Economica Internazionale*, Vol. 48, No. 2, pp. 209-244, May.

KOJIMA, K. (1978)
Direct Foreign Invetsment: A Japanese Model of Multinational Business Operations, Croom Helm, London.

LEAMER, E. (1992)
"Testing trade theory", NBER Working Paper, No. 3957.

LEVINE, R. and RENELT, D. (1992)
"A sensitivity analysis of cross-country growth regressions", *American Economic Review*, Vol. 82, No. 1, pp. 49-53.

LIM, D. (1982)
"Fiscal incentives and direct foreign investment in less developed countries", *The Journal of Development Studies*, April.

LUCAS, R.E. (1990)
"Why doesn't capital flow from rich to poor countries?", *American Economic Review*, Vol. 80, pp. 92-96.

MacMILLAN, S. (1995)
"Foreign direct investment in Ghana and Côte d'Ivoire", in S. Chan (ed.), *Foreign Direct Investment in a Changing Global Economy*, MacMillan Press, New York.

MUNDELL, R.A. (1957)
"International trade and factor mobility", *American Economic Review*, No. 47, June.

OECD (1997a)
International Direct Investment Statistics Yearbook, Paris.

OECD (1997b)
Activities of Foreign Affiliates in OECD Countries, Statistical Data 1985-1994, Paris.

REUBER, G., CROKELLE, H., EMERSEN, M. and GALLIAS-HAMONO, G. (1973)
Private Foreign Investment in Development, OECD Development Centre, Clarendon Press, Oxford.

RIEDEL, J. (1975)
"The nature and determinants of export-oriented direct investment in a developing country: a case study of Taiwan", *Weltwirschaftliches Archiv*, Vol. 3, pp. 505-528.

ROOT, F.R. (1978)
International Trade and Investment, 4th Edition, South-Western Publishing Co., Cincinnati.

SCHNEIDER, F. and FREY, B.S. (1985)
"Political determinants of foreign direct investment", *World Development*, No. 13, Vol.2, pp. 161-175.

SEVEN, S. (1992)
"Private investment and macroeconomic adjustment: a survey", *The World Bank Research Observer*, Vol. 7, No. 1, January.

SUMMERS, R. and HESTON, A. (1994)
The Pen World Table: an Expanded Set of International Comparisons, Cambridge, MA.

SWANSBROUGH, R.H. (1972)
"The American investor's view of Latin American economic nationalism", *Inter-American Economic Affairs*, No. 26, Vol. 3, pp.61-82.

UNCTAD (1996)
Incentives and Foreign Direct Investment, UN, Geneva and New York.

UNCTAD (1997)
World Investment Report 1997: Transnational Corporation, Market Structure and Competition Policy, UN, Geneva and New York.

UNITED NATIONS (1991, 1994)
Rapport mondial sur le développement humain, PNUD, New York and Geneva.

VERNON, R. (1966)
"International investment and international trade in the product cycle", *Quarterly Journal of Economics*, No. 80, pp.190-207.

WANG, J.Y. (1990)
"Growth, technology transfer, and the long-run theory of international capital movements", *Journal of International Economics*, Vol. 29, pp. 255-271.

WHEELER, D. and MODY, A. (1992)
"International investment location decisions: the case of US firms", *Journal of International Economics*, Vol. 33, pp. 57-76.

WORLD BANK (1994)
World Tables, Washington D.C.

WORLD BANK (1997)
World Development Indicators, Washington D.C.

Table 1. Direct investment flows 1986, 1990 and 1996

Millions of dollars

	1986	1990	1996
Algeria	5	12 *(1991)*	13
Egypt	1 217	734	636
Israel	137	101	2 110
Morocco	60 *(1987)*	165	311
Tunisia	64	76	253
Turkey	125	684	722
Hungary	..	1 462 *(1991)*	1 982
Poland	16	89	4 498
Czech Rep.	..		1 435
Spain	3 451	13 984	6 396
Greece	471	1 005	1 058
Portugal	238	2 610	708
China	1 875	3 487	40 180
Korea	460	788	2 325
Hong Kong (China)	..	1 728	2 500
Indonesia	258	1 093	4 348 *(1995)*
Malaysia	489	2 332	4 132 *(1995)*
Philippines	127	530	478 *(1995)*
Thailand	263	2 444	2 336
Singapore	1 710	5 575	9 440
Argentina	574	1 836	4 218
Brazil	345	989	4 859 *(1995)*
Chile	316	590	4 091
Colombia	674	500	3 322
Mexico	2 036	2 549	7 619

Sources: IMF (1998); UNCTAD (1997) for Hong Kong (China).

Table 2. **Manufacturing multinationals in Mexico and Turkey, 1993**

(ISIC Rev. 3)	Mexico			Turkey		
	Number of companies	Number of employees	Value added	Number of companies	Number of employees	Value added
Total	1 927	906 614	18 398	183	38 392	4 500
Food, beverages, tobacco	171	105 189	2 897	30	5 548	760
Textile, clothing, leather, footwear	137	59 779	335	33	2 995	118
Chemicals, rubber and plastics products	404	128 532	5 232	32	7 578	882
Electrical and electronic equipment	346	272 473	2 421	16	6 272	500
Motor vehicles	123	112 844	2 648	10	9 271	660

Sources: OECD (1997*b*).

Table 3. Determinants of direct investments

	1.1	1.2	1.3	1.4	1.5	1.6	1.7	1.8	1.9
LOPEN								**4.96**	**4.66**
								(8.08)	**(12.9)**
LGGDPC	-6.56	-0.94	-0.005		-10.99			-1.69	
	(-0.48)	(-0.84)	(-0.005)		(-0.95)			(-0.20)	
LGOUV	-0.09	-0.04	-0.04		-0.04			-0.012	
	(-1.24)	(-0.60)	(-0.60)		(-0.65)			(-0.27)	
LPLVL	-0.03	**-0.08**	**-0.08**	**-0.08**	**-0.08**	**-0.07**	**-0.07**	-0.007	_-0.014_
	(-1.37)	**(-4.05)**	**(-4.05)**	**(-4.58)**	**(-3.10)**	**(-3.44)**	**(-3.30)**	(-0.37)	_(-1.6)_
LGDFI	_0.07_	0.03	0.03		0.045		_0.05_	-0.04	_-0.04_
	_(1.44)_	(0.72)	(0.72)		(1.06)		_(1.40)_	(-1.35)	_(-1.55)_
MANUF	**2.24**	**1.61**	**1.61**	**1.37**	**1.95**	**1.43**	**1.25**	0.17	
	(2.50)	**(2.09)**	**(2.08)**	**(2.05)**	**(2.52)**	**(2.15)**	**(1.85)**	(0.28)	
PRIM	-0.25	-0.26	-0.26		-0.54			-0.26	
	(-0.24)	(-0.28)	(-0.28)		(-0.58)			(-0.39)	
SERV	1.18	0.33	0.33		0.40			0.29	
	(1.14)	(0.35)	(0.35)		(0.45)			(0.45)	
ASIE	1.0	_1.25_	_1.25_	1.51	1.47	1.50	1.24	-0.44	
	(1.16)	_(1.69)_	_(1.70)_	**(2.36)**	**(1.99)**	**(2.35)**	**(1.88)**	(-0.77)	
AMSUD	-0.17	0.47	0.47		0.52			0.51	_0.50_
	(-0.21)	(0.65)	(0.65)		(0.73)			(1.00)	_(1.46)_
LLgGDP	**-0.66**		**-0.93**	**-0.93**	**-0.94**	**-0.93**	**-0.93**	_0.36_	**0.31**
	(-2.31)		**(-3.66)**	**(-4.14)**	**(-3.80)**	**(-4.15)**	**(-4.17)**	_(1.49)_	**(2.04)**
LGDPC		**0.001**	**0.001**	**0.001**	**0.001**	**0.001**	**0.001**	-0.0001	
		(4.29)	**(4.29)**	**(7.10)**	**(4.71)**	**(5.48)**	**(5.10)**	(-0.54)	
LlgPOP		**-0.94**							
		(-3.66)							
ETUD	-0.117	**-0.39**	**-0.39**	**-0.37**	**-0.41**	**-3.7**	**-0.32**	0.03	
	(-0.75)	**(-2.62)**	**(-2.62)**	**(-3.16)**	**(-2.86)**	**(-3.19)**	**(-2.61)**	(0.31)	
LVAIND	**0.13**	_0.10_	_0.10_	0.08	**0.10**	0.08	0.06	0.004	
	(2.44)	_(1.74)_	_(1.74)_	**(2.62)**	**(2.21)**	**(2.68)**	**(1.99)**	(0.11)	
LVASERV	**0.12**	0.03	0.03		0.03			-0.001	
	(3.19)	(0.64)	(0.64)		(0.91)			(0.06)	
LGEX	1.26	1.27	1.28		-1.72			-0.008	
	(0.36)	(0.55)	(0.55)		(-0.43)			(-0.00)	
Constant	9.03	**23.4**	**10.3**	**25.6**	**24.2**	**25.9**	**25.0**	-7.7	_-6.27_
	(1.1)	**(2.28)**	**(2.28)**	**(4.45)**	**(3.2)**	**(4.7)**	**(4.3)**	(-1.16)	_(-1.62)_
Constant 1					-0.13	-0.38	-0.30	-1.05	**-0.94**
					(-0.16)	(-0.54)	(-0.43)	(-1.8)	**(-2.42)**
Constant 2					**-1.46**	_-0.96_	_-1.01_	-1.20	_-1.11_
					(-2.10)	_(-1.74)_	_(-1.83)_	(-2.4)	_(-3.06)_
Constant 3					0.0	0.0	0.0	0.0	0.0
					(.)	(.)	(.)	(.)	(.)
R²	0.39	0.55	0.55	0.52	0.58	0.54	0.55	0.79	0.78
Adjusted R²	0.27	0.45	0.45	0.48	0.48	0.49	0.50	0.73	0.76
CV	130	112	112	110	110	109	108	79	74
Nb obs	87	87	87	87	87	87	87	87	87

Note: Significance degree: 5% for bold results, 10% for italic bold results and 15% for italic underlined results.

Table 4. **Correlation with FDI and with LOPEN**

Variables	Correlation with FDI Pearson's coefficient (critical probability)	Correlation with LOPEN Pearson's coefficient (critical probability)
FDI	1	**0.84 (0.0001)**
LOPEN	**0.84 (0.0001)**	1
LGGDPC	**0.21 (0.05)**	**0.26 (0.01)**
LGOUV	**-0.21 (0.05)**	**0.21 (0.05)**
LPLVL	0.14 (0.18)	**0.33 (0.001)**
LGDFI	**0.38 (0.0003)**	**0.48 (0.0001)**
MANUF	**0.32 (0.003)**	**0.37 (0.0004)**
PRIM	-0.13 (0.23)	-0.11 (0.31)
SERV	-0.05 (0.65)	-0.04 (0.66)
ASIE	**0.36 (0.0007)**	**0.46 (0.0001)**
AMSUD	-0.127 (0.24)	-0.22 (0.04)
LLgGDP	-0.16 (0.13)	-0.32 (0.002)
LGDPC	**0.47 (0.0001)**	**0.56 (0.0001)**
ETUD	0.05 (0.66)	0.0008 (0.99)
LVAIND	-0.008 (0.94)	-0.027 (0.80)
LVASERV	**0.25 (0.01)**	**0.33 (0.002)**
LGEX	0.06 (0.59)	0.05 (0.67)

Table 5. **Collinearity diagnostics for the regression 1.9**

Variable	DF	Parameter Estimate	Standard Error	T for H0 : Parameter=0	Prob > |T|	Variance Inflation
INTERCEP	1	-7.694687	6.65029325	-1.157	0.2513	0.00000000
LOPEN	1	4.957441	0.61329217	8.083	0.0001	5.21721748
LGGDPC4	1	-1.696718	8.36385639	-0.203	0.8398	2.70139853
LGOUV	1	-0.012106	0.04459103	-0.271	0.7868	2.82067011
LPLVL	1	-0.007389	0.02009649	-0.368	0.7143	5.84948106
LTXGDFI	1	-0.043813	0.03254640	-1.346	0.1827	2.26514159
MMANUF	1	0.168351	0.59647060	0.282	0.7786	2.71508711
MPRIM	1	-0.261660	0.67184401	-0.389	0.6981	2.68412733
MSERV	1	0.294520	0.64829169	0.454	0.6511	2.08269599
ASIE	1	-0.449273	0.58271679	-0.771	0.4434	2.32209039
AMSUD	1	0.516056	0.51399867	1.004	0.3189	2.35657612
LLGDP4	1	0.358501	0.24067489	1.490	0.1410	3.62591244
LGDPC3	1	-0.000126	0.00023350	-0.538	0.5922	8.56182874
METUD	1	0.036442	0.11643810	0.313	0.7553	2.45863125
LVAIND	1	0.003835	0.03417090	0.112	0.9110	3.49267838
LVASERV	1	-0.001498	0.02726571	-0.055	0.9564	3.62058075
LGEX2	1	-0.008298	2.89145047	-0.003	0.9977	3.82791887
PER2	1	-1.045875	0.57684634	-1.813	0.0742	3.08168848
PER3	1	-1.199477	0.50335417	-2.383	0.0200	2.34647423

Table 5. Collinearity diagnostics for the regression 1.9 (cont.)

Collinearity diagnostics

Number	Eigenvalue	Condition Index	Var Prop INTERCEP	Var Prop LOPEN	Var Prop LGGDPC4	Var Prop LGGOV	Var Prop LPLVL	Var Prop LTXGDPI	Var Prop MMANUF	Var Prop MPPIM	Var Prop MSERV	Var Prop ASIE	Var Prop AMSUD	Var Prop LLGDP4	Var Prop LGDPC3	Var Pro METUD	Var Prop LVAIND	Var Prop LVASERV	Var Prop LGEX2	Var Prop PER2	Var Prop PER3
1	11.44576	1.00000	0.0000	0.0005	0.0194	0.0002	0.0001	0.0000	0.0007	0.0004	0.0007	0.0007	0.0006	0.0000	0.0000	0.0007	0.0005	0.0001	0.0005	0.0006	0.0006
2	2.00861	2.38712	0.0000	0.0015	0.0081	0.0002	0.0000	0.0000	0.0232	0.0264	0.0021	0.0287	0.0261	0.0000	0.0000	0.0002	0.0005	0.0000	0.0016	0.0006	0.0055
3	1.40205	2.85720	0.0000	0.0031	0.0001	0.0006	0.0000	0.0002	0.0065	0.0015	0.0061	0.0093	0.0041	0.0010	0.0010	0.0002	0.0140	0.0000	0.0140	0.0447	0.0590
4	1.07340	3.26544	0.0000	0.0001	0.0000	0.0029	0.0000	0.0003	0.0068	0.0569	0.0003	0.0103	0.0134	0.0000	0.0000	0.0000	0.0002	0.0000	0.0002	0.0008	0.0057
5	0.64254	4.22059	0.0000	0.0192	0.0053	0.0062	0.0007	0.0001	0.0103	0.0032	0.1691	0.0638	0.0001	0.0000	0.0000	0.0005	0.0021	0.0001	0.0004	0.0111	0.0536
6	0.51845	4.69859	0.0000	0.0240	0.0459	0.0000	0.0007	0.0002	0.0000	0.1648	0.0962	0.0962	0.0147	0.0004	0.0004	0.0044	0.0003	0.0004	0.0242	0.0242	0.0191
7	0.42388	5.19639	0.0000	0.0107	0.1039	0.0044	0.0008	0.0001	0.0531	0.1663	0.0007	0.0918	0.2941	0.0006	0.0006	0.0043	0.0111	0.0000	0.0092	0.0092	0.0002
8	0.39822	5.36121	0.0000	0.0279	0.4291	0.0002	0.0002	0.0002	0.2805	0.0000	0.0096	0.1419	0.1045	0.0000	0.0000	0.0000	0.0011	0.0000	0.0029	0.0564	0.0003
9	0.30767	6.09926	0.0000	0.0019	0.0077	0.0023	0.0008	0.0019	0.1043	0.0109	0.0259	0.0005	0.0629	0.0000	0.0015	0.0055	0.0021	0.0000	0.0041	0.2355	0.0565
10	0.24602	6.82081	0.0000	0.1422	0.1156	0.0195	0.0025	0.0122	0.1111	0.0115	0.0206	0.0328	0.0018	0.0000	0.0015	0.0184	0.0005	0.0001	0.0021	0.0149	0.3140
11	0.18044	7.96449	0.0000	0.0213	0.0000	0.1196	0.0022	0.0312	0.0062	0.0686	0.1090	0.1513	0.0080	0.0000	0.0324	0.0668	0.0003	0.0012	0.0116	0.0116	0.0229
12	0.12322	9.63790	0.0000	0.1311	0.0112	0.0048	0.0007	0.0438	0.0196	0.0018	0.0080	0.1230	0.0026	0.0000	0.0097	0.0442	0.0127	0.0090	0.0623	0.0623	0.0886
13	0.08553	11.56811	0.0000	0.0053	0.1311	0.1196	0.0007	0.0871	0.0107	0.0263	0.0115	0.0684	0.0489	0.0000	0.0048	0.0003	0.0111	0.0124	0.4653	0.0325	0.1472
14	0.07158	12.64546	0.0000	0.0125	0.0112	0.0048	0.0198	0.3262	0.0184	0.0190	0.0023	0.1023	0.0793	0.0001	0.0548	0.2991	0.0044	0.0004	0.0672	0.0020	0.1123
15	0.03144	19.07991	0.0000	0.0386	0.0112	0.0796	0.0004	0.1739	0.0241	0.0941	0.0060	0.0087	0.1745	0.0001	0.0555	0.0445	0.1525	0.1055	0.0112	0.0042	0.0142
16	0.02332	22.15636	0.0003	0.0386	0.0386	0.1686	0.3564	0.2754	0.0258	0.0559	0.0004	0.0460	0.0082	0.0000	0.4299	0.0037	0.0107	0.0157	0.0218	0.3719	0.0905
17	0.01234	30.45178	0.0030	0.0224	0.0278	0.5289	0.3135	0.2754	0.0269	0.3025	0.2377	0.0038	0.1440	0.0068	0.0379	0.2446	0.0432	0.2077	0.0989	0.0837	0.3140
18	0.00523	46.76353	0.0241	0.0664	0.0178	0.0179	0.0155	0.0061	0.1554	0.0252	0.0853	0.0158	0.0076	0.0327	0.0035	0.0007	0.6918	0.6327	0.0163	0.0089	0.0011
19	0.0003035	194.19938	0.9724	0.4122	0.0075	0.0233	0.2855	0.0410	0.1165	0.0146	0.0571	0.0047	0.0045	0.9602	0.3286	0.2623	0.0689	0.0146	0.0041	0.0250	0.0040

Collinearity diagnostics (intercept adjusted)

Number	Eigenvalue	Condition Index	Var Prop LOPEN	Var Prop LGGDPC4	Var Prop LGGOV	Var Prop LPLVL	Var Prop LTXGDPI	Var Prop MMANUF	Var Prop MPRIM	Var Prop MSERV	Var Prop ASIE	Var Prop AMSUD	Var Prop LGDPC4	Var Prop LGDPC3	Var Prop METUD	Var Prop LVAIND	Var Prop LVASERV	Var Prop LGEX2	Var Prop PER2	Var Prop PER3
1	3.44830	1.00000	0.0079	0.0157	0.0033	0.0021	0.0070	0.0136	0.0052	0.0010	0.0139	0.0074	0.0000	0.0030	0.0002	0.0009	0.0026	0.0026	0.0050	0.0008	0.0026
2	2.67967	1.13439	0.0029	0.0079	0.0036	0.0088	0.0014	0.0027	0.0055	0.0005	0.0047	0.0086	0.0105	0.0074	0.0091	0.0010	0.0164	0.0164	0.0033	0.0034	0.0034
3	2.61036	1.14935	0.0014	0.0029	0.0035	0.0017	0.0188	0.0019	0.0012	0.0039	0.0005	0.0034	0.0066	0.0002	0.0025	0.0283	0.0229	0.0229	0.0013	0.0181	0.0184
4	1.83208	1.37192	0.0022	0.0022	0.0401	0.0004	0.0001	0.0019	0.0349	0.0174	0.0004	0.0012	0.0100	0.0000	0.0302	0.0254	0.0131	0.0131	0.0045	0.0088	0.0184
5	1.39032	1.57487	0.0104	0.0000	0.0065	0.0018	0.0363	0.0104	0.0349	0.0492	0.0246	0.0012	0.0004	0.0047	0.0145	0.0446	0.0131	0.0131	0.0000	0.0057	0.0004
6	1.19509	1.69865	0.0016	0.0000	0.0106	0.0032	0.0019	0.0241	0.0829	0.1116	0.0347	0.0347	0.0004	0.0145	0.0048	0.0054	0.0001	0.0001	0.0011	0.0011	0.0011
7	0.99891	1.85797	0.0061	0.0018	0.0273	0.0177	0.0055	0.0049	0.0017	0.0492	0.0464	0.0603	0.0586	0.0081	0.0305	0.0027	0.0078	0.0078	0.0008	0.0013	0.0179
8	0.81398	2.05823	0.0006	0.0064	0.0060	0.0078	0.0038	0.0145	0.0013	0.0111	0.0551	0.0818	0.0376	0.0022	0.0460	0.0018	0.0194	0.0194	0.0083	0.0248	0.0179
9	0.70799	2.20693	0.0003	0.0184	0.0005	0.0098	0.0162	0.0145	0.0314	0.0160	0.0031	0.0075	0.0000	0.0065	0.1076	0.0061	0.0014	0.0014	0.0854	0.0854	0.0850
10	0.54821	2.50800	0.0284	0.0410	0.0011	0.0205	0.0205	0.1587	0.0314	0.0951	0.0268	0.0583	0.0082	0.0004	0.0219	0.0076	0.0233	0.0233	0.0114	0.0248	0.1108
11	0.40445	2.91990	0.0402	0.3582	0.0104	0.0008	0.0003	0.1923	0.0001	0.0267	0.0181	0.0030	0.0050	0.0006	0.0064	0.0142	0.0391	0.0391	0.0000	0.0090	0.1542
12	0.33322	3.21689	0.0013	0.0015	0.0249	0.0149	0.0149	0.0059	0.0143	0.0654	0.2804	0.0331	0.0574	0.0170	0.1306	0.0000	0.0233	0.0233	0.0333	0.1207	0.0030
13	0.29218	3.43539	0.0921	0.1128	0.0077	0.0192	0.2858	0.0376	0.0331	0.0679	0.1068	0.0265	0.0389	0.0016	0.0584	0.0506	0.0585	0.0585	0.0062	0.0124	0.0561
14	0.24860	3.72435	0.0624	0.0007	0.0409	0.0061	0.2275	0.0006	0.0720	0.0456	0.0693	0.0868	0.1184	0.0052	0.0405	0.0827	0.0558	0.0558	0.0417	0.2017	0.0109
15	0.18015	4.37503	0.0239	0.2525	0.0009	0.0409	0.0036	0.0001	0.0352	0.0306	0.0097	0.0868	0.0112	0.0010	0.0567	0.0264	0.0484	0.0484	0.6788	0.0059	0.4415
16	0.14980	4.79782	0.1054	0.0688	0.0864	0.0864	0.0093	0.2621	0.3398	0.0024	0.0074	0.1336	0.1070	0.0421	0.0067	0.3857	0.1001	0.1001	0.0535	0.1846	0.0352
17	0.11572	5.45885	0.0015	0.0741	0.4948	0.0294	0.1822	0.1210	0.1296	0.0137	0.0074	0.0005	0.5098	0.0849	0.0393	0.3655	0.1561	0.1561	0.0199	0.0233	0.0233
18	0.05094	8.22729	0.6117	0.0373	0.0127	0.7186	0.0303	0.1388	0.0044	0.0057	0.1185	0.0005	0.5098	0.8149	0.3706	0.1676	0.0161	0.0161	0.0108	0.2984	0.0048

Table 6. **Factors explaining growth, OLS method (III-1)**

	2.1	**2.2**	**2.3**	**2.4**
LLgGDPC	0.0067 (0.775)	0.0045 (0.53)	0.005 (0.60)	0.007 (0.87)
ETUD	-0.003 (-1.32)	-0.003 -1.35	***-0.004 (-1.64)***	*-0.003 (-1.57)*
GOUV	-0.0006 (-0.82)	-0.0006 (-0.81)	-0.0006 (-0.77)	-0.0005 (-0.68)
PLVL	***-0.0004 (-1.93)***	*-0.0003 (-1.58)*	*-0.0003 (-1.50)*	**-0.0004 (-1.87)**
GPOP	***-0.97 (-1.89)***	***-0.93 -1.84***	**-1.14 (-2.2)**	**-1.20 (-2.25)**
MANUF	**0.035 (4.26)**	**0.034 (4.16)**	**0.030 (3.52)**	**0.031 (3.52)**
GDFI	***0.00065 (1.87)***	***0.0007 (1.76)***	0.0004 (1.02)	0.0004 (1.18)
SERV	0.0045 (0.46)	0.0035 (0.36)	0.0056 (0.57)	0.0066 (0.67)
PRIM	0.0084 (0.84)	0.0074 (0.75)	0.010 (1.03)	0.011 (1.11)
ASIE			0.014 (1.44)	*0.015 (1.48)*
Constant	-0.004 (-0.05)	0.008 (0.11)	0.014 (0.18)	-0.004 (-0.05)
Constant 1		-0.007 (-0.89)	-0.009 (-1.1)	
Constant 2		0.01 (1.23)	0.008 (0.97)	
Constant 3		0.0 (.)	0.0 (.)	
R^2	0.36	0.41	0.42	0.38
Adjusted R^2	0.28	0.32	0.33	0.29
CV	167	163	162	166
Nb obs	87	87	87	87

Table 7. Factors explaining growth, two-stage least squares method (III-2)

	FDI projection on exogenous variables		GGDPC OLS	GGDPC 2SLS	GGDPC 2SLS	GDPC 2SLS	GGDPC 2SLS	GGDPC 2SLS
	3.0	3.01	3.1	3.2	3.3	3.4	3.5	3.6
FDI				0.0012 (0.75)	-0.0010 (-0.55)	-0.0004 (-0.21)	-0.0008 (-0.43)	-0.0009 (-0.46)
LFDI	**1.10** **(9.13)**	**1.07** **(8.58)**						
LVAIND	0.011 (0.49)	0.0006 (0.024)						
ASIE	0.19 (0.33)	-0.0060 (-0.10)			**0.020** **(2.10)**		_0.015_ _(1.52)_	
PER1	**-1.24** **(-2.81)**	**-0.98** **(-1.99)**			*-0.15* *(-1.83)*			-0.008 (-0.98)
PER2	**-1.11** **(-2.63)**	*-0.83* *(-1.73)*			0.0022 (0.28)			0.009 (1.12)
LLgGDPC	-0.0091 (-0.02)	0.074 (0.13)	0.0069 (0.79)	0.0043 (0.46)	0.007 (0.75)	0.0075 (0.78)	0.0093 (0.97)	0.0063 (0.67)
ETUD	0.05 (0.37)	0.082 (0.59)	_-0.0035_ _(-1.56)_	_-0.0033_ _(-1.46)_	**-0.0047** **(-2.10)**	-0.0030 (-1.32)	_-0.0036_ _(-1.59)_	-0.0032 (-1.39)
GOUV	-0.031 (-0.71)	-0.011 (-0.24)	-0.0011 (-1.45)	-0.0010 (-1.36)	-0.0009 (-1.27)	-0.0006 (-0.78)	-0.0005 (-0.62)	-0.0006 (-0.80)
PLVL	0.0026 (0.22)	0.00034 (0.03)	*-0.00037* *(-1.79)*	*-0.00037* *(-1.76)*	-0.00027 (-1.35)	*-0.0004* *(-1.93)*	*-0.00038* *(-1.89)*	_-0.00032_ _(-1.58)_
GPOP	-8.26 (-0.26)	-8.36 (-0.26)	*-0.93* *(-1.78)*	*-0.98* *(-1.84)*	**-1.17** **(-2.24)**	*-0.96* *(-1.85)*	**-1.18** **(-2.21)**	*-0.89* *(-1.76)*
MANUF	0.47 (0.89)	0.31 (0.56)	**0.040** **(5.14)**	**0.037** **(4.28)**	**0.033** **(3.76)**	**0.035** **(4.11)**	**0.031** **(3.52)**	**0.035** **(4.07)**
SERV	-0.019 (-0.03)	-0.074 (-0.13)	0.0051 (0.51)	0.0043 (0.42)	0.0074 (0.75)	0.004 (0.47)	0.007 (0.72)	0.004 (0.41)
PRIM	0.10 (0.17)	0.15 (0.25)	0.0074 (0.73)	0.0077 (0.76)	0.011 (1.07)	0.008 (0.83)	0.011 (1.11)	0.007 (0.74)
GDFI		0.032 (1.13)				_0.0007_ _(1.64)_	0.0005 (1.23)	*0.0008* *(1.78)*
Constant	1.20 (0.25)	-0.37 (-0.07)	0.018 (0.25)	0.037 (0.46)	0.024 (0.31)	-0.012 (-0.14)	-0.020 (-0.24)	-0.0065 (-0.08)
R^2	0.73	0.73	0.33	0.33	0.42	0.36	0.38	0.41
Adj. R^2	0.68	0.68	0.26	0.26	0.32	0.28	0.29	0.31
CV	85.9	85.7	170.1	171.6	162.8	168.2	166.5	163.8
Nb obs	87	87	87	87	87	87	87	87

Table 8. **Collinearity diagnostics for regressions 3.2 and 3.4**

Factors which inflate the variance

Regression 3.2

Variable	DF	Parameter Estimate	Standard Error	T for H0: Parameter=0	Prob > |T|	Variance Inflation
INTERCEP	1	0.045561	0.07512312	0.606	0.5461	0.00000000
LLGDPC4	1	0.007536	0.00896745	0.840	0.4034	3.55442145
METUD	1	-0.010288	0.00304861	-3.375	0.0012	5.32419061
MGOUV	1	-0.001139	0.00072539	-1.570	0.1207	2.22979900
MPLVL	1	-0.000389	0.00020021	-1.943	0.0559	2.18882609
MGPOP	1	-1.316326	0.50609700	-2.601	0.0112	2.65790678
MMANUF	1	0.030254	0.00861090	3.514	0.0008	1.78751537
MSERV	1	0.007116	0.00954159	0.746	0.4582	1.42519410
MPRIM	1	0.012464	0.00961326	1.296	0.1989	1.73602178
PER2	1	-0.005900	0.00876276	-0.673	0.5029	2.24645583
PER3	1	0.011056	0.00817748	1.352	0.1806	1.95638632
ASIE	1	0.020382	0.00939294	2.170	0.0333	1.90596151
IDEHAT	1	-0.013833	0.00523473	-2.643	0.0101	20.30451784
IDETUHAT	1	0.003307	0.00126878	2.606	0.0111	25.46662030

Regression 3.4

Variable	DF	Parameter Estimate	Standard Error	T for H0: Parameter=0	Prob > |T|	Variance Inflation
INTERCEP	1	0.024370	0.08303001	0.294	0.7700	0.00000000
LLGDPC4	1	0.007896	0.00918976	0.859	0.3931	3.64212101
METUD	1	-0.008818	0.00320884	-2.748	0.0076	5.75520870
MGOUV	1	-0.000926	0.00079433	-1.166	0.2474	2.60879792
MPLVL	1	-0.000377	0.00020199	-1.869	0.0657	2.17362703
MGPOP	1	-1.241568	0.51517961	-2.410	0.0185	2.68722828
MMANUF	1	0.029862	0.00871149	3.428	0.0010	1.78506059
MSERV	1	0.007126	0.00966494	0.737	0.4633	1.42674236
MPRIM	1	0.011053	0.00971817	1.137	0.2592	1.73100326
MTXGDFI	1	0.000297	0.00046686	0.637	0.5263	2.79316047
PER2	1	-0.005294	0.00893617	-0.592	0.5554	2.27946976
PER3	1	0.011810	0.00844579	1.398	0.1663	2.03615857
ASIE	1	0.017738	0.01001775	1.771	0.0809	2.11527365
IDEHAT	1	-0.011525	0.00511279	-2.254	0.0272	19.02097875
IDETUHAT	1	0.002648	0.00125381	2.112	0.0382	24.92077538

Table 8. Collinearity diagnostics for regressions 3.2 and 3.4 (cont.)

Belsley, Kuh and Welsch indicators, regression 3.2

Collinearity diagnostics

Number	Eigenvalue	Condition Index	Var Prop INTERCEP	Var Prop LLGDPC4	Var Prop METUD	Var Prop MGOUV	Var Prop MPLVL	Var Prop MGPOP	Var Prop MMANUF	Var Prop MSERV	Var Prop MPRIM	Var Prop PER2	Var Prop PER3	Var Prop ASIE	Var Prop IDEHAT	Var Prop IDETUHAT
1	7.92686	1.00000	0.0000	0.0000	0.0004	0.0006	0.0009	0.0010	0.0023	0.0013	0.0013	0.0015	0.0018	0.0021	0.0003	0.0002
2	1.72290	2.14497	0.0000	0.0000	0.0000	0.0012	0.0001	0.0016	0.0420	0.0253	0.0345	0.0076	0.0018	0.0462	0.0027	0.0018
3	1.02317	2.78341	0.0000	0.0000	0.0000	0.0001	0.0000	0.0004	0.0107	0.0640	0.0053	0.1336	0.1106	0.0108	0.0004	0.0003
4	1.00652	2.80634	0.0000	0.0000	0.0001	0.0001	0.0000	0.0009	0.0001	0.3054	0.1770	0.0174	0.0172	0.0000	0.0000	0.0000
5	0.80014	3.14752	0.0000	0.0000	0.0000	0.0004	0.0008	0.0009	0.0650	0.0158	0.0529	0.0033	0.1121	0.0513	0.0066	0.0055
6	0.51158	3.93634	0.0000	0.0001	0.0075	0.0001	0.0069	0.0214	0.0010	0.1554	0.1945	0.0099	0.0022	0.2012	0.0006	0.0003
7	0.38381	4.54455	0.0000	0.0000	0.0013	0.0023	0.0000	0.0007	0.6713	0.0389	0.0536	0.0075	0.0065	0.2806	0.0000	0.0000
8	0.23616	5.79354	0.0000	0.0000	0.0286	0.0085	0.0018	0.0907	0.0261	0.2544	0.1790	0.0035	0.0122	0.1721	0.0176	0.0001
9	0.20620	6.20021	0.0003	0.0001	0.0048	0.0389	0.0064	0.0162	0.0001	0.0445	0.0609	0.4234	0.4188	0.0151	0.0113	0.0006
10	0.07970	9.97308	0.0001	0.0000	0.0317	0.0184	0.5659	0.0074	0.0018	0.0000	0.0147	0.1843	0.0775	0.0420	0.0070	0.0074
11	0.07409	10.34390	0.0000	0.0000	0.0029	0.2912	0.0079	0.4141	0.0728	0.0083	0.0263	0.0119	0.0065	0.1386	0.0097	0.0027
12	0.02042	19.70149	0.0000	0.0129	0.0366	0.2541	0.0402	0.1582	0.0374	0.0581	0.1008	0.1687	0.1973	0.0009	0.2478	0.3382
13	0.00773	32.01318	0.0232	0.0287	0.8843	0.1891	0.1391	0.1852	0.0000	0.0225	0.0914	0.0267	0.0293	0.0082	0.6909	0.6407
14	0.0007177	105.09443	0.9664	0.9581	0.0017	0.1951	0.2300	0.1020	0.0695	0.0062	0.0078	0.0007	0.0064	0.0310	0.0051	0.0021

Collinearity diagnostics (intercept adjusted)

Condition Number	Eigenvalue	Condition Index	Var Prop LLGDPC4	Var Prop METUD	Var Prop MGOUV	Var Prop MPLVL	Var Prop MGPOP	Var Prop MMANUF	Var Prop MSERV	Var Prop MPRIM	Var Prop PER2	Var Prop PER3	Var Prop ASIE	Var Prop IDEHAT	Var Prop IDETUHAT
1	3.68953	1.00000	0.0117	0.0053	0.0153	0.0106	0.0084	0.0051	0.0044	0.0020	0.0021	0.0001	0.0049	0.0018	0.0020
2	2.05817	1.33889	0.0131	0.0098	0.0026	0.0092	0.0174	0.0550	0.0000	0.0111	0.0000	0.0011	0.0624	0.0027	0.0009
3	1.53937	1.54815	0.0021	0.0010	0.0005	0.0040	0.0040	0.0002	0.0009	0.0059	0.1259	0.1453	0.0001	0.0000	0.0000
4	1.36186	1.64596	0.0059	0.0100	0.0200	0.0316	0.0338	0.0215	0.0455	0.0666	0.0254	0.0011	0.0149	0.0047	0.0022
5	1.22880	1.73279	0.0000	0.0002	0.0061	0.0000	0.0187	0.0027	0.2707	0.1752	0.0004	0.0110	0.0119	0.0002	0.0002
6	0.80233	2.14442	0.0198	0.0211	0.0657	0.0924	0.0331	0.2451	0.0132	0.0402	0.0366	0.1591	0.0218	0.0034	0.0034
7	0.75443	2.21145	0.0043	0.0043	0.1588	0.1077	0.0505	0.0545	0.0200	0.0003	0.0003	0.0114	0.0344	0.0005	0.0004
8	0.54962	2.59091	0.0134	0.0890	0.0008	0.0139	0.0020	0.3931	0.3762	0.1682	0.0094	0.0073	0.1200	0.0035	0.0000
9	0.35226	3.23632	0.0034	0.0006	0.2610	0.0592	0.0576	0.0126	0.0426	0.0132	0.0042	0.0021	0.5963	0.0006	0.0004
10	0.27577	3.65772	0.0441	0.0030	0.0452	0.3009	0.1193	0.1838	0.0113	0.0967	0.4953	0.3190	0.0191	0.0018	0.0018
11	0.18586	4.45547	0.8764	0.0002	0.0810	0.2960	0.0780	0.0193	0.0336	0.0001	0.0730	0.1044	0.0465	0.0067	0.0067
12	0.18120	4.51237	0.0012	0.2794	0.3231	0.0028	0.5536	0.0072	0.1810	0.4089	0.1068	0.1036	0.0832	0.0088	0.0088
13	0.02080	13.31801	0.0087	0.5764	0.0201	0.0546	0.0235		0.0008	0.0116	0.1200	0.1344	0.0036	0.9549	0.9732

Table 8. Collinearity diagnostics for regressions 3.2 and 3.4 (cont.)

Belsley, Kuh and Welsch indicators, regression 3.4

Collinearity diagnostics

Number	Eigenvalue	Condition Index	Var Prop INTERCEP	Var Prop LLGDPC4	Var Prop METUD	Var Prop MGOUV	Var Prop MPLVL	Var Prop MGPOP	Var Prop MMANUF	Var Prop MSERV	Var Prop MPRIM	Var Prop MTXGDFI	Var Prop PER2	Var Prop PER3	Var Prop ASIE	Var Prop IDEHAT	Var Prop IDETUHAT
1	8.83994	1.00000	0.0000	0.0000	0.0003	0.0004	0.0007	0.0008	0.0019	0.0010	0.0010	0.0005	0.0011	0.0013	0.0015	0.0002	0.0002
2	1.73353	2.25819	0.0000	0.0000	0.0001	0.0011	0.0002	0.0018	0.0397	0.0260	0.0347	0.0001	0.0078	0.0020	0.0398	0.0028	0.0018
3	1.02322	2.93928	0.0000	0.0000	0.0001	0.0000	0.0000	0.0004	0.0104	0.0437	0.0015	0.0000	0.1380	0.1126	0.0095	0.0004	0.0004
4	1.00729	2.96243	0.0000	0.0000	0.0000	0.0001	0.0000	0.0000	0.0000	0.3225	0.1844	0.0000	0.0100	0.0099	0.0000	0.0000	0.0000
5	0.80578	3.31219	0.0000	0.0000	0.0000	0.0004	0.0007	0.0009	0.0679	0.0176	0.0494	0.0001	0.0031	0.1083	0.0477	0.0067	0.0055
6	0.51171	4.15634	0.0000	0.0001	0.0068	0.0001	0.0068	0.0212	0.0014	0.1570	0.1978	0.0001	0.0092	0.0020	0.1807	0.0006	0.0003
7	0.38713	4.77857	0.0000	0.0000	0.0009	0.0020	0.0000	0.0008	0.6756	0.0418	0.0551	0.0010	0.0046	0.0045	0.1584	0.0000	0.0000
8	0.23841	6.08926	0.0000	0.0000	0.0247	0.0101	0.0034	0.0924	0.0208	0.2684	0.1911	0.0022	0.0012	0.0005	0.1584	0.0133	0.0003
9	0.21572	6.40149	0.0001	0.0001	0.0058	0.0209	0.0065	0.0037	0.0017	0.0128	0.0220	0.0090	0.4138	0.3933	0.0153	0.0192	0.0011
10	0.08133	10.42537	0.0001	0.0000	0.0227	0.0608	0.4741	0.0201	0.0090	0.0019	0.0076	0.0169	0.1594	0.0568	0.0055	0.0097	0.0092
11	0.07561	10.81251	0.0000	0.0000	0.0341	0.2362	0.0782	0.2679	0.0630	0.0167	0.0039	0.0276	0.0009	0.0012	0.1899	0.0070	0.0024
12	0.05391	12.80507	0.0000	0.0000	0.0282	0.0027	0.0493	0.2540	0.0036	0.0198	0.1197	0.5330	0.0344	0.0418	0.0305	0.0002	0.0116
13	0.01929	21.40514	0.0056	0.0009	0.0117	0.1354	0.0161	0.0570	0.0438	0.0287	0.0503	0.0877	0.2142	0.2632	0.0112	0.4143	0.4333
14	0.00648	36.92390	0.0288	0.0575	0.8425	0.2658	0.1378	0.1599	0.0078	0.0388	0.0716	0.2241	0.0004	0.0025	0.0650	0.5243	0.5184
15	0.0006519	116.45125	0.9652	0.9324	0.0221	0.2641	0.2264	0.1191	0.0536	0.0034	0.0098	0.0977	0.0017	0.0001	0.0032	0.0011	0.0156

Collinearity diagnostics (intercept adjusted)

Condition Number	Eigenvalue	Condition Index	Var Prop LLGDPC4	Var Prop METUD	Var Prop MGOUV	Var Prop MPLVL	Var Prop MGPOP	Var Prop MMANUF	Var Prop MSERV	Var Prop MPRIM	Var Prop MTXGDFI	Var Prop PER2	Var Prop PER3	Var Prop ASIE	Var Prop IDEHAT	Var Prop IDETUHAT
1	4.03092	1.00000	0.0073	0.0028	0.0100	0.0072	0.0047	0.0063	0.0034	0.0021	0.0099	0.0017	0.0002	0.0063	0.0020	0.0019
2	2.32440	1.31688	0.0164	0.0115	0.0050	0.0118	0.0217	0.0271	0.0006	0.0044	0.0172	0.0003	0.0019	0.0326	0.0012	0.0002
3	1.54386	1.61584	0.0026	0.0008	0.0003	0.0230	0.0037	0.0017	0.0004	0.0088	0.0005	0.1191	0.1371	0.0010	0.0000	0.0000
4	1.37207	1.71401	0.0058	0.0076	0.0160	0.0283	0.0293	0.0317	0.0440	0.0730	0.0015	0.0301	0.0022	0.0194	0.0039	0.0018
5	1.22743	1.81219	0.0000	0.0002	0.0052	0.0001	0.0182	0.0031	0.2738	0.1734	0.0000	0.0003	0.0103	0.0113	0.0003	0.0002
6	0.81670	2.22162	0.0177	0.0220	0.0041	0.1599	0.0110	0.0546	0.0041	0.0292	0.0127	0.0349	0.1431	0.0108	0.0002	0.0023
7	0.78379	2.26778	0.0023	0.0001	0.1830	0.0227	0.0593	0.2211	0.0232	0.0098	0.0157	0.0018	0.0075	0.0267	0.0001	0.0005
8	0.55576	2.69312	0.0108	0.0005	0.0000	0.0036	0.0069	0.0423	0.3698	0.1538	0.0119	0.0100	0.0035	0.1323	0.0015	0.0002
9	0.38296	3.24433	0.0282	0.0850	0.0000	0.1658	0.0343	0.0001	0.0084	0.0147	0.0085	0.0527	0.0045	0.0007	0.0242	0.0000
10	0.35170	3.38543	0.0078	0.0003	0.2351	0.0325	0.0473	0.3973	0.0481	0.0165	0.4350	0.0004	0.0007	0.5526	0.0000	0.0000
11	0.25598	3.96826	0.0017	0.0240	0.0030	0.1549	0.3356	0.0160	0.0423	0.2393	0.1124	0.3985	0.3041	0.0043	0.0085	0.0133
12	0.18622	4.65247	0.6873	0.0493	0.0010	0.2891	0.0054	0.1949	0.1194	0.0780	0.0008	0.1231	0.1552	0.0830	0.0093	0.0094
13	0.14658	5.24401	0.2089	0.2054	0.4827	0.0675	0.3956	0.0000	0.0587	0.1908	0.3163	0.1611	0.1611	0.0998	0.0094	0.0011
14	0.02162	13.65442	0.0031	0.5906	0.0543	0.0338	0.0270	0.0036	0.0040	0.0061	0.0576	0.0661	0.0687	0.0190	0.9394	0.9700

155

Table 9. **Introducing a crossed effect (III-2)**

GGDPC 2SLS	4.1	4.2	4.3	4.4
FDI	**-0.011**	**-0.014**	*-0.0081*	*-0.011*
	(-2.10)	**(-2.64)**	*(-1.71)*	*(-2.25)*
FDI.ETUD	**0.0029**	**0.0033**	*0.0021*	*0.0026*
	(2.44)	**(2.61)**	*(1.75)*	*(2.11)*
ASIE		**0.020**		*0.018*
		(2.17)		*(1.78)*
PER1		-0.006		-0.005
		(-0.67)		(-0.59)
PER2		0.011		0.011
		(1.35)		(1.40)
LLgGDPC	0.0057	0.0093	0.0072	0.0079
	(0.62)	(0.97)	(0.76)	(0.86)
ETUD	**-0.008**	**-0.010**	**-0.007**	**-0.009**
	(-2.80)	**(-3.75)**	**(-2.19)**	**(-2.75)**
GOUV	*-0.0014*	<u>*-0.0011*</u>	-0.0010	-0.0009
	(-1.83)	<u>*(-1.57)*</u>	(-1.28)	(-1.17)
PLVL	**-0.0004**	*-0.0004*	**-0.0004**	*-0.0004*
	(-2.21)	*(-1.94)*	**(-2.16)**	*(-1.87)*
GPOP	**-1.08**	**-1.32**	**-1.03**	**-1.24**
	(-2.10)	**(-2.60)**	**(-2.00)**	**(-2.41)**
MANUF	**0.037**	**0.030**	**0.035**	**0.030**
	(4.35)	**(3.51)**	**(4.17)**	**(3.43)**
SERV	0.004	0.007	0.005	0.007
	(0.46)	(0.75)	(0.51)	(0.74)
PRIM	0.009	0.012	0.008	0.011
	(0.94)	(1.29)	(0.86)	(1.14)
GDFI			0.0004	0.0003
			(0.93)	(0.64)
Constant	0.06	0.04	0.02	0.02
	(0.76)	(0.61)	(0.28)	(0.29)
R^2	0.38	0.46	0.38	0.46
Adj. R^2	0.30	0.37	0.29	0.35
CV	165.3	157.1	166.2	159.0
Nb obs	87	87	87	87

Table 10. **Factors explaining domestic investment (III-3)**

	5.1	5.2	5.3	5.4	5.5
LLgGDPC	**-9.39**	**-8.31**	**-8.48**	**-7.21**	**-7.92**
	(-3.77)	**(-3.26)**	**(-3.84)**	**(-3.23)**	**(-3.50)**
ETUD	-0.34	-0.34	**-0.84**	**-0.85**	*-0.73*
	(-0.78)	(-0.78)	**(-2.07)**	**(-2.15)**	*(-1.82)*
GOUV	**-0.77**	**-0.71**	**-0.89**	**-0.80**	**-0.76**
	(-4.10)	**(-3.6)**	**(-5.24)**	**(-4.33)**	**(-4.14)**
MANUF	**7.29**	**5.35**	**8.52**	**6.51**	**6.08**
	(3.56)	**(2.37)**	**(4.65)**	**(3.28)**	**(3.05)**
PRIM	-0.69	0.32	-0.65	0.21	-0.51
	(-0.31)	(0.13)	(-0.34)	(0.09)	(-0.23)
SERV	**6.08**	**6.27**	**6.48**	**6.69**	**6.11**
	(2.28)	**(2.38)**	**(2.74)**	**(2.92)**	**(2.64)**
VAIND	**0.84**	**0.77**	**0.86**	**0.79**	**0.81**
	(5.4)	**(4.85)**	**(6.27)**	**(5.73)**	**(5.95)**
VASERV	**0.59**	**0.57**	**0.57**	**0.54**	**0.53**
	(4.13)	**(4.05)**	**(4.43)**	**(4.37)**	**(4.26)**
FDI	**1.36**	**1.19**	**0.85**	**0.65**	
	(4.35)	**(3.73)**	**(2.85)**	**(2.17)**	
OPEN					**3.25**
					(2.5)
ASIE		*4.60*		**5.16**	*4.02*
		(1.91)		**(2.46)**	*(1.82)*
AMSUD		-0.82		-0.52	0.066
		(-0.38)		(-0.27)	(0.03)
Constant	52.6	46.1	55.6	47.6	51.7
	(3.36)	(2.7)	(4.01)	(3.19)	(3.43)
Constant 1			**-7.03**	**-7.20**	**-7.56**
			(-3.99)	**(-4.20)**	**(-4.63)**
Constant 2			**-7.58**	**-7.74**	**-8.02**
			(-4.51)	**(-4.74)**	**(5.10)**
Constant 3			0.0	0.0	0.0
			(.)	(.)	(.)
R^2	0.59	0.61	0.69	0.71	0.72
Adj. R^2	0.54	0.56	0.64	0.66	0.67
CV	25.2	24.8	22.3	21.6	21.4
Nb obs	87	87	87	87	87

ECONOMIC INTEGRATION OF PORTUGAL IN THE EUROPEAN UNION: EFFECT ON DIRECT INVESTMENT, MIGRATION AND EMPLOYMENT

by
Maria da Conceição Pereira Ramos
University of Porto

Introduction

Portugal entered the European Community with the severe economic and social burden of poor infrastructure, a high rate of illiteracy, a disproportionately large and inefficient agricultural sector, an unwieldy and relatively ineffective public sector, a low level of technology, shortcomings in business methods and organisation which depressed productivity, and living standards below the community average.

The demands of convergence raised a number of issues: how to improve human resource skills and introduce a new competitive spirit, new education and training systems, new organisational patterns, new workforce management methods, a new industrial relations system, new collective bargaining practices and new productive factor mobility within the context of the single market. The prospects for convergence were clearly conditioned by two sets of factors: institutional policies at the domestic and community level (accommodation arrangements) and domestic production structures.

What impact has Portugal's entry to the European Community had on foreign direct investment (FDI), migration and employment? What has been the end-result of the community's efforts to promote economic and social cohesion in Portugal and encourage convergence between its economy and those of the other member states?

Section 1 of the paper looks at the effects of fund transfers and productive factor mobility. Section 2 considers FDI and the way it has developed since Portugal's entry into the EU. Section 3 shows that Portugal is a both an emigration and immigration country and explains how regional economic integration has affected the flow of migrants to Portugal. Section 4 deals with changes in the labour market following entry into the EU. Finally, Section 5 looks at the challenges posed by economic and monetary union in the context of converging European economies.

1.   The effects of fund transfers and productive factor mobility

Structural funds will certainly be the principal vehicle for sustaining the necessary readjustment process to build Europe and encourage productivity in the least developed economies so as to close the gap with the most competitive EU economies as quickly as possible.

Portugal has had the benefit of a "Community Support Framework", involving the allocation of considerable sums which have served to bring about a real measure of convergence, for example, in transport and telecommunications infrastructure, in agricultural and industrial activity, in the area of innovation and in education and vocational training. EU transfers have helped to improve Portuguese infrastructure and raise the skill level of its human resources. Since 1988, the annual gross amount of funds has amounted to over 2.5% of GDP. Net inputs from the EU in 1996 came to 3.1% of Portuguese GDP, as against 0.6% in 1986.[1] They derive mainly from various European structural funds aimed at reducing regional imbalances, such as ERDF (European Regional Development Fund), ESF (European Social Fund), EAGGF (European Agricultural Guidance and Guarantee Fund), PEDIP (Special industrial development programme for Portugal) and the Cohesion Fund for member states with a per capita GDP of less than 75% of the EU average. For 1994-99, the amount of EU (the Europe of Twelve) structural funds targeting regions lagging in development made up three-quarters of all EU funds. Some of them have gone to Portugal.

Under the first Community Support Framework (1989-93), EU structural funds provided resources amounting to some 5% of Portuguese GDP (see Table 1). The second Community Framework (1994-99) made a provision for spending on education and training, including national co-financing, of up to 6% of 1993 GDP (OECD, 1996). This Framework is devoting 835 billion escudos to measures for "improving the knowledge base and innovation capacity"[2] and for strengthening "vocational training and employment".[3] In 1996, investment funded by the EU made up 10% of total investment, the majority of structural funds going to projects to improve infrastructure and human capital (OECD, 1998).

The European integration inaugurated a faster pace of structural reform as far as institutions, regulations and economic machinery were concerned. It was between 1985 and 1991, in particular, that Portugal showed a considerable capacity for swift and stable acceptance of reform and radical change aimed at ensuring convergence with Europe, improving competitiveness and promoting employment.

On the threshold of the birth of a single currency and the gradual introduction of an optimal monetary zone,[4] the closer economic structures are to each other, the lower the relevant adjustment costs will be. Structural funding is the preferred system for achieving convergence and redistribution. The adjustment costs may also be offset by labour market flexibility (labour mobility and wage flexibility) (Erkel-Rousse, 1997).

The degree of productive factor mobility will have an impact on the real rate of convergence. High labour mobility will speed up convergence of per capita income. FDI in less developed regions will accelerate convergence in three ways: by increasing production capacity through injection of capital, by transfer of technology and by imparting new skills in spheres such as management.

---

1. Net flows of 26 000 million escudos in 1986 and some 500 000 million in 1995 and 1996 (OECD, 1996).

2. The "education" sub-programme aims to increase the school enrolment rate at all levels; the "science and technology" sub-programme seeks to improve the scientific system in Portugal with a view to raising spending on R&D to 12-15% of GDP in 1999.

3. This programme is concerned with initial qualifications and the transition from school to work, improvement of the level and quality of employment, support for human resource training and management and training for the public service.

4. According to Mundell's theory (1968), an optimal monetary zone is distinguished by perfect labour mobility, which means that a shock in any part of the zone can be overcome by workers moving from areas in crisis to more prosperous areas; the lack of the adjustment provided by unemployment is made up for by labour mobility. Monetary union without labour mobility would require specific national policies to be put in place to cope with shocks.

Despite all the talk of mobility and measures to promote free movement of workers, labour mobility is still very low in Europe. Factors such as labour cost differentials and different employment conditions, however, promote greater international sub-contracting and temporary mobility of Portuguese nationals (Ramos, 1990, 1995, 1997). Since the introduction of the single market, some types of migration have been found to be on the increase in the EU, such as professionals with advanced technical and linguistic skills (senior staff), young workers who are highly mobile, and cross-frontier workers. On the whole, such migration is temporary rather than permanent.

2. The magnitude of FDI in Portugal following entry to the European community

The tradition in Portugal has been to achieve international adjustment by exporting labour (Ramos, 1990) rather than by importing capital. Joining the EEC, however, has led to a radical change in capital flow. FDI has increased considerably since 1986, rising to 3.8% of GDP in 1990, the highest rate in any OECD Member country. While total investment in 1986 was US$166 million, it shot up subsequently to thirteen times that figure.

After entry, Portugal also realised that its FDI was procured mainly (some 80%) from its EC partners. Investment was principally directed to the tertiary sector, mainly financial services, property and business services, followed by the manufacturing industry (transport equipment, machinery, electrical equipment, chemicals, and so forth). In industry, FDI was primarily aimed at the more capital-intensive sectors, although recently some labour-intensive sectors have begun to take a larger share of such funds. There has been strong growth in traditional exporting sectors (textiles, clothing and footwear) and in industries associated with natural resources. The industrial jobs created by foreign capital in 1990-92 were concentrated in the metal product, machinery and transport equipment industries (40% of all jobs in industry are attributable to injection of foreign capital),[5] the textile, clothing and footwear industries (25%),[6] the chemical and oil industries (12%) and the agri-food industry (8%) (Gonçalves and Guimarães, 1997).

Foreign investors take advantage of tax benefits and a continuing favourable level of labour costs to set up local export bases or to enjoy high profit levels, particularly in the non-tradable goods area (to some extent as a result of lack of competition). The impetus for foreign investment in Portugal has come from low labour costs, available natural resources and the existence of a protected local market. The growth in the motor vehicle, machinery, electrical equipment and electronic equipment industries, however, has been largely due to the flow of FDI in recent years, which has helped to diversify manufacturing industry. Foreign investment and its associated technology have helped in the restructuring of industry, and in giving impetus to Portuguese exports and making them more diversified.[7] Such investment – encouraged by the liberalisation of financial markets and attendant privatisation – has promoted the spread of cutting-edge technology and a change in traditional attitudes to training.[8] Contact with multinational companies has given greater insight into modern

---

5.   Transport equipment industries represent some 80% of the employment created with the help of foreign capital in this sub-sector.

6.   The clothing industry has the highest proportion.

7.   Foreign investment has helped to change the structure of external trade. There has been an increase in exports of manufactures, such as machinery and transport equipment, products that made up 27.6% of the whole in 1995 as against 15.6% in 1985. Another development has been the considerable rise in imports of machinery and transport equipment (34.3% of the whole in 1995) (INE, 1998b).

8.   Thus, in the case of AutoEuropa – a joint venture by Ford and Volkswagen – the importance of personnel skills has led to considerable efforts being devoted to training workers.

production processes and allowed an "international mindset" to develop that has encouraged Portuguese entrepreneurs to invest abroad.[9]

External trade within the community has greatly increased and the share of trade with EU partners has grown substantially, particularly in the case of trade with Spain (see Table 2).[10] The principal exports are from labour-intensive industries (textiles, clothing and leather), which made up 32% of the total in 1995, but the growing importance of exports of machinery and transport equipment should also be noted.

There was tremendous growth in FDI in Portugal between 1987 and 1991 (see Table 3). This trend was due to the opportunities offered to foreign investors following Portugal's entry to the EEC as well as to the stable political, economic and social conditions prevailing in the country. Other noteworthy factors include the liberalisation of procedures relating to FDI, the increasing number of foreign investors after 1989, notably in the financial sector as a result of the liberalisation of the economy and privatisation,[11] improved infrastructure, in particular with respect to transport and telecommunications as a result of community funding, and the proximity of the principal European markets. A further inducement was the nature of the labour market, which had an attractive wages to productivity ratio, few strikes or social demands, considerable real wage flexibility and many market opportunities for profit.

What has been the effect of this large foreign investment? To start with, it has increased the number of businesses with majority foreign capital in almost all sectors of the economy. Between 1989 and 1982, the number of businesses involved (among the 500 largest companies based in Portugal) has risen from 108 to 148 (see Table 4). During this three-year period, the proportion of the workforce employed by them rose from 15 to 21% (Saraiva, 1993).

Next, since the mid-1980s, foreign capital has been decisive in the progress of the manufacturing industry. Of the 500 largest companies in this sector, the proportion of employees in businesses with a majority of foreign capital rose from 24% to some 36% (Saraiva, 1993). The largest industrial projects were promoted by multinationals (such as the Ford-Volkswagen project in the motor industry). Such projects allowed Portuguese products to play a greater part in international production and distribution networks, and were the major factor in the rapid growth of Portuguese exports of manufactured goods since 1986. The export share of businesses with a majority of foreign capital was 47% in 1989 (as compared to 37% in 1973) (Lopes, 1996). That share is particularly large in clothing and footwear, minerals (copper), petrochemicals, electrical goods and the products of the motor vehicle industry.

It was the financial sector (banking and insurance), property and trade, however, that attracted most foreign investment in Portugal between 1986 and 1992. The importance of the trading, catering, hotel and property sectors, to some extent, reflects the importance of tourism in Portugal.

---

9.   There has been a substantial increase in direct investment from Portugal to other countries since it joined the EC (halted only by the 1993 economic recession), in particular as a result of adjustments following the liberalisation of financial markets. In 1996, for the first time in many years, direct investment abroad was greater than FDI in Portugal.

10.   On the basis of the share of GDP represented by external trade, Portugal's opening up was, even in 1980, comparable to that of the major European countries. It is explained by its membership to EFTA and a long tradition of trade with its African colonies and with Brazil. Upon entry to the EEC, tariff barriers were already low. Import licences and quotas, however, were still in force.

11.   Portugal is one of the OECD countries most active in privatisation. Some forty public enterprises were privatised in 1990-96 for a sum amounting to some 14% of GDP. Further progress was made in 1997 with the partial sale of major state enterprises in the energy sector.

Foreign capital is largely concentrated in the five most densely industrialised areas of the country (Lisbon, Porto, Setúbal, Aveiro and Braga), where 86% of the jobs in companies benefiting from the injection of foreign capital, in 1990-92, are found. The areas around Lisbon and Porto hold 53% of these jobs. It should be noted that FDI has not worsened regional imbalances in the distribution of industry dependent exclusively on domestic capital.

FDI comes principally from the EU (from two-thirds to three-quarters of the whole). Spain has significantly increased its share in recent years. The large share by the United Kingdom derives from the fact that a considerable part of multinational investment by the United States is channelled through its British subsidiaries. This factor also applies in the case of investment from Spain, although most Spanish investment has arisen from the expansion of major Spanish businesses, in particular banks, to the Portuguese market.

In 1986, Portugal and Spain established the institutional framework for a gradual strengthening of bilateral economic relations. The gradual dismantling of measures to protect their domestic markets led to a rapid increase in the movement of goods and capital within the peninsula. Spain has become Portugal's major partner with regard to movement (both inward and outward) of FDI. Following the entry of Portugal and Spain into the European Community, integration of the Iberian market has become a key factor in the economic advancement of the two countries. The peninsula has begun to be perceived as a sub-regional market within the internal European market. As the dismantling of the systems formerly in place in both markets began to take place, multinational companies started to regard the region as a single area for investment and the pursuit of bilateral trade.

As an intermediary in trade and financial proceedings, Spain was perceived as a useful interface between Portugal and other EU countries. This was also due to the great improvements it had made in its access infrastructure (land, sea and air) and because it could offer major facilities in support of international goods traffic. Other features that make co-ordination of activities on the Iberian peninsula attractive are clearly in Spain's favour, such as the greater size of its market, the higher skill level of its human resources and its scientific and technological capabilities.

Corado and Leite (1991), after considering the changing pattern of FDI in Portugal and Spain during the period, came to the conclusion that both countries have attracted considerable external resources, noting however, "that Spain appears to attract relatively more FDI than Portugal and also attracts businesses that have a greater potential for technology transfer since they specialise in high quality products. Portugal, on the other hand, seems to attract smaller businesses in traditional sectors with much less opportunity for transfer of innovative technology".

3.   Portugal, a country of emigration and immigration in the European Area

Emigration was very high in Portugal between 1965 and 1973 (Ramos, 1990). It began to slow down in 1974 as a result of restrictive policies adopted by the countries of destination, the end of colonial wars and the political and social changes taking place in Portugal. In the 1980s and 1990s, migratory movement to countries such as Switzerland and Luxembourg replaced traditional destinations (France and Germany). Although the rate of permanent emigration has slowed down,[12] temporary emigration has increased.

---

12.   Persons leaving the country with the intention of living abroad for a period exceeding one year (INE, 1998c). In 1990, 18 000 permanent departures were recorded in contrast to a mere 9 500 in 1988. For the period 1980-88, the figures come from statistics for an administrative procedure, the issue of an emigrant passport. Since 1992, data have been obtained from a sample survey of family housing carried out by the INE (*Inquérito aos movimentos migratórios de saída*).

Since the mid-1970s, Portuguese have emigrated mainly on a temporary or seasonal basis, but with a large number becoming "permanent" residents in the host country, notably in France and Switzerland (see Table 5). They have benefited from measures to regularise their situation (in France and Spain) and from the principle of free movement. In France in 1981-82, Portuguese made up 13% of those regularising their positions. In Spain in 1985-86, they made up 9% of all applicants (Ramos, 1991). Before the implementation of community regulations on free movement in 1992, Portuguese accounted for a large share of the clandestine labour force in the *Ile de France* region especially.

The economic sectors in which migrants work in Europe are mainly construction, agriculture and the hotel trade, where demand for labour is subject to marked fluctuations for seasonal and economic reasons. Portugal, traditionally a country of emigration, has in recent years also become a country of immigration.

Portugal has been recording immigration from EU countries in the form of highly skilled personnel (executives, scientists and technologists engaged in the modernisation of business and industry). On the other hand, it supplies via emigration a contingent of relatively unskilled workers to the most developed European countries. Portugal also receives unskilled workers from developing countries, notably from its former African colonies (a flow of economic immigrants, which has significantly increased since the 1980s, filters into the construction industry and the major public works launched by entry into the community). It in turn sends senior personnel and skilled professionals (equivalent to those it is receiving from the EU) to these Portuguese-speaking African countries (PALOP).

The initial influx of immigrants dates from the 1960s, with the recruitment of Cape Verde nationals to work in the construction sector, which had been badly hit by a decline of the working age male population (as a result of emigration and colonial wars). The process of de-colonisation in 1974-75, the social and political changes taking place in the former seat of colonial power, and the restrictions placed on immigration by other European countries, have together turned Portugal into a country with a certain attraction for immigrants, especially those from PALOP countries (Cape Verde, Angola, Mozambique, Guinea-Bissau and Sao Tome and Principe) (Ramos, 1990, 1995). Portuguese-speaking Africans, most of them unskilled, have similar characteristics to Portuguese immigrants in Europe in the 1960s and 1970s.

The gradual increase in the average skill level of the Portuguese population in the past twenty years, the demand in Portugal for labour for major public works and the continuation of seasonal Portuguese emigration and sub-contracting in Europe has led to a shortage of labour in some parts of the Portuguese labour market, where a low-skills level is required (construction, domestic service). The employment, sometimes illegally, of immigrants, and particularly Africans, in the above-mentioned sectors, still continues today, despite tighter immigration controls provided by the 1993 Act. Portugal is currently the EU country with the highest relative proportion of African immigrants (47% of all foreigners in 1997, as against 28% from Europe and 15% from South America).

In addition to the two operations aiming to regularise the situation of illegal immigrants in 1993 and 1996 (Table 6), a High Commissioner for Immigration and Ethnic Minorities has been established. Immigration has thus become a significant factor for employment and for migration, education and development policies (Ramos, 1995).

The number of foreigners doubled between 1986 and 1997 (rising from 87 000 to 175 000, according to the Department of Foreign Nationals and Frontiers, Portugal). Foreign nationals currently make up 1.8% of the total population. A large proportion of new foreign residents in Portugal in recent years have come from EU countries, mainly the United Kingdom, Spain and Germany.[13] Such immigration is associated with the increase in foreign investment, with the entry of multinational companies and with an influx of retirees.[14] European workers are mainly found in scientific occupations and in the service sector; many are self-employed. The entry of highly skilled personnel from other community countries with high rates of unemployment is likely to continue. At present, there is a fairly large influx of Spanish doctors, notably in the north of Portugal. In 1997, of the European citizens seeking a residence permit in Portugal for the first time, two-thirds had no family in Portugal. The number of young people of Portuguese origin graduating from Portuguese universities, or, if educated in France, seeking temporary or permanent residence in Portugal, is tending to rise.

a)   *Portuguese workers in the European Economic Area (EEA)*

The impact of Portugal's entry to the EEC on migration is difficult to assess. In view of the country's low unemployment rate, compared to the European average and to social, cultural and linguistic barriers, the flow of migrants is fairly limited. The impetus to emigrate is very low, except in some occupations, such as workers in the building industry.

Portuguese immigrants welcomed the country's entry to the EU. Portuguese nationals constitute one of the largest contingents of EU nationals living outside their country of origin (see Table 7), numbering about a million, or a sixth of all EU citizens living outside their own countries (Eurostat, 1997*b*[15]). In France, they represent the largest foreign national group, while very few French nationals live in Portugal.

b)   *Migration and European integration*

Has Portugal become a country of immigration? Admittedly, unlike long periods of its history, the flow of entries and departures seems fairly balanced. In the future, migration movements will be an indicator of Portugal's new status in the international arena.

The effect of regional economic integration on international migration may be viewed, theoretically, from the dual standpoint of international economic relations and the place where economic activity is carried out. In the first case, one must consider the effect of trade patterns on factors influencing the decision to emigrate and, in the second, the transfer of labour brought about by the relocation of activity – the reference point being international trade theory. The creation of a single market, characterised by the free movement of goods and services, capital and persons, is bound to have an impact on migration. On the one hand, the lifting of legal obstacles to mobility encourages migration while, on the other, the tendency to level out the remuneration of productive factors, labour in particular, ought to reduce the incentive to migrate between EU countries.

---

13.   Of the initial requests (3 644) from foreign nationals for residence permits in 1996, 55.3% came from EU citizens. Of the EU residents in the foreign workforce in Portugal in 1997, the largest contingents were British (5 842), Spanish (5 269), German (4 572) and French (3 250) (Department of Foreign Nationals and Frontiers, Portugal).

14.   The European contingent includes an unusually high number of retirees, mainly settled in the south of the country (Algarve).

15.   29.5% of all Portuguese residing abroad in 1997 live in Europe and 25.9% in the EU (data from embassies and consulates abroad, DGACCP, Ministry of Foreign Affairs). In trying to assess the size of foreign communities in various EU countries, the only data available are composite data made up of information supplied by the OECD (SOPEMI) and by the Statistical Office of the European Communities (Eurostat, 1997*b*).

The question for Portugal is whether the establishment of a common market has brought living standards closer to a common level and reduced the incentive to emigrate. EU entry led to a substantial increase in trade with community members and to foreign investment, in particular between 1986 and 1991. Incentives for Portuguese to emigrate declined, because economic convergence helped increased employment and diminished wage differentials. Portugal is now also a receiving country.

The rate of migration to the EU is relatively low. In 1995, less than 0.5% of the working age population migrated (Eurostat, 1997*b*). The number of entries to member countries has fallen considerably since the early 1990s. As far as immigrants are concerned, only half come from countries outside the European Union. Trade liberalisation and the establishment of a single market has to some extent been able to balance differences in national living standards and thus reduce migration within the community. Converging population trends – in particular, the birth rate decline in Southern countries, such as Portugal – have deterred incentives to migrate. Portugal and Ireland are the only two EU countries to have recorded net emigration in recent years.[16] Clear disparities in unemployment and living standards, however, still remain between countries.

The increasing integration of European economies within the framework of the Economic and Monetary Union (EMU) should give labour mobility an important part to play in absorbing regional stresses. In practice, there has been little change in labour mobility within the EU, and it is seldom used as a mechanism for restoring regional balance. Capital, on the other hand, has become more mobile. Specific factors tend to influence the choice of location for economic activity. Differences in wage levels within the EU are buttressed by a build-up of specialisation that leads to asymmetries.

Trade, investment and sub-contracting flows generate a mix of labour opportunities that strengthen links between national labour markets. In recent years, in Portugal, but also in other countries of southern Europe, illegal forms of labour have been on the rise. They include clandestine labour, unlawful employment of foreigners, child labour, fraudulent international sub-contracting and labour trafficking. Mobility and clandestine practices in the EU appear to stem from distortions of competition, relocation and wage bargaining associated with social dumping and the spread of the underground economy (Ramos, 1991, 1995, 1997). Playing on differences in living standards and disparities in social legislation and labour, some business have developed extremely flexible approaches to labour management that, even if they cannot always be legally defined as clandestine, are very close to it.

The Treaty of Rome (1957), in affirming the principle of the free movement of goods and persons, prepared the way for the establishment of a common migration area. The Schengen Agreement and the Dublin Convention signal the "Europeanisation" of the debate on immigration. While some northern European countries have taken steps to review their legislation, southern European countries – which have a tradition of emigration (Portugal, Spain, Italy and Greece) – must deal with the recent creation of new immigration countries and the imperative for at least some harmonisation of standards and procedures. The March 1993 decrees, regarding the entry and residence of foreign nationals in Portugal, decrees such as that of May 1998, regulating work by nationals of EEA member countries, and the procedures provided in the Schengen Agreement[17] (which Portugal signed on 25 June 1991) all advocate a more common regulating policy rather than a social

---

16. In 1986-94, Ireland alone had a net negative migration flow (except in 1991); the same was true for Portugal in 1986-92 (Eurostat, 1997*b*).

17. This agreement, signed in 1985, but not brought into force until 1995, provides for the complete abolition of border controls between the signatory states. It marked an important step towards harmonising migration policies with respect to third-party countries.

policy. European immigration policy should not be limited to controlling migratory movements. The EU should also seek a common plan to integrate population groups of immigrant origin.

4.   Changes in the labour market in Portugal following entry to the community

In addition to measures aimed at liberalising the Portuguese economy, since 1986 policy priority has been to restore macroeconomic equilibrium by controlling inflation and reducing the wide gap between real per capita income in Portugal and in other countries of the EU. A structural adjustment programme for the external deficit and unemployment (PCEDED) was set up in 1987 to reduce major imbalances affecting the Portuguese economy (public sector deficit, current account deficit and unemployment). A medium-term adjustment plan, the QUANTUM, was drawn up in July 1990 to smooth the way for entry of the escudo into the exchange-rate mechanism of the European Monetary System. It was amended in 1991 to allow Portugal to become part of the EMU.

Between 1986 and the early 1990s, under the impetus of growing domestic demand and as a result of new export capacities, Portugal's gross domestic product increased more rapidly than that of its EC partners.[18] Job creation was likewise more rapid. During this period, Portugal profited from comparative advantages deriving from its low wage levels in order to increase its exports (footwear, textiles, and clothing), while a substantial rise in wages fuelled strong growth in domestic demand. Thus, while its partners were facing persistent unemployment, Portugal was heading for full employment. Between 1986 and 1991, the unemployment rate dropped from 8.2 to 4.1%.

Between 1993 and 1995, however, progress towards the convergence of real incomes was halted, recession then giving way to a fairly slow recovery in 1995. Unemployment rose to a higher level than in the EU as a whole. Despite the worsening of unemployment, contractual wages rose in 1995, as they had the previous year, with somewhat larger increases in minimum wages and average earnings. This development was accompanied by a marked improvement in labour productivity. Labour market policies led to a rise in the overall productivity of economic factors, reaching an annual level of 3% between 1985 and 1994, thus strengthening GDP growth (OECD, 1995). In 1996, hourly productivity (real GDP/No. of hours worked) rose faster than it had in 1995 and unit labour costs halted their downward slide, which began in 1991 (see Table 8).

The economic improvement following Portugal's entry to the EEC occurred against a backdrop of remarkable structural change. Reform of the labour market sought to ease restrictions on employment but was above all targeted at improving the educational and training system. The wider opening of the economy might have caused frictional unemployment by altering the way jobs were distributed among the different economic sectors. There were wide swings in the employment share of each sector, with a steep rise in the numbers working in the service sector after 1986 and a fall in employment in the agricultural sector, from 24% in 1985 to 12.2% in 1996.[19] But this was still more than double the average for the EU (5% according to Eurostat, 1997a). There was a steep increase in agricultural employment in 1997 (+13.7%), which made up 13.6% of total employment, followed by industry (+2.6%), which made up 31.6% of the same total. The service sector showed a drop during the year (-1%) and accounted for 54.8% of employment (INE, 1998a). In 1997, sectoral factors continued to have an important effect on the labour market. Although employment rose steeply in agriculture and construction, the latter sector having benefited from investment in major infrastructure

18.   However, disparities still exist. In 1994, Portuguese per capita GDP at market prices was 11 432 as against 16 641 on average for the 15 EU member countries, at current prices and purchasing power (Eurostat, 1997a).

19.   Employment in 1996 in Portugal was divided between industry, 31.4% and services, 56.4% (INE, 1998a).

and housing projects, employment continued to decline in the textile and clothing industries, the sectors most affected by competition from non-EU member countries.

In 1993, the decline in paid employment affected all major economic sectors, leaving only a few sub-sectors unaffected (machinery and machine tools, textiles, electricity, education and health). Redundancies, more frequent in industry, where workers were generally male, led to a greater decline in male employment. Unemployment needs to be addressed through a redeployment of part of the workforce of traditional labour-intensive industries, which are now less competitive.

Employment shrank by 0.6% in 1995, the decline being more salient in agriculture and industry, whereas employment increased in the tertiary sector. These cuts, which came as losses in permanent contract work, affected wage earners. They were compensated, in part, by offers of fixed-term contracts.[20] In 1996, economic recovery was strengthened, with a 0.6% increase in overall employment over the previous year, but a 0.4% decline in paid employment. In 1997, employment rose as the economy picked up further, with overall employment up 1.9% and paid employment up 1.4%. Self-employment and fixed-term contracts increased.

Although economic factors affected employment trends, the shedding of jobs was attributable, in part, to the structural adjustment of Portuguese businesses to new technologies and the strengthening of foreign competition, particularly from countries with low wage levels.[21] The relationship between employment and production points to a structural change at the expense of traditional labour-intensive industries. It is difficult to determine the relative influence of economic cycle factors and structural factors, but the simultaneous increase in unfilled job vacancies and unemployment gives evidence of skill incompatibilities and labour adjustment difficulties. The Strategic Social Pact[22] (CES, 1996) reaffirms the aim to raise the level of teaching and acquired skills in Portugal to the European average via the pursuit of active training and education policies: career guidance inside and outside schools and provision of training.

EU funding has played a key role in the expansion and modernisation of training structures. Thus vocational training programmes were greatly expanded in Portugal during the 1990s, with an annual workforce participation rate of 8% in 1993 as against 4.7% in 1990, and public spending of 0.67% in 1993 (OECD, 1995). Some positive, albeit modest, results were made, such as an improvement in career prospects for those following continuing training programmes and for young people on initial training courses. In both cases, unemployment has fallen, despite a downturn in the labour market.

Average attendance at education and training courses for wage earners has been much lower in Portugal than in EU countries. Priority given to adult retraining courses is visible in its share of general education in Portugal, where it accounts for over 40% of all training provided (as against the

---

20. Fixed-term contracts as a percentage of all wage earners (INE, 1998a): 1985, 14.2%; 1994, 10.7%; 1996, 12.4%; 1997, 14.2%.

21. According to a survey of the labour market in the EU carried out in 1994, the proportion of industrial enterprises giving "rationalisation" and "adoption of new technologies" as the main reason for anticipated workforce reductions was much higher in Portugal than in other EU countries (OECD, 1996).

22. Signed in December 1996 by the Prime Minister, the General Workers' Union (UGT), the Portuguese Farmworkers' Confederation (CAP), the Portuguese Confederation of Trade and Services (CEP) and the Confederation of Portuguese Industry (CIP). It was the first time such a pact had been concluded between the government and the social partners. However, the main trade union group, the CGTP-IN, did not sign it.

European average of 7.3%). A high level of attendance by better-educated worker is reflected in the greater proportion of advanced skill courses (OECD, 1995).

5.   Progress of convergence[23] in Portugal and the EMU challenge

Portugal's economic progress since 1986 has been remarkable, with growing participation in the world economy, reform of the public sector, expansion of the social and economic infrastructure, a high rate of job creation, better economic efficiency, structural reform that has strongly stimulated investment and expansion of financial networks.

Although the performance of the education and training system improved during the first half of the 1990s, it still remains below that of most other EU countries. Providing for adult education, including vocational training, is still insufficient and businesses invest very little in this field. The economic crisis of the 1990s did not disrupt the Portuguese labour market as much as other European economies. There has nevertheless been a rise in unemployment among young people and growth of long-term unemployment, as well as a steep rise in insecure forms of employment.

As far as the social sector is concerned, it is particularly interesting to note the readjustment of salary scales and the high proportion of low wages in total income. This especially affects women and young people and encourages both emigration and immigration. Other essential factors include the modest increase in real wages, the part played by co-operation between the social partners and the existence of large pockets of poverty.[24]

Reviewing the main components of the economic growth that followed entry to the EEC shows that the Portuguese economy, despite a growth rate above those of other EU countries, is taking some time to converge towards average European levels of productivity, wages and living standards. What entry to the EEC did bring were guarantees of stability and means of access to the major European markets likely to attract foreign investment.

Some structural imbalances persist in the Portuguese economy. Fears exist that the economic growth triggered by EU entry might accentuate the two-tier structure of Portuguese society.[25] It is essential for economic growth to fuel income distribution if social cohesion is to be strengthened. Questions are currently being asked about the effects of Portugal joining the single European currency. Barbosa's study (1998) anticipates positive effects on the whole. With regard to Portugal's capacity for cushioning external shocks, the study shows the importance of adjusting the labour market via variations in real wages. Real wage flexibility gives the Portuguese economy additional capacity for

23.   Real convergence is assessed in terms of the removal of economic disparities and the financial and budgetary measures assisting that process (structural funds). Indicators: per capita GDP and comparison with the European average; degree of openness of economies; structure of employment; share of the various economic sectors; vigour of investment; levels of education and vocational training; levelling out of growth rates, unemployment rates, real remuneration rates, productivity, and so forth. Nominal convergence refers to changes in cost and price variables and their underlying determinants (public funding ratios, long-term interest rates)

24.   The inadequacy of social welfare is still a major cause of the persistence of poverty. Portugal voted in June 1996 to establish a national minimum income. In July 1997, the guaranteed minimum income system was introduced nation-wide after a one-year pilot period.

25.   This is quite visible in the coastal region/interior region dualism. Expenditure on R&D, the supply of training and investment are concentrated in the most developed industrial coastal regions of the country (districts of Lisbon, Porto, Setúbal, Aveiro and Brag), reinforcing regional productive specialisations as far as distribution and economic activity is concerned.

adjustment to counter potential shocks. Real wage flexibility is a substitute for international labour mobility and is an essential element in cushioning crises, according to a study by Gaspar and Luz (1997), based on data for the period 1983-96.

In the current EU context, one cannot expect inequalities in job availability in the different zones to be compensated via worker migration; national barriers are still important. The adjustment can take place at the labour level, that is, at the level of real wages, provided that wages are flexible in their response to variations in the demand for labour. This has proven to be the case in Portugal. Policies for change and budgetary policy have not played a major role in this area in the past; the adjustment of real wages remains the principal instrument of adaptation.

According to the scenarios envisaged by Barbosa (1998), if Portugal did not adhere to the euro-founding group but maintained budgetary discipline, after 10 years an accumulated difference of 1% of per capita GDP would be obtained comparatively to the situation resulting from Portugal's participation in the euro-zone. However, if Portugal were not to enter the European Monetary Union and abandoned budgetary discipline, the accumulated difference of per capita GDP would increase rapidly, reaching 7% in cases of great instability. Adoption of the euro would not seem to generate any significant job creation. According to the above study, there could even be a slight increase in unemployment in the short-term, although in the medium-term, employment should rise thanks to opportunities for growth offered by the single currency. The euro's effects on employment will thus be indirect. It is possible, however, that the public accounting discipline required by the euro will limit the funds available to promote employment and create jobs. It may, for example, oblige the Portuguese government to change its policies with regard to the public service. The same study, however, considered that integration, comparability and "transparency" of labour markets might well reduce the margin for manoeuvre in collective bargaining, which could result in a wage freeze or at least a slowdown in rate of wage growth. The fact that harmonisation of wage discipline takes place much more rapidly than harmonisation of real wages will help to keep wages in Portugal low in comparison with the European average.

The euro will therefore not affect income and wage levels and will have even less impact on social inequalities. There has been no shrinkage of social inequalities in recent years despite economic growth. The euro's contribution to economic growth, however, could help to raise middle-level incomes, although increased competition could promote greater real wage flexibility. Budgetary constraints could affect social policies, while trans-national or intra-community collective bargaining, especially in terms of wage policy, is difficult to achieve.

Conclusion: some useful pointers

Entry to the EEC has undoubtedly given Portugal a unique opportunity to solve some of its structural problems and thus to improve its long-term macroeconomic performance. The country has benefited from financial resources from European structural funds. Entry has led to the establishment of an institutional and legislative framework that is more favourable to growth. It has given the players in the economic sphere a strong incentive towards development, and the structural reforms implemented have led to vigorous growth in foreign investment in Portugal and an increase in trade with the rest of the community.

Although progress in terms of nominal convergence is unquestionable, innovation in the areas of real convergence is still important in the context of furthering economic and monetary union. Conditions will have to be created to allow Portugal to strengthen its capacity to participate in the construction of Europe. Macroeconomic developments have favoured growth and employment despite disparities in productivity and incomes between Portugal and the EU. Although mobility of capital and trade has increased, labour mobility within the EU and free movement of labour has not yielded the results expected. On the social front, much remains to be done, such as improving the quality of employment and social welfare, enhancing the collective bargaining process,[26] reducing inequalities and poverty, increasing real wages and reducing working hours. Surely something should be done to ease the criteria for budgetary convergence in the interests of achieving social convergence.

Since 1995, Portugal has been pursuing active employment policies. New programmes have been introduced to promote the inclusion of the long-term unemployed and the poor into the social welfare system and the job market.[27] The 1996 Strategic Social Pact points to the need to rework active employment policies in order to support structural adjustment and strengthen social cohesion. The pact also advocates social welfare reform.

In the future, Portugal must create conditions favourable to the emergence of further comparative advantages, not only by maintaining competitiveness in existing sectors but also by developing other productive sectors. In this respect, much remains to be done in the education and training field to ensure that existing skills are enhanced and to increase comparative labour costs and skill level advantages. This, in turn, will stimulate investment and employment. The difficulty in attaining such real convergence lies in the capacity to ensure virtuous interaction between enhancing competitiveness and promoting human resources.

---

26.   The Permanent Social Consultation Council was only set up in Portugal in 1984. The first real social consultation pact was signed on 29 July 1986 (see the review by Rodrigues, 1996).

27.   According to the Statistics Department of the Ministry of Employment and Qualifications, 18.3% of the Portuguese (continental) population was below the poverty line in 1997 (persistent and severe shortage of essential needs such as food, housing, consumption, social welfare, health care, and so forth).

BIBLIOGRAPHY

BANCO DE PORTUGAL (1996, 1997)
Relatório anual, Lisbon.

BARBOSA, A.P. (co-ord.) (1998)
O impacto do euro na economia portuguesa, Ministério das Finanças, Universidade Nova de Lisboa, Lisbon.

BARRETO, A. (co-ord.) (1996)
A situação social em Portugal 1960-1995, Instituto de Ciências Sociais da Universidade de Lisboa, Lisbon.

BUZELAY, A. (1996)
Intégration et désintégration européennes, Economica, Paris.

CAIRE, G. (1997)
"Convergences internationales des relations de travail", in J.P Faugère *et al.* (eds.), *Convergence et diversité à l'heure de la mondialisation,* Economica, Paris.

CERDEIRA, M.C. (1997)
A evoluçao da sindicalização portuguesa de 1974 à 1995, Ministério para a Qualificação e o Emprego, CICT, Lisbon.

COMMISSION OF THE EUROPEAN COMMUNITIES – CEC (1993)
Growth, Competitiveness, Employment: the Challenges and Ways Forward into the 21st Century: White Paper, Supplement No. 6/93 of the Bulletin of the European Communities.

CONFRARIA, J. (1995)
Desenvolvimento económico e política industrial, Universidade Católica Editora, Lisbon.

CONSELHO ECONOMICO E SOCIAL – CES (1996)
Acordo de concertação estratégica 1996–1999, Lisbon.

CORADO, C. and LEITE, A. (1991)
"Inversión directa extranjera y localización de la industria en la Península Ibérica", *Información Comercial Española*, Nos. 696-697.

DIRECÇÃO GERAL DO EMPREGO E FORMAÇÃO PROFISSIONAL – DGEFP (1995)
Relatório sobre Portugal elaborado no âmbito da informação sobre políticas de emprego. MISEP, Lisbon.

ERKEL-ROUSSE, H. (1997)
"Labour market flexibility, adjustment to asymmetric shocks and European Monetary Union", *Economie et prévision*, No. 128, April-June, pp. 79-100.

EUROPEAN COMMISSION (1995)
Livro verde sobre a inovação, Brussels.

EUROPEAN COMMISSION (1997)
L'emploi en Europe, 1997, Office des publications officielles des Communautés européennes, Luxembourg.

EUROSTAT (1997*a*)
Statistiques de base de l'Union européenne, 33 ed./1996, Office des publications officielles des Communautés européennes, Luxembourg.

EUROSTAT (1997*b*)
Statistiques sur la migration 1996, Office des publications officielles des Communautés européennes, Luxembourg.

FARINHA, L and MATA, J. (1996)
"The impact of foreign direct investment on the Portuguese economy", *Estudos e documentos de trabalho,* Working Paper 16-96, Banco de Portugal, Lisbon.

FRANCO, A.S. (1996)
"Portugal e as grandes questões da União Europeia", *Anuário da economia Portuguesa – O economista,* Associação Portuguesa de Economistas, Lisbon, No. 9, pp. 17-25.

GASPAR, V. and LUZ, S. (1997)
"Desemprego e salários em Portugal", *Boletim económico,* Banco de Portugal, Lisbon, December, pp. 27-32.

GONCALVES, O.M.D. Figueiredo and GUIMARAES, P. de Freitas (1997)
"O investimento directo estrangeiro na indústria transformadora portuguesa: uma abordagem sectorial e regional através do emprego para o período 1982-1992", *Estudos de economia,* Vol. 16-17, No. 3, pp. 333-358.

INSTITUTO NACIONAL DE ESTATÍSTICA – INE (1998*a*)
Estatísticas do emprego, Lisbon.

INSTITUTO NACIONAL DE ESTATÍSTICA – INE (1998*b*)
Estatísticas do comércio externo e do comércio internacional).

INSTITUTO NACIONAL DE ESTATÍSTICA – INE (1998*c*)
Estatísticas demográficas, Lisbon.

LOPES, J. da Silva (1996)
A Economia Portuguesa desde 1960, Grádiva, Lisbon.

MARSDEN, D. (1993)
"Existera-t-il un grand marché européen du travail ?", *Formation-Emploi,* No. 43, pp. 5-13.

MATEUS, A., *et al.* (1995)
Portugal XXI – Cenários de desenvolvimento, Bertrand Editora, Lisbon.

MENDONÇA, A. (1997)
"O investimento directo estrangeiro em/de Portugal (1980-1996)", *ICEP – Comércio e investimento internacional,* ICEP, Lisbon, pp. 153-198.

MINISTÉRIO DO EMPREGO E DA SEGURANÇA SOCIAL (1997)
Inquérito às necessidades de formação profissional 91-93 e 93-95, DEMESS, Lisbon.

MINISTÉRIO DO TRABALHO E DA SOLIDARIEDADE (1998)
Quadros de Pessoal, 1996, Departamento de Estatística, Lisbon.

MINISTÉRIO PARA A QUALIFICAÇÃO E O EMPREGO – MQE (1996*a*), *Programa plurianual do emprego até 1999,* Lisbon.

MINISTÉRIO PARA A QUALIFICAÇÃO E O EMPREGO – MQE (1996b)
Quadros de Pessoal, 1994, Departamento de Estatística, Lisbon.

MINISTÉRIO PARA A QUALIFICAÇÃO E O EMPREGO – MQE (1997)
O semprego de longa duração em Portugal: Situação actual e tendências de evolução, Lisbon.

MOREIRA, B.F. (1997)
Políticas de geminação e interculturalidade, Masters' Thesis in Intercultural Relations, Universidade Aberta, Porto.

MUNDELL, R.A. (1968)
International Economics, MacMillan, New York, N.Y.

NGUYEN, K. (1996)
"La convergence réelle en Europe", *Problèmes économiques,* No. 2475, Vol. 5, pp. 7-14, June.

OECD (1994)
The OECD Jobs Study: Evidence and Explanations, Vol. 2, Paris.

OECD (1995, 1996, 1998)
OECD Economic Survey – Portugal, Paris.

OECD (1997a)
The OECD in Figures, supplement to the OECD Observer, No. 206, June-July, Paris.

OECD (1997b)
Employment Outlook, Paris.

OECD (1997c)
Trends in International Migration, Annual Report 1996, OECD, Paris.

PANDA, M.C.S. (1997)
Percursos migratórios de caboverdianos em Portugal, Masters' Thesis in Intercultural Relations, Universidade Aberta, Porto.

PETERS, T. (1995)
"Marchés du travail : que faut-il attendre de l'Union monétaire européenne?", *Revue internationale du travail,* Vol. 134, No. 3, pp. 347-368.

POCHET, P. (1997)
"L'union européenne et l'emploi", *Problèmes économiques,* No. 2521, pp. 12-16, May.

PORTER, M. (dir.) (1994)
Construir as vantagens competitivas de Portugal, Monitor Company, Ed. do Forum para a competitividade, Lisbon.

RAMOS, M.C.P. (1990)
"Marchés du travail et migrations internationales : croissance, crise et marché unique, Cas du Portugal et de la France", Ph.D. dissertation, Université de Paris I, Sorbonne.

RAMOS, M.C.P. (1991)
"L'immigration clandestine : élément structurel du phénomène migratoire et donnée permanente du système d'emploi des pays européens", Communication à la Conférence de l'Association européenne des économistes du travail, Madrid, 26-29 September.

RAMOS, M.C.P. (1995)
"Desafios da mobilidade internacional do trabalho em Portugal", in M. Brandão Alves *et al.* (eds.), *Por onde vai a economia portuguesa?,* pp. 129-176, ISEG, Lisbon.

RAMOS, M.C.P. (1997)
"Mobilité du travail et marché unique – l'exemple du Portugal", *Congrès de l'Association internationale des économistes de langue française*, Porto and Evora, 28-31 May.

RAMOS, M.C.P. (1998)
"Evolution du marché du travail au Portugal suite à son intégration communautaire : transformations et défis", in M. Dusautoy (ed.), *Intégration européenne et emploi – le cas des pays semi-périphériques de l'Europe : Bulgarie, Grèce, Portugal*, Presses Universitaires de la Sorbonne Nouvelle, Paris.

RODRIGUES, H.N. (1996)
"Os acordos de concertaçao social", in A. Barreto (ed.), *A situaçao social em Portugal 1960-1995*, ICS, Lisbon, pp. 499-510.

SARAIVA, A.M. (1993)
"Investimento directo estrangeiro em Portugal no período de 1986 a 1992", *Boletim trimestral*, Banco de Portugal, Lisbon, December, pp. 103-124.

SILVA, A.C. (1996)
"Portugal e a transição para a moeda única", *Anuário da economia Portuguesa – O Economista*, Associação Portuguesa de Economistas, Lisbon, No. 9, pp. 27-35.

SIMÕES, V.C. (1996)
Inovação e gestão em PME industriais portuguesas, GEP, Lisbon.

SOUZA, F.F. de and FERREIRA, E.G. (1993)
"Fonds structurels, cohésion et convergence en Europe", in P. Maillet (ed.), *Trois défis de Maastricht : convergence, cohésion, subsidarité,* L'Harmattan, Paris, pp. 93-104.

TAPINOS, G. (1994)
"Regional economic integration and its effects on employment and migration", *Migration and Development*, OECD, Paris, pp. 213-228.

VAZ, I.F. (1997)
As formas atípicas de emprego e a flexibilidade do mercado de trabalho, Ministério para a qualificação e o emprego, Lisbon.

WERNER, H. (1993)
"Migration movements in the perspective of the single European market", *The Changing Course of International Migration*, OECD, Paris, pp. 79-85.

Table 1. Spending under the Community Support Framework (CSF), 1989-1999

Per cent of GDP

	1989-1993	1994-1999
Infrastructure	0.74	0.90
Human resources	0.91	0.81
R&D	0.07	0.08
Productive sector	0.99	1.08
Total EU funding	**2.70**	**2.86**
Infrastructure	0.64	0.55
Human resources	0.39	0.26
R&D	0.03	0.03
Productive sector	0.47	0.41
Total public funding	**1.53**	**1.25**
Infrastructure	0.02	0.02
Human resources	0.02	0.02
R&D	-	-
Productive sector	0.98	1.29
Total private funding	**1.11**	**1.43**
Total CSF funding	**4.98**	**5.76**

Source: OECD (1998).

Table 2. Changes in the geographical distribution of external trade in Portugal, 1986 and 1996

	1986	1996
Exports (billion escudos)	1 082.3	3 795.9
Percentage of total		
EU	*68.0*	*80.6*
Spain	*6.6*	*14.6*
Imports (billion escudos)	1 442.5	5 427.1
Percentage of total		
EU	*52.8*	*76.3*
Spain	*10.9*	*22.7*

Source: INE (1998*b*).

Table 3. **Changing FDI in Portugal, 1986-1997**

Year	FDI (billion escudos)	FDI (net) (billion escudos)	FDI/GFCF (%)	FDI/GDP (%)
1986	38.0	35.9	3.1	0.7
1987	72.9	65.5	4.6	1.2
1988	139.1	133.1	7.1	2.0
1989	286.6	273.3	12.8	3.5
1990	421.1	371.2	16.1	4.4
1991	490.2	354.9	17.3	4.4
1992	427.9	265.8	14.1	3.4
1993	475.5	249.2	15.9	3.6
1994	344.5	208.2	10.4	2.4
1995	648.9	104.2	18.1	4.3
1996	717.6	109.1	18.6	4.5
1997	1 330.6	302.9	30.0	7.4

Sources: Mendonça (1997) and Banco de Portugal (1996 and 1997).

Table 4. **Businesses with foreign and domestic capital among the 500 largest companies, 1989 and 1992**

	Number of companies		Number of employees (thousands)	
	1989	**1992**	**1989**	**1992**
Businesses with foreign capital				
Manufacturing industry	66	82	42.6	53.3
Chemicals	26	32	10.0	10.8
Machinery and transport equipment	20	21	18.8	24.6
Trade and hotels	33	54	9.0	13.4
Other sectors	9	12	5.5	7.9
Total	**108**	**148**	**57.1**	**74.6**
Businesses with domestic capital				
Total	**391**	**352**	**324.6**	**273.2**

Source: Saraiva (1993).

Table 5. **Portugal: Temporary Emigration (TE), 1976-1988 and 1992-1996**

Year	TE	% of total emigration	TE to France	% of emigration to France	TE to Switzerland	% of emigration to Switzerland
1976	1 976	10.1	858	32.5	..	..
1977	2 317	11.9	1 059	42.5	..	..
1978	3 453	15.6	2 091	56.6	..	..
1979	5 744	21.8	3 401	61.2	..	..
1980	7 136	28.3	3 905	67.7	..	..
1981	6 634	28.7	3 386	68.4	3 087	98.4
1982	6 859	40.0	3 734	86.4	2 910	98.4
1983	6 584	48.1	3 708	84.8	1 888	97.7
1984	7 407	53.0	3 649	84.5	2 062	98.5
1985	7 795	52.2	3 386	74.2	2 980	99.1
1986	7 437	54.3	3 762	80.3	2 749	98.0
1987	8 120	50.0	3 812	95.8	3 076	97.1
1988	8 762	47.9	4 516	92.4	2 848	96.2
1992-96	88 724	57.9	21 193	57.6	19 103	58.9

Note: In 1989-91, by virtue of Legislative Decree 438/88, which abolished mandatory possession of a passport by emigrants, it was not possible to obtain statistics on emigration. INE data do not coincide with those of the Secretary of State to the Portuguese Communities and are much lower than those provided by host countries.

Source: INE, Inquérito aos Movimentos Migratórios de Saída.

Table 6. **Foreigners undergoing special regularisation measures in Portugal, by country of origin**

	1993	1996[1]
Angola	12 525	9 155
Brazil	5 346	2 330
Cape Verde	6 778	6 872
China	1 352	1 608
Guinea-Bissau	6 877	5 328
Pakistan	-	1 754
Sao Tome and Principe	1 408	1 363
Senegal	1 397	-
Other	3 483	6 702
Total	**39 166**	**35 082**

1. Figures from 11/6/96 to 11/12/96.

Source: Serviço de Estrangeiro e Fronteiras, Ministry of the Interior.

Table 7. EEA (European Economic Area) citizens living in an EEA country that is not their own, 1 January 1994

Thousands

Host country	Citizens of EU 15	Of which: Portuguese
Belgium	548.5	21.9
Denmark	42.4	0.4
Germany	1 750.2	105.6
Greece	42.9	0.3
Spain	200.5	32.3
France[1]	1 321.5	649.7
Ireland[2]	70.4	-
Italy	120.1	10.1
Luxembourg	115.6	47.1
Netherlands	193.9	9.6
Portugal	38.8	-
Finland	12.5	0.1
Sweden	182.6	1.4
United Kingdom[3]	827.0	30.0
Total EU 15	**5 546.3**	**908.6**
Iceland	2.4	-
Liechtenstein	5.0	0.3
Norway	58.9	0.5
European Economic Area	**5 612.6**	**909.3**
Switzerland	828.5	122.1

1. 1990 census results, metropolitan France.
2. Provisional data, Labour Force Survey (Spring 1994).
3. Labour Force Survey (Spring 1994), figures rounded to the nearest thousand.

Source: Eurostat (1997*b*).

Table 8. Productivity and labour costs, 1975-1996

Variation in %, annual mean

	1975-85	1985-90	1990-94	1994-95	1995-96
Portugal					
GDP/number employed	2.3	3.3	1.6	2.6	2.3
GDP/number of hours worked	-	3.9	2.3	1.8	2.5
Mean real labour costs	0.5	2.9	3.9	- 0.5	3.1
Real unit labour costs	- 5.7	- 0.9	2.1	- 3.3	0.7
EU					
GDP/number employed	2.1	1.8	1.9	1.7	1.3
GDP/number of hours worked	-	2.1	2.3	1.9	1.5
Mean real labour costs	1.2	1.3	1.0	0.3	0.9
Real unit labour costs	- 1.0	- 0.6	- 0.8	- 1.5	- 0.6

Source: European Commission (1997).

PART III

WHAT DIRECTION SHOULD EMPLOYMENT AND MIGRATION POLICIES TAKE IN ORDER TO STRENGTHEN REGIONAL INTEGRATION?

THE GEOPOLITICAL DIMENSION OF REGIONAL INTEGRATION

by
Ghazi Hidouci
Economist, Former Algerian Minister for the Economy

The question of the opportunities that the combination of free trade and regional integration may offer is addressed in much the same way in North America, Europe and Asia. However, while approaches to free trade are analogous or even the same, the general strategic, political and economic conditions that shape regional-integration objectives and public practice with regard to the management of migration policies remain different, both historically and cyclically.

1. Overall trends in the demo-economic constraints facing OECD countries

OECD countries must contend with challenges posed by development and migration within the framework of a "triangle" of constraints. First, aside from a sudden and as yet unforeseen economic depression, the globalisation of trade in the present neo-liberal context limits the magnitude and range of the main (that is to say, governmental) decisions regarding development inequalities, at both the national and regional level.

Monopolistic competition between firms generated by major concentrations and trans-border engagements complicates – when it does not actually prevent – the drawing up and application of public rules at regional and international levels. What is more, the slowdown in growth, which has become structural, now coincides in these same countries with reduced space for budgetary manoeuvres. This, in turn, stifles and/or limits the possibility to adopt pro-active policies to absorb excess resident labour, leaving little hope, in the short and medium term, for an easing of pressures on employment.

Finally, wealthy OECD countries are commencing the long-term process of what the demographers have called the "grey revolution", which in various ways is making them structurally short of labour at the close of the present demographic transition, which began at the end of the Second World War. The temporal proximity of this transition varies from one country to another. The overall shortage of labour is already preceded in Japan and Europe by sectoral imbalances that are only amended via deregulation and the use of surplus immigrant labour. Even if improved productivity is temporarily easing labour demand, future equilibrium is not guaranteed.

Looking forward to 2005, the potential for renewal by means of immigration will no doubt, for want of an alternative, serve to cushion crises (except a deep and unforeseen economic recession). In the more immediate future, the trend towards more flexible management of recruitment and wages will see to it that there is constant pressure for immigration, perhaps of a more selective, reduced and professional nature, whenever labour-intensive activities cannot be transferred to wherever labour is least expensive.

2.   Differences in regional trends

Within the above context, it would seem that, if there are more constraints on Japan and Europe than on North America, it is for demographic reasons. Economic, indeed ethical, behaviour is operating in favour of the United States and Canada which have historically done more to encourage selective immigration and, albeit to a lesser extent in Canada, job insecurity and deregulation. The wealth of information deriving from earlier seminars stresses this point sufficiently.

It is Europe, in particular, that is having to contend with new immigration flows stemming from changes brought about by globalisation (Central and Eastern Europe) and pervading political instability. At the same time, immigration linked to colonial factors (the Mediterranean area and Africa) remains a real and evolving phenomenon. It is apparently also in Europe and Japan, more so than in North America and the rest of Asia, that behaviour linked to population ageing is reinforcing Malthusian attitudes. Trends towards isolation are all the more harmful when at the same time internal economic forces are structurally affected by ageing.

This is why it is in Europe that the cultural, political and economic outlines of the precepts for regional integration between emigration and immigration areas are enforcing the most decisive strategic choices in the medium and long term.

The fact that migration phenomena are subjectively over-represented in the present disorders affecting the world economy points, over and above economic factors, to the existence of political, cultural and even strategic resistance. It is everywhere indicative of isolationist attitudes exacerbated by the transition difficulties prompted by globalisation. In reality, of course, the populations that emigrated before wealthy countries closed their frontiers (with varying degrees of effectiveness) are not concerned by migration policies aiming to control flows. Their problems are almost entirely attributable to the way in which domestic policies are implemented. In this context, current flows are not very substantial and have slowed down overall. The nature of these flows is changing rapidly under the impact of the international differentiation of labour, which is contributing to job insecurity and selective flows, whether it be skilled or unskilled labour. These flows, in fact, are only worrisome from the viewpoint of the fragility and likelihood of instability in emigration countries, which the skill drain is accentuating.

3.   Macroeconomic impediments to regional integration

Against the background of the wide-ranging liberalisation of movements of capital, goods and services and the convergence of fiscal and financial policies, the behaviour of investors, firms and markets is by no means promoting lasting recovery and regional integration. It is not far-reaching enough to cope with the challenges posed by demographic pressures, poverty and increasing inequalities between partners. Economists, in fact, expect a downward alignment of probable equilibria rather than any upward trend.

Most empirical studies conclude that international trade will increase between highly developed countries and will involve similar goods and services – paradoxically, because of increasing returns. The results of industrial relocation to poor countries with surplus labour are of relatively little significance: in the area of R&D, these countries suffer from both a weak surrounding infrastructure and a lack of funds. Moreover, the importance of economies of scale operates against them due to the undeveloped nature of their markets. Today, increasing set-up costs are leading to the concentration of investment according to the concentration of information. The "Ricardian" comparative advantage of the poor countries is, therefore, increasingly confined to activities that can be moved offshore, involving a large amount of relatively immobile labour. This being the case, the increasingly abundant savings of rich consumers going to emerging market economies is partly speculative, not really aimed at productive accumulation and, in reality, liable to magnify cyclical financial shocks and thereby generate new forms of unemployment and emigration pressure, which are politically destabilising for the middle classes.

In the final analysis, all these constraints mean that present efforts at integration remain minimal, both in North America and Europe, and take the form of free-trade agreements whose results are differentiated, modest and sometimes unjust. The economic restructuring, which such agreements inevitably involve, is causing severe social strains in situations where the economic capacity for compensation, by countries engaged in the integration process, is reduced by the exigencies of financial markets. Can these trends be reversed?

4.   Short- and medium-term integration and migration management policies

Pending a return to a more favourable equilibrium, the options available for the control of movements of people remain characterised by a host of administrative obstacles and the preference for constraint, which renders discussion more confused and thus makes it painfully difficult to find satisfactory equilibria. In the present context, moreover, the agreements reached would seem, for reasons already indicated, to be marginal for the major economic powers and strategic for the emigration countries involved.

The explanation as to their strategic importance for emigration countries is that, to some extent, their political regimes are more and more clearly controlled by those social categories that benefit from export-oriented economic policies, whose interests coincide nowadays with the requirements of attempts at integration within the context of globalisation. Yet the idea that regional integration, between similar poor countries and between neighbours with differing levels of development, reduces uncertainty and political costs in the context of inevitable integration into world markets is one that has nowadays prevailed over all other alternatives. It has the advantage of better organising transition stages and of targeting the objectives more clearly. These phenomena should logically open up new opportunities to further regional co-operation; unfortunately this is still not the case.

The reasons for this are, of course, due mainly to the fact that investor behaviour is consistent with the logic of the system. Another factor is the reduced room for public policy manoeuvre. The sluggishness or even reversal of the modernisation and democratisation of institutions in poor countries also plays a decisive role in the blatant lack of initiatives taken. Proof of this is found in the glaring weakness of domestic accumulation and growth and the low internal credibility of the regimes.

5.   What trends should be encouraged?

Recent examples (the case of certain countries of Central and Eastern Europe and to a lesser degree, of the Mediterranean area) show clearly that when business in the domestic markets of emigration countries is buoyant, and when the rules governing the modernisation and democratisation of political and economic systems converge as they should, integration agreements move forward at a sufficient pace towards a cumulative increase in mutual benefits, the release of substantial public resources and the acceleration of trade and productive capital movements. Against such a background, agreements concerning the circulation and settlement of people become less complicated to draft, while at the same time they can be part of a long-term view of co-operation and in turn become more human.

For those countries whose economic growth poses problems and whose progress towards integration in regional entities remains inadequate or uncertain (in the case of political crises, for example), these trends undoubtedly show the way forward. It is important to be convinced beforehand that there is no direct causal link for the future between the divergence of demographic transitions in young and old countries, labour supply pressures and migration. The strained relations between these phenomena are the result of inappropriate policies that encourage them. Migration policies based on convergent strategic interests are possible, necessary and useful to all parties. Possible acts, combining economic, political and demographic interests, should, in order to have a chance of success, be ranked in order of priority without losing sight of their overall coherence.

- With this in mind, great emphasis should be given to modernising the political and economic rules of the game in the countries in question. It is only when this level of institutional convergence exists that cumulative processes of improved productivity, resource saving and stability truly begin.

- Regional integration has to be seen as a stage in the total liberalisation of markets. The parties to the contract must have the capacity to innovate as far as organising deadlines and targets is concerned. This can be achieved by equipping themselves temporarily with sufficient budgetary resources and by moderating the pace of deregulation just enough to protect themselves against the harmful effects of speculation, to guarantee domestic growth and to tackle the subsequent stages more successfully, but without finding themselves outside the dynamic of the market and overall world developments.

- Finally, integration policies must be part of agreed and transparent frameworks and pro-active public policies, which encourage positive and converging behaviour and expectations in the societies of the host and emigration countries concerned.

Impediments to the progress of regional economic integration, like those concerning the implementation of migration policies, are in fact located at the level of immigration countries' distrust of the inefficient political and economic systems of emigration countries. The search for durable solutions must necessarily begin with the recognition of this reality rather than by the limited endeavours of free-trade agreements. Were the problems posed at this level, everyone would gain – as they would from the search for lasting solutions that incorporate the strategic preoccupations of peace and war (domestic or regional) and that integrate them in democratic control processes.

THE SOCIAL DIMENSION OF REGIONAL INTEGRATION

by
John Evans
Trade Union Advisory Committee (TUAC), OECD

There are significant differences between the processes of regional integration that are taking place in different areas of the world and consequently very different attitudes and responses from trade unions. One central concern is the form of "social dimension" that accompanies investment and trade integration and this has relevance to the general OECD policy discussion on globalisation and regionalisation.

In Europe the process of economic integration has been supported by virtually all national trade union confederations affiliated to the European Trade Union Confederation (ETUC). This has involved difficult decisions with regard to some aspects of the process, notably the impact of the Maastricht criteria and some features of the Single European Act. However the support has been conditional on making progress with a broad "social agenda" at European level. Some key features of this are: *i*) the need to give priority to employment, particularly to use the greater scope for macro economic policies to encourage growth following the completion of Economic and Monetary Union (EMU); *ii*) the extension of employee rights to information, consultation and negotiation at the European level through measures such as the European Works Council directive, which gives consultation and information rights to workers in larger European enterprises; *iii*) the encouragement of European level collective bargaining following EMU through the development of the Social Dialogue negotiations between the ETUC and their employers' counterpart UNICE; and; *iv*) the strengthening of European political institutions to correct the "democratic deficit".

In the Americas the process of economic integration has been dominated by trade and investment liberalisation and a satisfactory social dimension has not been in place. As a result the political dynamics of regional integration have been completely different. Trade unions in both North and South America have in general been critical of the process. In the United States this came to a head a year ago with the American labour movement's opposition to the continuation of Fast Track negotiating authority for the US Administration on the Free Trade Agreement of the Americas.

The recent history of Asian economic development could be more accurately described as one of disintegration rather than integration. But even before the current economic and financial crisis the APEC process was a rather limited development with most of the APEC members wishing to expand trade on a multilateral basis rather than to develop regional integration. In that process Asian trade unions themselves have called for a more developed social agenda.[1] One of the lessons of the Asian crisis was the development of social systems did not keep pace with economic development.

---

1.   See conclusions of TUAC/ICFTU-APRO/RENGO Symposium on "Trade Unions in an Increasingly Interdependent World", Tokyo, 30 November 1992.

The first conclusion that can be drawn from the brief sketch of different processes of integration is that a social dimension is crucial if there is to be broad support. The imbalance between European developments and those elsewhere in the world is also a cause for concern as there is always the risk of Europe and the European workers turning inwards as the process of globalisation intensifies.

A second general feature of the current process of globalisation is that it has been accompanied by growing inequality and poverty both between and within countries. The latest UNCTAD human resources report points to the appalling increase in the gap between the poorest and the richest countries since 1960. Recent OECD work has also shown the growth of poverty in OECD countries. Not all these developments can be blamed on globalisation but there has been a tendency by both companies and governments to say that they have no responsibility for their actions because outcomes are determined by global markets over which they have no control. Recent events, notably the crisis in Asia, the failure of the MAI, and political change in Europe may suggest that this is no longer a satisfactory response and governments now have to develop effective public policy responses to problems created by their own policies and by global markets.

There would appear to be four priorities in such a policy response. Firstly, the need to establish binding and effective enforcement at international level of core labour standards as defined in the recent ILO Declaration on fundamental labour rights. Secondly, to encourage a model of competitiveness that is both economic and efficient and socially just. One aspect of this model which has been touched on in this conference has been the potential role of local development and tripartite approaches (a feature of the success of the Irish economy). Thirdly, the need to develop more expansionary macro-economic policies and a new framework for achieving more stable international financial markets. Fourthly, a more dynamic view of the role of the public sector at the national level which still accounts for an average of 40% of GNP in OECD countries.

To conclude this brief review of globalisation from a trade union viewpoint I would say that the policy agenda has changed from the 1980s and the central objective of policy must now be to re-link the potential of global markets with the achievement of social progress. The failure to achieve this may lead to a rejection by many parts of society of the globalisation process itself.

LABOR MOBILITY AND HUMAN RESOURCES DEVELOPMENT POLICIES

by

Demetrios G. Papademetriou

Carnegie Endowment for International Peace, Washington D.C.

Introduction

It is fitting that we should be in Lisbon to take stock of what we have learned about the relationship among regional economic "integration," and particularly trade and investment liberalisation agreements, development, and international migration for at least two reasons. The first one is that Portugal falls in a relatively new category of states that have made the transition from countries of emigration to countries of immigration in what amounts to record time, at least by historical standards. Spain, Italy, and Greece, as well as a number of other countries in other regions, have experienced a similar change in status and, as we all know, they are all trying to understand and manage their new status as best they can – and with predictably mixed (really, poor) results.[1] Of course, an even larger number of states throughout the world (Mexico is but one example) are simultaneously significant sending *and* receiving states – a status that poses its own challenges and creates additional opportunities.

The second reason that Lisbon is such a good fit as the site for concluding this phase of the OECD's work on these issues is that our five year long journey started in the other great Iberian capital city, Madrid. What have we learned in this journey that has taken us through Vienna, Tokyo, Athens, and, earlier this year, Mexico City? And how should one think *now* about labour mobility and human resources development policies *in the context of regional integration efforts*?

I will organise my remarks, my sense of the "lessons learned," into three broad categories. The first one focuses on the seminar's main theme, the relationship between regional integration and migration. The second explores briefly the burdens and opportunities labour mobility (in the context of a regional integration scheme) places on policy making in the human resources development area *both* for labour senders and labour receivers. The third one reflects on a handful of "rules of the game" for societies that choose to or are considering engaging in regional integration arrangements in some part as a means of relieving regional migration pressures.

1. Regional integration and migration

The overarching lesson about the relationship between regional integration and migration is one that we sort of knew already in Madrid, although some were politically too committed to a

---

1. The related issue of Portugal's standing as the "metropolis" of a former empire is also important in that it complicates the calculus about the admission and treatment of the foreign-born even further.

strongly positive relationship between these two concepts even to acknowledge uncertainty, let alone entertain much scepticism about it. In fact, by the time we reached Madrid, a significant gap had developed already between the *political* euphoria about liberalisation's ability (promise?) to reduce substantially pressures for migration and the much more nuanced and conditional conclusions of the analytical literature. Japan's policy of extensive foreign direct investments (really, a policy with only a tangential relationship to migration), the North American Free Trade Agreement (NAFTA), and the European Union's projected expansion to the east and intent to negotiate a free trade agreement with many countries to the south (what eventually became the Mediterranean Initiative) all rested in some part on the assumption that the opening of substantial and sustained trade and investment opportunities would gradually relieve emigration pressures.

Now, a mere few years later, the optimism (or was it escapism?) of Madrid has given way to a pronounced and broad scepticism about the robustness of the syllogism's underlying premise. First, as the proposition moved from whether regional integration would lead to the abatement of migration pressures to how it might do so, the twin issues of the length of the transition period and depth (or amount) of investments and trade required to arrest the forces of emigration undermined much political support for further regional integration. ("Globalisation," the seminar's "other" theme has fared even worse.) At the same time, as the domestic consequences for certain industries and segments of the labour market of liberalising the international trade and investment regimes have become clearer, domestic political support for further integration both in industrial countries and in some segments of the less developed countries has waned. In fact, the reaction to these consequences has been so strong, *and the public policy remedies so inadequate,* that advocates for further liberalisation have had to tread very carefully while the political elite that had supported liberalisation initiatives in a mantra-like manner now waver in their support at least for the pace of liberalisation, if not the concept itself.

Underlying this growing scepticism has been a rather simple reality that was largely overlooked in the political excitement about the promise of trade and investment liberalisation as *the* engine of further development and development's role in stemming the pressures for emigration. Namely, that in order for liberalisation to lower such pressures in significant ways, it must lead to large scale and sustained investments that promote steady growth and it must be accompanied by fundamental changes in the way the immigrant-sending societies that are party to these initiatives are organised socially and economically, as well as in the way in which they govern themselves.

Before I list some of these changes, I wanted to acknowledge that instituting fundamental change is difficult because those who would "lose" are among a society's most powerful actors. As a result, the architects of change must show the political courage to be honest about the complexity of the issues, the uncertainty of outcome, and the sacrifices fundamental change will entail. Furthermore, they must show steady nerves, and the strongest possible political and management skills. These are clearly attributes that are in short supply in any part of the world.

Among the changes that appear to be most essential are the following:

- A political vision around which people can rally, especially one that treats equity and social responsibility as critical public policy aims.

- Transparence in both decision-making processes and the implementation of initiatives (lack of transparence leads to credibility gaps and contributes to difficult-to-bridge democratic deficits).

- The development and nurturing of public and civil society institutions that can assist the government to exercise its powers responsibly and with full accountability.

## 2.	Migration and human resources development policies

The second broad category of my remarks focuses on the nexus between employment policies and migration policies. It is important to acknowledge up front that international migration is a key element of human progress and that in all but the most extraordinary circumstances it can be neither responsible for a state's labour market problems (real or imagined) nor can it solve all of them. This aphorism holds largely true for both migrant receiving and migrant sending societies.

From the perspective of the former, for immigration policy to make the greatest positive labour market contribution it must meet the following tests.

–	First, it must be consonant with human resources development policies. This means that immigration should be seen as a supplement to the domestic labour force and as the means to redress qualitative and quantitative imbalances between domestic labour supply and labour demand. Policies (or lack thereof) that violate this simple rule may reinforce a country's labour force shortcomings and are likely to create labour-market-based political problems.

–	Second, immigration policy must "walk" a fine line between too much and too little regulation. Inflexible immigration policies (just like inflexible labour market policies), by limiting the employment options of immigrants, interfere with their ability to play out their creative potentials and aspirations and thus diminish the overall value of immigration for the receiving society. Within reason, immigration succeeds most as a policy when immigrants succeed.

–	Third, countries engaged in immigration must endeavour to create and maintain social and labour market level playing fields (both in law *and in practice*) for both natives and immigrants. Nothing undermines the legitimacy of a decision to participate in the migration system faster than placing immigrants in direct competition with domestic workers or allowing the presence of immigrants to lower workplace standards for anyone.

–	Finally, and in a somewhat contrarian tack, a state's decisions about immigration must be realistic about the fact that such decisions typically entail political and economic trade-offs, in other words, that they are not made either abstractly or only through the lens of labour market policy. An immigration decision, for instance, that chooses to emphasise dimensions other than employment policy may appear to be less than fully "rational" when judged from the parochial perspective of a ministry of labour or social affairs. Yet, such a policy may be addressing another set of national interests that are dominant at that time. Those may be of a foreign policy nature, a long-term demographic or economic nature, a humanitarian nature, or, simply meeting the terms of a legal or moral obligation. Certainly, few negotiators of global liberalisation and regional integration initiatives would assign high priority to the concerns of their domestic labour markets, although policymakers can ill afford to ignore the labour market implications of their decisions. Balance, again, is at the foundation of stable liberalisation initiatives.

Similarly, from the perspective of sending societies, engaging the migration system in a significant way – within or outside the context of globalisation and regional integration – must be accompanied by a number of actions if emigration is to contribute in an orderly and systematic way to the sending area's well-being. Among those actions are the following:

- Determined initiatives in areas of economic and political reform.

- Actions that address uneven economic, social, and cultural development among regions (in order to create alternative *internal* migration attraction poles than those of the capital city and change locational migration habits).

- Hard-nosed investments in physical and human infrastructure (in order to make oneself attractive to investors and make regional integration a "race to the top," rather than to the bottom).

- Creating an environment conducive to the emergence and take-off of civil society.

3. Migration "rules of the game" in regional integration schemes

The migration system is unforgiving of the inattentive. If a receiving country decides to participate in it, it must commit to managing it closely - and then be able to live with great uncertainty. In what follows, I have developed a small number of "do's" and "don'ts" - a few rules of the game - that apply equally to the experienced and to the neophyte.

One must demystify the migration process, err consistently on the side of transparency, and spare no effort to educate the public on the value (and challenge) of immigration. In that last regard, one must acknowledge the complex social and cultural issues immigration entails, discourage irresponsible rhetoric regardless of source, refuse quick fixes of any type, and, above all, be consistent in policies and patient about results.

Effective management requires credible and persistent control efforts. Yet, in matters of control, one must be always mindful of the costs (political, social, and economic) – and especially their tendency to quickly approach diminishing returns. Constantly evaluating control initiatives for their effectiveness would allow for midterm corrections that may address the issue in contention at another, more productive point. For instance, after a while, border controls without a concomitant serious effort to seek the co-operation of your neighbouring country (by engaging it in a conversation that seeks to identify appropriate incentives for such co-operation – viz. the US/Mexico case) become an exercise in futility.

One must be constantly aware of a policy's perverse effects and act swiftly to address them. For instance, enhanced border enforcement, by making re-entry more difficult, can encourage permanence – by turning unauthorised migrants who may be circular migrants into long-term stayers – and creates immense incentives for organised criminal networks to expand into the business of smuggling people. (The United States/Mexico situation is again a case in point.). Similarly, the aggressive enforcement of employer sanctions clearly contributes to the growth of underground economies. These may in fact be a much larger problem for OECD countries than illegal immigration *per se* – at least in terms of employment and taxation policy. (Of course, illegal immigration contributes to the vitality and tenacity of the underground economy.) Likewise, denying foreign-born persons a legal means for immigrating to join their families or join employers who seek their skills creates extraordinary pressures on a state's asylum and immigration control systems. Finally, the wilful decision not to offer realistic and fair opportunities for citizenship to long-term foreign-born residents not only leads to the marginalization of immigrant minorities but also undermines societal cohesion.

One must be mindful of ensuring that basic employment standards are observed. Doing so guarantees that immigrants will make the greatest long-term contribution to their hosts' economies and societies (if they choose to stay) – and that they will be the transmitters of significant physical, social, and cultural capital to their countries of origin (if they choose to return).

Conclusion

Regional integration agreements – with or without significant movement of labour provisions – are not for the faint of heart. They require a great deal of attention, a strategic sense of direction, the flexibility to adapt to changing on the ground conditions, a sense of what is politically feasible at any given point in time, a vision that is larger than a single agency's parochial interests, and extraordinary management skills. I know of no OECD member state that can claim more than qualified success in more than one or two of these areas. Doing better in this regard, then, should become the call and the lesson we should all take away from this exercise that started and now ends in the Iberian Peninsula.

CONCLUSION

The question of the links between migration, free trade and economic integration has been the dominant theme of the regional seminars on North America, Asia, the Mediterranean Basin and Central and Eastern Europe, organised by the OECD over the past two years. The central working hypothesis was that within the framework of international integration increases both in openness to trade and in foreign investment flows should over the long term reduce incentives to emigrate and so make it easier to exercise control over immigration flows. Neither the theoretical analyses nor the empirical studies conducted under the auspices of this seminar series have provided us with the magic formula that would produce this result. The regional integration programmes currently underway are without doubt insufficiently mature for any firm conclusions to be drawn from them. However, the regional seminars and the Lisbon International Conference brought to light elements that could play a fundamental role in successful strategies, and proposals were formulated to accelerate the economic convergence, and over the longer term, reduce incentives to emigrate in those countries of high migration potential.

1.   The key factors of a successful economic integration

The integration of developing countries into regional groupings of industrialised countries can have beneficial effects for the former only if integration is accompanied by sufficient financial inflows to build up their human and physical capital. Along with market size and the internal dynamic of investment growth, human and physical capital are two key factors in attracting foreign direct investment. The experience of countries like Ireland and Portugal over the past twenty years shows that economic openness and regional integration alone cannot produce dynamic effects of convergence towards the average European per capita income. This can only be attained if the process is accompanied by structural and institutional reforms including the adoption of credible macroeconomic policies, a more equitable distribution of the fruits of growth and the greater enhancement and use of human resources. Among the other frequently highlighted key elements are political stability, the quality of investment (including the optimal use of structural funds and migrants' transfers), and the existence of basic infrastructure. Concern for the human and social side of the process also plays an essential part in ensuring that the inevitable adjustments are better accepted at the political level, both domestically and internationally. In this regard, governments have here an important regulatory role to play in setting not only labour but also social standards.

The different forms of regional integration involve a wide variety of participants: governments, national and multinational enterprises and the labour force. Co-ordinated assistance and multinational co-operation are required to attenuate the disruptive effects of the structural adjustments that opening to trade and insertion into the world economy necessitate. In addition to stability and social equity, determining factors underlying the success of the economic opening process and the integration of the newly developing countries into international trade include the dissemination of innovation and technological progress, as well as the implementation of policies which promote employment and the use of modern business management methods.

The place of international migration flows in the on-going process of economic globalisation was the subject of much discussion during the conference. Trade liberalisation has advanced considerably compared with the liberalisation of labour movements, especially in the case of

North-South relations. One should therefore abstain from talk of a globalisation of migration flows. Yet the increasing diversity of migrants' nationalities and the migration channels used, and the growing proportion of movements of temporary workers and skilled workers in total migration flows, does indeed indicate that developments in migrational phenomena are being strongly influenced by economic globalisation.

That sending and receiving countries are becoming increasingly interdependent was frequently underlined. In the origin countries, debate on migration has become inseparable from the issues of human rights, political organisation and economic development. In host countries, the integration of immigrants is one of the main goals of migration policy. These countries are faced with the problem of ageing populations; in the medium term it is quite possible that migration might feature among the solutions adopted to maintain or reform the welfare state.

Over the past decade, the efforts accorded to regional integration strategies have intensified. The degree to which economic convergence processes have accelerated has been dependent on the level of integration chosen. The announcement effect produced by the prospect of certain central and eastern European countries joining the European Union was of crucial importance in attracting foreign capital and favouring these countries' transition towards a market economy. In the cases of Ireland and Portugal, often mentioned during the conference, the judicious use of the European Community's structural funds made it possible for them, once they had joined, to modernise their infrastructure and to increase investment in human capital. Together, these two elements enabled them to attract foreign capital. Their economic and technological catch-up was accompanied by a reversal in migration flows.

2.   Proposals to accelerate economic convergence

Among the measures proposed at the conference to accelerate economic convergence, participants stressed the need to promote the existence of efficient public and financial institutions, the launching of training and manpower skilling programmes, as well as the inflow of foreign capital to projects (including those carried out by emigrants in their home countries) that would ensure sustainable development.

In this context of accelerating economic convergence, migration policy could play a critical role. One objective of this policy is to combat illegal immigration by better controlling flows within the regionally integrated area and granting legal immigrants and their families the same status as native citizens. Another objective is to encourage the exchange of skilled manpower and to facilitate the free movement of persons, in particular business executives and employees. The current discussions in the WTO on the GATS dealing with the international mobility of persons in connection with the provision of services are deadlocked; this is penalising the developing countries the most heavily. Bilateral or multilateral agreements in this field are possible, however, as are an increased use of service contracts permitting labour movements and the adoption of measures facilitating the settlement of self-employed workers. Lastly, the enhancement of human resources should form an important part of migration policy.

The present situation of economic globalisation and accelerating regional integration would seem to favour a productive return home for migrants. Moreover, where regional integration is successful, the initial brain drain can be expected to taper off thereby allowing the emigration countries to benefit more fully from the skills their migrants have acquired.

During the Lisbon conference, as during the earlier regional seminars, policy makers were invited to integrate migration issues into the broader context of international economic and political relations. The effort to place this subject in its geopolitical setting shows that the issue of the relationship between globalisation, migration and development deserves to be further investigated and revisited when current experiences of regional integration have reached more advanced stages.

OECD PUBLICATIONS, 2, rue André-Pascal, 75775 PARIS CEDEX 16
PRINTED IN FRANCE
(81 2000 02 1 P) ISBN 92-64-17166-5 – No. 50991 2000